TACKLING THE INNER CITIES

TACKLING THE INNER CITIES

*The 1980s Reviewed, Prospects
for the 1990s*

———

EDITED BY

SUSANNE MACGREGOR AND BEN PIMLOTT

CLARENDON PRESS · OXFORD
1990

Oxford University Press, Walton Street, Oxford OX2 6DP

Oxford New York Toronto
Delhi Bombay Calcutta Madras Karachi
Petaling Jaya Singapore Hong Kong Tokyo
Nairobi Dar es Salaam Cape Town
Melbourne Auckland

and associated companies in
Berlin Ibadan

Oxford is a trade mark of Oxford University Press

Published in the United States
by Oxford University Press, New York

British Library Cataloguing in Publication Data
Tackling the inner cities: essays on the 1980's
and prospects for the 1990's
1. Great Britain. Cities. Inner areas.
Social planning. Policies of government
I. MacGregor, Susanne   II. Pimlott, Ben, 1945–
307.120941
ISBN 0–19–827737–7

Library of Congress Cataloging in Publication Data
Tackling the inner cities: essays on the 1980s
and prospects for the 1990s / edited by
Susanne MacGregor and Ben Pimlott.
1. Urban policy—Great Britain.   2. Inner cities—Great Britain.
3. Great Britain—Social conditions—1945- .
I. MacGregor, Susanne.   II. Pimlott, Ben, 1945- .
HT133.T33 1990   307.3'42176'0941—dc20   90–6733
p. cm.
ISBN 0–19–827737–7

Set by Hope Services (Abingdon) Ltd.
Printed and bound in
Great Britain by Biddles Ltd,
Guildford & King's Lynn

To

Greg and Sarah Jane

Acknowledgements

This collection of essays has grown from a series of seminars held at Birkbeck College in 1987–8, principally arranged and chaired by Susanne MacGregor, which focused on research on the inner cities question and related policy issues. The volume is also linked through Ben Pimlott with the Birkbeck Public Policy Centre, which provides a forum for discussion of current issues in public policy. Some of the essays were however written separately. A range of opinions are expressed. Though each chapter is very much an individual contribution, an important stage was a lively and expert discussion in the seminar group, composed of professionals and researchers in the field with a wide knowledge of policy problems in London and other urban centres. We would like to thank all those who came to the series and helped to make it a success. We would like to record our special debt to Harriet Lodge whose cheerfulness, quiet efficiency, and creative enthusiasm were vital ingredients both in the organization of the series and in the production of the manuscript. We are also grateful to Adam Crosier and David Grey, who helped as research assistants.

We should like to thank the Controller of Her Majesty's Stationery Office for permission to reprint the diagramme in Chapter 4, 'Exhibit 1', reprinted from Audit Commission Paper No. 2 (1987), *The Management of London's Authorities: Preventing the Breakdown of Services*; and Penguin Books Ltd. for permission to quote at length in Chapter 1 from *Inside the Inner City: Life under the Cutting Edge* by Paul Harrison (1983).

We've got a big job to do in some of those inner cities . . .
and politically, we've got to get back in there—we want to
win those too.

(Mrs Thatcher, election night 1987)

Contents

Figures

Tables

Abbreviations

ARC	Arts and Recreation Committee
BMA	British Medical Association
BCS	British Crime Survey
BES	Business Expansion Scheme
BIC	Business in the Community
CBI	Confederation of British Industry
CDP	Community Development Project
CEPR	Centre for Economic Policy Research
CIPFA	Chartered Institute of Public Finance and Accountancy
CLES	Centre for Local Economic Strategies
CPAG	Child Poverty Action Group
CSO	Central Statistical Office
CTC	City Technology College
DES	Department of Education and Science
DHSS	Department of Health and Social Security
DoE	Department of the Environment
EEC	European Economic Community
EPG	Economic Policy Group
ET	Employment Training
FIS	Family Income Supplement
GDC	Glasgow District Council
GGTB	Greater Glasgow Tourist Board
GHS	General Household Survey
GLC	Greater London Council
GLEB	Greater London Enterprise Board
GRE	Grant Related Expenditure
HAT	Housing Action Trust
HRA	Housing Revenue Account
ICA	Invalid Care Allowance
IEC	Industry and Employment Committee
ILEA	Inner London Education Authority
IMF	International Monetary Fund
LDDC	London Docklands Development Corporation
LEA	Local Education Authority
MXD	Mixed Use Development
NCC	National Curriculum Council

NCVO	National Council for Voluntary Organizations
OECD	Organization for Economic Co-operation and Development
OPCS	Office of Population Censuses and Surveys
RCCO	Revenue Contributions to Capital Outlay
RFC	Rate Fund Contributions
RPI	Retail Price Index
RSG	Rate Support Grant
SDA	Scottish Development Agency
SMR	Standardized Mortality Ratio
UDC	Urban Development Corporation

List of Contributors

editors Susanne MacGregor and Ben Pimlott

SUSANNE MACGREGOR is Senior Lecturer in Political Sociology in the Department of Politics and Sociology, Birkbeck College, University of London. She has researched widely in the field of politics and social policy, focusing on responses to homelessness, unemployment, drug-taking, and poverty. She has written *The Politics of Poverty* (1981), *Dealing with Drug Misuse: Crisis Intervention in the City* (1984) (with Anne Jamieson and Alan Glanz), and *The Poll Tax and the Enterprise Culture* (1988), and has edited *Drugs and British Society* (1989).

BEN PIMLOTT is Professor of Politics and Contemporary History in the Department of Politics and Sociology, Birkbeck College, University of London. He is the author of *Labour and the Left in the 1930s* (1977) and *Hugh Dalton* (1985) which won the Whitbread Biography Award. He has edited, or joint edited, several collections of essays, and he was researched and written on the politics of unemployment. He has been a political columnist on *The Times*, the *Sunday Times* and the *New Statesman*.

JOHN BENYON is Senior Lecturer in Politics and Public Administration in the Departments of Adult Education and Politics at the University of Leicester, and Director of the Centre for the Study of Public Order. He has carried out research on public order, policing, and race relations. He has co-edited *Scarman and After* (1984), *The Police: Powers, Procedures and Proprieties* (1986), and *The Roots of Urban Unrest* (1987).

FRANCO BIANCHINI is the co-author of *City Centres, City Cultures* (1988) and the author of various articles and book chapters on the urban cultural policy of the Left in Italy and Britain since the late 1970s. He is currently working at the Centre for Urban Studies, University of Liverpool, on a major research project (funded by the Leverhulme Trust) on economic regeneration in post-industrial cities.

JOHN GIBSON is a Lecturer at the Institute of Local Government Studies, University of Birmingham and he is the author of *Block Grant: A Study in Central–Local Relations* (1986) and numerous articles in the field of local government finance, including several on the poll tax.

HILARY LAND is Professor of Social Policy at Royal Holloway and Bedford New College, University of London. Her main research and teaching interests involve the political economy of social policy and in particular feminist analysis of the relationship between the family and the state.

DAVID MALLEN is the Education Officer of the Inner London Education Authority. He has also worked as an officer in Coventry, having earlier taught in Rochdale and Salford. He is the author of *Local Government and Politics* (1978; 2nd edition, 1987) with M. Cross.

DOREEN MASSEY is Professor of Geography, Faculty of Social Science at the Open University. She has researched and written extensively on unemployment, regional problems, and economic policy. She was a Member of the Board of the Greater London Enterprise Board.

NICK RAYNSFORD, Member of Parliament for Fulham 1986–7, is probably best known for his work and expertise in the housing field. Before becoming an MP he was Director of SHAC for ten years and played a leading role in the campaign for legislation to extend homeless people's rights. Since the 1987 General Election he has been working as a housing consultant.

ROBERT REINER teaches criminology in the Law Department of the London School of Economics and Political Science. He was formerly Reader in Criminology at Bristol and Brunel Universities. He is author of *The Blue-Coated Worker* (1978) and *The Politics of the Police* (1985).

JOHN SOLOMOS is Lecturer in Public Policy in the Department of Politics and Sociology, Birkbeck College, University of London.

He has researched widely in the field of the politics of racial inequality, youth unemployment, equal opportunity, urban unrest,
and local politics. He has written *Black Youth, Racism and the State*
(1988) and *Race and Racism in Contemporary Britain* (1989), and has co-
edited *Racism and Equal Opportunity Policies in the 1980s* (1987) and
The Roots of Urban Unrest (1987).

PETER TOWNSEND has been studying poverty and inequality for
over thirty years. He is the leading writer in this field in the United
Kingdom. His many books include *The Poor and the Poorest* (1965)
(with Brian Abel-Smith), *Poverty in the United Kingdom: A Study of
Household Resources and Standards of Living* (1979), and *Inequalities in
Health. The Black Report* (edited and with an introduction) (1982)
(with Nick Davidson). He is Professor of Social Policy at the
University of Bristol.

Action and Inaction in the Cities

Susanne MacGregor and Ben Pimlott

The essays in this book do not amount to a programme: but they are intended to provide a springboard for one. The aim is to analyse a problem which economic growth alone has failed to cure—and to consider possible new forms of public action.

The biggest single difficulty in drawing attention to urban poverty is that it is not new, but simply—in some of its most worrying manifestations—getting worse. Like the poor themselves, the inner city has long been with us. Ever since the Industrial Revolution created a mass urban society, the conditions of the poorest city dwellers have given rise to anxiety among the better off. The inner city has been variously regarded as a cause for moral outrage, a threat to public order, or as a stain on the nation's conscience. Meanwhile bad housing, bad sanitation, lack of education, and other perennial ills associated with overcrowding and poverty have been routinely denounced by political leaders and social reformers.

A central objective of the post-war welfare state was, indeed, to alleviate the problems of the urban poor, over whom Beveridge's Five Giants (Want, Disease, Ignorance, Squalor, and Idleness) had for so long held sway. In the early 1940s and 1950s, the belief was widely held that a combination of government intervention—in the form of town planning, housing and health programmes, and the provision of social security—and permanent male full employment, together with an increase in real wages, would reduce suffering due to poverty to manageable proportions. The 1964 Labour Government was elected on a tide of impatience at the slackening pace of social reform, but also of optimism that little more than economic growth, fuelled by technological change, was needed to remove the main causes of urban deprivation (MacGregor, 1981).

Disillusion swiftly followed. The work of Peter Townsend and others showed that, far from presiding over the elimination of poverty, the Wilson Government actually failed to prevent some of its features from worsening (Townsend and Bosanquet, 1972). Evidence began to mount that much of the social welfare paternalism of the post-war period had created almost as many problems as it solved. Neither the Butler Education Act of 1944, nor the introduction of comprehensive schools, prevented a high proportion of children from under-achieving. Post-war reconstruction and housing programmes seemed to do nothing to prevent, and seemed even to encourage, a rise in crime and mental illness. Meanwhile, in many parts of the country, a problem as old as cities themselves—tension between cultural groups, between earlier immigrants and newer ones, between black, brown, and white, and (increasingly) between large sections of urban youth and the police—came to be identified as the key inner-city issue.

Rising unemployment turned a lingering and growing malaise into a crisis. As in the United States, so in Britain it was an outbreak of violence that dramatically brought the plight of the inner cities to public notice. In the early 1980s, at a time when manufacturing industry was collapsing and the outlook for the unskilled looked particularly bleak, frustration boiled over in a series of riots in London, Bristol, Birmingham, Liverpool, and elsewhere. All were spontaneous outbursts: none, contrary to some claims, were politically inspired or orchestrated (except in Northern Ireland where urban problems existed on a grander, more devastating scale, and where there was a unique heritage). Many had an 'ethnic' dimension, in the sense that many of the rioters were black. Unlike, however, the 1958 Notting Hill riots, few of those involved were immigrants—the vast majority were British born. And the disturbances could not strictly be called racial: the most prominent feature was that of violent clashes between young people and the police.

The problems, however, were not confined to violent upheavals of this kind. Paul Harrison's *Inside the Inner City: Life under the Cutting Edge* focused on Hackney, a London borough ranked among the worst off on any scale of urban deprivation

(Harrison, 1983). Harrison describes (p. 369) the way in which the inner urban powder-keg leads to a vicious circle, with many victims, but few individual villains:

The police force face the virtually impossible task of keeping the lid on the explosive mixture of ingredients that the dynamics of British society have assembled in the inner city. This mixture, heated by recession and high unemployment, inevitably generates a high level of crime. This necessitates, in turn, a far more numerous and ubiquitous police presence than in other kinds of area, far more frequent unpleasant contact with the public as potential suspects, and far greater opportunities for police misjudgment or abuse.

The inevitable sufferers, of course, are the poor, of whom those who actually commit the offences that concern the police are a tiny minority and whom, indeed, it should be the purpose of the police to protect. Not only are the most disadvantaged on the receiving end of most crime, argues Harrison, they also have to put up with the heaviest police presence. They are more likely to be stopped and searched, and to be the victim of mistaken arrest or conviction. At the same time, the residents of the poorest areas have to suffer, in a way that is not true of those who live elsewhere, a growing fear of attack on themselves or their property. Improved police methods might help, writes Harrison, to contain the problem. But, without other changes, the result is likely to be a 'society of barricaded self-defence, and a steady erosion of civil liberties'. And he concludes, 'of all the warnings that the inner city has to offer for the direction British society is taking, this is perhaps the most sinister'.

Harrison's vision of a nightmarish future for inner cities, locked in a cold or hot war between have-nots and the forces of public order, was echoed by Robert Chesshyre (1987, p. 95), who concluded that by the late 1980s:

The basic social contract, whereby citizens enjoy certain rights—including health care, decent education and housing and a job—in return for which they observe the rule of law, was breaking down. As a consequence an underclass was evolving—football hooligans, muggers, inner city rioters—somewhat more frightening than their Dickensian forebears because they were mobile and all too visible.

Recently, of course, there has been an added dimension—part media-and-politician inflated, part real: drugs. The spiral in drug abuse and trafficking, with direct consequences for the AIDS epidemic, has created a new kind of alarm. The early 1980s witnessed a radical change in patterns of heroin taking, alongside the global increase. Smoking heroin ('chasing the dragon') was one feature of the upsurge. Another was the increased availability of, and demand for, cocaine. Sensational media and police reports in 1989 seemed to suggest an increased use of 'crack' among young people in parts of south London, Liverpool, and Birmingham—with attendant fears that this particularly dangerous substance might become widespread, as it was reported to be in parts of the United States. For the moment, however, the pattern of drug abuse in Britain remains as varied as ever—with home-produced drugs such as amphetamines as serious a problem as those that hit the headlines. It is a symptom of public anxiety about urban squalor—and, less creditably, of class and racial prejudice—that 'drugs' and 'inner cities' are automatically linked in the popular consciousness (MacGregor, 1989*a*). Nevertheless, drug-taking and more particularly the disruptive social consequences of addiction, are especially serious in areas of city poverty (Burr, 1989).

In short, if life was always harder in the inner cities than elsewhere, and if conditions may temporarily have been alleviated by the impact of the welfare state and rising incomes, the last decade has been widely represented as a period of deterioration. Moreover, few would dispute that this apparent decline is a reality: the first words of the Prime Minister herself, after the result of the 1987 election was known, were an acknowledgement of the challenge posed to Government by the 'inner cities'. What has been lacking however—as well as the political will to do something—has been any shared agreement on the cause. Can the problems of urban poverty be blamed on individual pathology? On feckless parents and grandparents? Or on the social or physical environment—the replacement of companionably unhygienic slums by soulless tower blocks with broken lifts (Coleman *et al.*, 1985)? Or would a simple injection of resources transform Kafkaesque honeycombs into happy living-spaces, with a consequent decline in inner-city ills? 'A duke can live comfortably in a castle, after all', the architect Cedric Price is quoted as saying. 'You and I would die of frostbite. Same building—just a matter of money and management' (Parkin, 1989).

The view that only 'outstanding management' could meet the problem was held by the Audit Commission (1987). The picture painted by the Commission's report on inner London is as gruesome as any ever presented (and is itself revealing of common prejudices in its choice of indicators of deprivation):

In some London boroughs, unemployment among young men exceeds 45%; in some places, among young blacks, it exceeds 60%. More than one child in three is born into a single parent family. Half the school leavers have no O levels or their CSE equivalents. Homelessness, housing conditions, crime are worsening year by year, as the cycle of urban deprivation becomes more established (p. 1)

Drawing on North American experience, the Commission concluded that 'poor management was an important contributory factor to New York's problems', and sought to apply the same lessons here (p. 2).

The Government's post-1987 initiatives have, to some extent, reflected a diagnosis based on the need for better management—though on the principle that central authorities can provide a firmer grip than local ones—but combined with an anti-collectivist belief in the restorative powers of capitalism. Leech and Amin (1988, p. 14) summarize this approach, not unfairly, in the following terms:

the encouragement of private investment and the liberation of the market; the containment of the forces of social discontent; the control of the powers of the local authorities; and the encouragement of the movement of the wealthy into the inner city thus creating buffer areas of Tory support, accentuating inequalities and injustice and (hopefully though not necessarily) reducing the potential for conflict among the urban poor.

The main thrust of the Government's policy is contained in the January 1988 White Paper on Regional Policy and the Enterprise Economy, in the new Employment Training Programme, and especially in the March 1988 *Action for Cities* programme—all resting on wider reforms to local government structure and finance, and to education and housing. The most striking feature of this package, apart from its aim actively to involve employers and entrepreneurs, is a sharp reduction in the role of local government.

Despite the contemporary tone of much of *Action for Cities*, the programme's heritage can be traced to the early 1960s studies which provided the basis for the 1965 Milner–Holland Report on housing and the 1967 Plowden Report on education, as a result of which general improvement areas and education priority areas were established. The 1970s 'Urban Programme' had a social, rather than economic, emphasis and was administered by the Home Office. It was initiated partly in response to the furore caused by Enoch Powell's 1969 'rivers of blood' speech, much as disturbances at the 1976 Notting Hill Carnival prompted further steps on the part of the Department of the Environment—'A riot makes a much bigger impact on government thinking', as Donnison (1987) has pointed out, 'than any amount of earnest and accurate research'. The Urban Programme consisted of grants and initiatives under the 1969 Local Government Grants (Social Need) Act, which was intended as a flexible instrument to provide supplementary help to local authorities in the fields of housing, education, and health. Originally, the Programme supplemented existing central and local government schemes designed to meet special needs in urban areas. The scope was extended in an 'enhanced' Urban Programme, which included economic and environmental as well as social projects, and was specifically directed at the inner urban areas where the problems were most severe. Earlier, the change of emphasis from a 'social' to an 'economic and environmental' focus had been reflected in a switch of responsibility for the Programme from the Home Office to the Department of the Environment.

The 'enhanced' Programme resulted from the 1978 Inner Urban Areas Act, based on a White Paper, published the previous year, on *Policy for the Inner Cities* (DoE, 1977), the first comprehensive policy statement on the subject to acknowledge it as a definable and cohesive problem. The White Paper drew on studies conducted earlier in the decade in Liverpool, Birmingham, and London which pointed to a debilitating flight of capital and skilled labour from the critical areas of deprivation.

A key aspect of the 1977 White Paper was the stress it placed on the wider effects of poverty: that it was not just those with acute needs who suffered. It argued that in talking about inner cities it was vital to think in terms not just of individuals, but of society; that the multiple deprivations of the worst hit areas affected all the residents; that the consequences included a pervasive sense of neglect and decay, a decline in community spirit, a low standard of neighbourhood facilities, and an increase in crime and vandalism; and that, without government intervention, the future was one of reduced job opportunities, deteriorating housing, and a decline in public services. The document, and the legislation that derived from it, pointed to a positively discriminatory approach: with both central and local government supplementing existing programmes in such a way as to strengthen local economies, as well as the physical and social environment.

Such measures constituted the present Government's heritage, when it took office in 1979. None of them, of course, anticipated the scale of the problems which were caused by the slump and collapse of much of what remained of inner urban manufacturing industry in the early 1980s. Neither, at first, did the incoming administration foresee the impact of rising unemployment, which was to be especially serious among the urban young. True, the new Secretary of State for the Environment laid stress, from the outset, on the need for economic regeneration, and indicated his sympathy for the voluntary sector in the tackling of urban problems. The previous Government, however, had already pointed to the need to revitalize urban economies, and at first the shift was more rhetorical than real.

Michael Heseltine (1987, p. 138) has since claimed that 'we set a new objective: to make the inner cities places where people would want to live and work and where the private investor would be willing to put his money'. *Partnership* became his slogan—the partnership of public and private brains and money. A new Urban Development Grant was devised, to pump-prime with public funds schemes which would then attract private investment. Heseltine's vision was of 'partnerships which recognise that there are some things that only governments can pay for, but also that the ingenuity and flexibility of the private sector is indispensable' (p. 156). He claims that serious work on inner-city policy began in 1979: but it was, undoubtedly, the riots of 1981, coinciding with the biggest drop in employment and job vacancies since the war, which gave impetus to the new approach. Urban Development Corporations were introduced in 1981 in London Docklands and Merseyside, and the Urban Development Grant came in late the following year.

Conservative instincts were, of course, to minimize—within the 'partnership'—state involvement and expenditure, relative to that of private enterprise. Yet, the irony of the early 1980s—as a deteriorating, but perennial, urban problem rapidly became the most acute aspect of the crisis of mass unemployment—was that a Tory government, willy-nilly, found itself presiding over an increase in state intervention through a variety of agencies. The increased scale of operations also ushered in another fashion of the 1980s—new management structures. Thus in 1985 City Action Teams were introduced to each 'Inner City Partnership' area to co-ordinate the work of the three government departments involved. Task Forces, meanwhile, were directed to tackle youth unemployment. By 1986/7 the Urban Programme was supporting 1,380 starter units and 400 business starts in enterprise workshops. It was providing 27,500 training places (often in conjunction with the Manpower Services Commission): some 2,500 buildings were being improved; estate action aimed to tackle run down housing; and a large number of new 'partnerships' (which some might see as subsidies, or discredited regional grants, in a new guise) were in operation, in an effort to bring private investment to run-down urban areas. By 1988 it was claimed that £200 million of Urban Development Grant and Urban Regeneration Grant had successfully 'levered' more than £800 million of private investment into the inner cities (although how much of the latter sum might have been invested in any case is difficult to say). Meanwhile, there were other incentive schemes—Enterprise Zones, for example, and simplified Planning Zones, which aimed to lift tax and planning 'barriers' in order to facilitate investment. Indeed, while with one hand trying to hold down expenditure by local authorities, the Government found itself by the late 1980s involved with the other hand in massive ear-marked spending on inner urban areas. The Department of the Environment alone by 1988 was spending half a billion pounds out of an Action for Cities total, involving most Home departments, estimated at £3 billion. Perhaps a Labour government would have spent even more: it would certainly have spent it in different ways. It is a curious comment on Thatcherism, however, that the administration most committed to a reduction in the role of the state, and in the need for an independent private sector, has spent more on *specific* urban regeneration and employment schemes and incentives to private investment in urban areas than any other in recent history.

One of the most bizarre aspects of government policy has been the effective murder of the voluntary sector, and its appropriation, by subterfuge, into the Tory version of the corporate state. Conservatives have always lauded the 'voluntarist' principle in welfare, and encouraged it from platforms. Faced, however, with the catastrophic increase in unemployment and the need to occupy large numbers of workless people without directly employing them (which would have run counter to the economic doctrine which had led to the redundancy of many of them in the first place), the Government poured money into any 'voluntary' agency willing to put in a bid for government-funded cheap labour. One result was the triumphant expansion of some charitable organizations, which rejoiced both at their new-found importance and at the Government's munificence. Another was the transformation of many such bodies, already heavily subsidized from public funds, into *de facto* agencies of the state, which financed them and indirectly determined their policy. Nowhere was the impact of this clumsy sleight of hand more evident than in the inner cities, where voluntary organizations had been most active, and where the Government was most anxious for them to mop up unemployment. However, the later withdrawal of government support, with the scrapping of the Community Programme as unemployment receded, left many of these voluntary organizations high and dry. The National Council for Voluntary Organizations (NCVO) has suggested from a recent survey that around 3,000 projects had been affected and had lost £285 million in funding (MacGregor, 1990).

There was, of course, a crucial element in the Government's anxiety: the high concentration of ethnic minorities in the areas of concern. In 1981 nearly 40 per cent of ethnic minorities in the UK lived in 'partnership' or 'programme' areas. There is a danger in reading back from this figure another stereotype, similar to the Pavlovian 'drug addiction/inner city' assumed link. Some urban areas have serious problems without a major ethnic dimension (Newcastle, Teesside); not all members of ethnic minorities are poor or deprived. Nevertheless, the high proportion of inner urban populations composed of people from ethnic minorities, and the high incidence among these groups of all the indices of poverty and social and environmental hardship—combined with the specific problem of inter-racial rivalry, harassment, and tension—make race and ethnicity an aspect that is central to any analysis of the inner cities and of any ameliorative approach.

It was with the aim of contributing to such an improvement, as the representative body of employers and business investors, that the 1988 Confederation of British Industry (CBI) Task Force on business and urban regeneration came to three conclusions: first (in line with the Government's own beliefs), that business must take the lead in reversing urban decline; second, that charity—governmental or voluntary—cannot in itself deal with problems, and any regeneration must spring from private investment, commercially motivated; and third, that the potential exists for such investment, provided that early projects are seen to succeed (CBI, 1988). Echoing the Government, the CBI stressed the 'partnership' theme, involving developers and (for the CBI) local authorities. Leadership in such ventures, however, should come from businessmen, not local government.

The essence of the CBI approach—as it admits, and as the Government approves—is enlightened self-interest: salvation will only come when investors want to invest, not when well-meaning local politicians and bureaucrats decide that they ought to do so. Notably absent from the CBI's understanding of the problems of inner cities was any notion that they should be met by national economic policy. The assumption, rather, was one of special, even isolated, blackspots that can be dealt with by localized attention.

As an organization of businessmen, the CBI—naturally perhaps—looked on the inner city primarily as a business opportunity. Thus a special report of the CBI London Region Urban Regeneration Task Force in October 1988 concluded that there was a need for partnerships in which government, local authorities, teachers, church leaders, and residents would all play a part, but with business taking the lead—helped by government subsidy or pump-priming. The bottom line to private investment remains, as always, the extent and nature of government funding.

One paradoxical consequence of central government limits to rate support grant was a real-money leap in business rates in some areas, and a sizeable increase in the proportion of local budgets paid through rates by the business community. This heightened business interest in local spending and revenue raising, and fermented anxiety about the operation of the uniform business rate and the community charge: the CBI, previously concerned about fluctuating rates, is now concerned about the commercial consequences of fluctuating services, as local authorities try to manage their finances. To the CBI's worries about the future of the inner city is added a very real concern that business services may be placed high on the list for cuts by budget-chopping local authorities. While echoing the Government's 'partnership' theme in its rhetoric, and paying dutiful lip service to the principle of *laissez-faire*, the coded message of the CBI is an urgent demand for more government funding, not less. So far, the Government has been unreceptive.

In addition to the Audit Commission and the CBI, Business in the Community (BIC) has taken up the theme of 'partnership'. The problem, however, is turning phrases that are warmly applauded at rotary club or chamber of commerce lunches into serious investment. Why should genuine money-makers bother? 'We all like to be liked', as one Northern businessman recently put it. 'But, in reality . . . what we are doing is serving our own best interests. . . . The more successful the town and country is the more chance we as individuals have of being successful.' The trouble is, however, that the linking of individual with group self-interest is not a sufficient incentive for smaller firms struggling to make a profit, nor indeed for large, profitable organizations. One of the causes of the inner-city crisis has, precisely, been the withering of the 'Victorian value' of civic philanthropy which once encouraged locally-based businesses to link commercial considerations with the welfare of the wider community. It is naïve to imagine that such an ethic can be revived by exhortation alone, or by the use of an uplifting but empty phraseology.

It is possible, indeed, to turn the logic of the opponents of traditional regional policy and incentives, and of the proponents of a 'partnership' approach, on its head. 'Partnership' is an acknowledgement that business will not invest without encouragement, combined with a view that long-term investment needs to be self-sustaining. But if the aim is to encourage serious investment, there is also a need for serious spending on infrastructure and services, as well as for start-up finance or subsidy. There is a need, above all, for an environment in which a fledgling (or established) business will feel comfortable and wish to remain, because of local amenities and because of the availability of a healthy, happy, well-equipped workforce.

It is certainly arguable (and many progressive employers would agree) that the wisest use of public money from a strictly economic point of view would be on schools, houses, and medical services, together with relevant training and measures to reduce discrimination; in short, that the agencies which most obviously have the capacity to produce strategic planning of a business-friendly kind are precisely those which this pro-business administration wishes to bypass—central government departments, and local government, properly funded.

That, more or less, was the conclusion reached by the 1985 report of the Archbishop of Canterbury's Commission on Urban Priority Areas, *Faith in the City* (1985), a remarkable document roundly condemned by some Conservatives for its alleged implicit Marxism. Focusing on economic decline, physical decay, and social disintegration as distinctive features of contemporary urban poverty, the report stressed the Commission's view—quite different from that of the Government, the Audit Commission, or even the CBI—that 'the inner city and the peripheral estates are creatures of the whole society, not simply of their inhabitants' (p. 24). It dared to question the assumption that the creation of wealth, at whatever social cost, was necessarily the first priority of an economic system. Contemplating 'the displaced fragments of inner city decline'—peripheral council estates—it suggested that wealth-creation 'must always go hand in hand with just distribution'—offering, thereby, an alternative interpretation of 'partnership' (p. 53). It commented, too, on the environmental and ecological consequences. For the Archbishop's commissioners, partnership needed to mean not just a link-up between business and the public or voluntary sectors, but a conscious attempt to meet the powerlessness felt by the 'people in the street' (p. 186). The Archbishop's investigators did not search for, or embrace, a fashionable solution. On the contrary. Their main call was for a return to the 1977 White Paper, namely: 'a specific commitment on the part of central and local government to the regeneration of the inner areas . . . both central and local government will be judged by their willingness to implement new priorities, to make funds available, to change policies and to adapt their organisations' (DoE, 1977, para. 25). *Faith in the City* concluded bluntly that the 1977 White Paper's 'policy proposals have not been tried and found wanting. They have not been tried' (Archbishop of Canterbury's Commission, 1985, p. 193). So far from treating the problems of the inner city as local difficulties which a bit of capitalist enterprise could clear up, it regarded them as evidence of systemic failure.

The retreat from the principles of the 1977 White Paper occurred in the context of the economic crisis of the 1970s, which culminated in the 1976 resort to the International Monetary Fund. The scale of expenditure on all aspects of local government, and the greatly increased proportion of total public expenditure which it represented, meant that, when the crisis came, some were led to blame local authorities, and in the cuts that followed inner cities inevitably suffered most acutely.

A serious blow, of course, was also dealt to the reputation of the Labour Party, which controlled many of the councils with the greatest needs and which made the heaviest demands on the public purse, and whose members were least apologetic about doing so. When Anthony Crosland declared that the 'party is over' he cannot have realized that the Government's cuts presaged a long period in which the Labour Party itself would be seriously threatened—partly because of its association with supposedly spendthrift urban policies. In the early and mid-1980s a handful of 'municipal socialist' Labour councils (triumphantly declared 'loony' by Norman Tebbit and the right-wing press) were used as a symbol of the party's alleged financial irresponsibility. With Labour welfarism out of fashion, and neo-liberalism in vogue, the scene was set, not only for the downgrading of local authority power (including the outright abolition of the Greater London Council and the metropolitan authorities which, though actually limited in their spending power, were nevertheless the co-ordinators and vocal champions of many inner urban schemes), but also for the injection of national party dogma into the management of local affairs.

'This Government is a radical government with a radical message . . .', wrote Secretary of State Nicholas Ridley (1988, p. 32). 'Conservatives have a strong localist tradition, but the danger of too much localism is that the Party's voice and through the Party the political interpretation of the Government's voice is not heard.' This was one 'problem', at least, which the present administration has proved highly successful at solving. So dramatic, indeed, has been the impact of privatization and contracting out of services, and of other local government changes, that a reduction of over a third in the total number of local authority employees over the next five years has been predicted by one senior official (Davies, 1988).

It remains to be seen whether the restructuring will save money, or merely shift essential expenditure between agencies, or simply reduce available services. What it will not do, of course, is tackle the inner-city problem—nor indeed is it designed to do so. If there ever was a Thatcherite economic miracle, it has, to an alarmingly divisive degree, passed the urban poor by. Jobless growth, changes in the composition of the workforce, increased 'flexibility' of labour's terms and conditions, have all contributed to an economic revival which has had minimal benefits where these are needed most. 'The effect has been to reinforce the concentration of unemployment in traditional inner city areas', the Centre for Local Economic Strategies (CLES) reported in *Local Work* (1988), 'and in the regions which were already suffering the worst unemployment before 1979.' Yet the critical question for the 1990s and the twenty-first century remains unanswered: is there an approach—through central government intervention, decentralization, the encouragement of participation, or any other method—which avoids the insensitivities of bureaucratic welfarism, and yet produces results?

PROGRAMME FOR THE 1990s

Responding to this question—by asking new questions as much as by offering solutions—is the purpose of this book. It is, indeed, a great deal easier to point out the irrelevance of much of what is happening at the moment than to have confidence in any particular alternative. Still, some things may be said with reasonable assurance.

Almost everyone agrees, for instance, that enterprise zones alone are of limited value, that tax incentives are relatively ineffective and deregulation is no solution. Despite government rhetoric, the impact of such measures on people rather than places—as several authors in this volume show—has been marginal. Contributors also agree on another point: that public expenditure and public services based on principles of universalism and citizenship for all are central to any real programme.

The chapters in this book deliberately provide a balance between experts with direct political or administrative experience of the areas they describe (such as Nick Raynsford and David Mallen) and academic observers. Several contributors have both political/administrative and academic credentials. The original intention was to provide a critical accompaniment to government promises of action on the inner cities made at the beginning of this Parliament. Out of them, however, has emerged the kernel of a view of the future. If there is a consistent bias in favour of public intervention and against inertia, there is also, we hope, little shirking of awkward issues—though the collection does not claim to be comprehensive, and there are aspects of a huge topic that are barely touched.

What the book does attempt to do is to provide a framework of problems and ideas, exploring major themes. Some chapters look at the manifestations of urban breakdown—John Benyon and John Solomos writing about racial conflict and disorder, for example—others, like Robert Reiner, at the evidence on rising crime rates and the complex ethical dilemmas which are often presented as simple. Several contributors are concerned with how urban dwellers actually live their lives: Peter Townsend, for example, shows the impact of social polarization upon health and well-being by indicating differential rates of mortality and morbidity, and the widening gap between the experiences of rich and poor.

Others look at local government and central–local relations in practice. Susanne MacGregor points to the impact of a growing climate of social conservatism, a climate that is encouraged by aspects of government policy. John Gibson highlights the regressive aspects of recent local government financial reform, and predicts dire consequences for the urban poor. The chances of the new system of local government finance surviving for long seem slim. Particular services are examined by two writers closely involved with implementation: Nick Raynsford looks at recent developments in policies on housing, and David Mallen considers how education might effectively be used as a key instrument of social improvement. Hilary Land examines women's systematic loss of rights and claims for social protection and its effect on the family and children during the 1980s. She demonstrates that policies of amelioration will do no more than touch the surface unless fundamental gender inequalities are addressed.

A consistent underlying theme is that a reliance on market forces cannot be the answer: in every area, public action is urgently needed. Alternative approaches are reviewed by Franco Bianchini, who points to the potential role of an adequately funded arts programme in fostering civic pride and countering alienation, and Doreen Massey who emphasizes the need for a combination of progressive national and local economic strategies.

She turns the Government's self-help approach around by arguing that urban recovery will only be achieved by empowering the people who live in cities. Her final essay, indeed, echoes the theme of the whole book: the focus must be on democracy and on a sensitivity to local and individual needs and aspirations.

In the early post-war period, the British welfare state was thought to be the envy of much of the industrialized world. Today, it is a cause for embarrassment, especially in the context of moves towards European integration. One reason is relative economic decline. Another is the failure of vision of successive governments, Labour and Conservative, since 1951. A third—since 1979—has been a conscious—and accelerating—ambition to limit public provision.

To a large extent, however, fashionable doctrine has been the excuse for actual incompetence and neglect. There has been a consistent failure to direct the fruits of growth to the areas, industries, and groups that need it most. Outside London and the South-East, mass unemployment persists even among 'prime-age males', and much of the increase in employment has taken the form of low-paid, so-called 'part-time' work usually undertaken by women in addition to their child-rearing and 'community care' activities. Contempt for the public sector has led to a deterioration of the infrastructure, and a visible collapse of key public services. Meanwhile, as Layard and Nickell (1989) have shown, Britain's recent record on education and training has been notably inadequate.

The pragmatic short-term remedies suggested by W. J. Wilson (1987) in his study of inner cities and public policy in the United States could serve as one starting-point for discussion of policy in Britain. Wilson warns of the long-term effects of discriminatory policies. 'Long periods of racial oppression', he writes, 'can result in a system of inequality that may persist for indefinite periods of time even after racial barriers are removed' (p. 146). Bad policies in the past may continue to cause problems, long after they have been replaced by good ones. Similar problems follow from centuries of unequal treatment of men and women. Conversely, positive policies should not be abandoned because they do not show immediate miraculous results. What the Right regards as wasteful—'throwing money at the problem'—in terms of, for example, income support to the unwaged, non-means-tested family and child benefits, may actually be a prudent investment in the future, with social and economic dividends. Wilson's conclusion—in favour of universal programmes—is one that needs to be reasserted for many areas of policy in Britain.

Here, too, Richard Titmuss's exposure of the inadequacies of the 'residual' model of the welfare state bears re-examination: so does his healthy disrespect for econometric models as a foundation for social policy. It is not just that a 'market' approach to the administration of services dehumanizes people and makes doubtful assumptions about the way organizations actually work. It also ignores the complexity and variability of social relations and human needs, 'chopping people up' into consumers of this, clients of that, institutionalized service. Thus, Titmuss ridiculed the contortions of some economists in trying to base models on unreal statistical categories, such as that of the ubiquitous 'average family' (Abel-Smith and Titmuss, 1987, p. 9).

In spite of their claims, 'targeted' programmes frequently miss some of their most needy would-be clients, and stigmatize those they do succeed in reaching: selectivist policies deepen social divisions rather than heal them. Such programmes treat people as consumers in a supermarket, an approach which is the hallmark of Thatcherite social policy best epitomized in their poll tax legislation. Another, more fundamental lack is the absence of a view of the recipients of services as social participants. An obsession with cutting costs and with theories of self-help has downgraded public services and re-evoked images of the poor law.

There is no simple way to turn local administration—which increasingly means delegated central administration—into what John Stewart and Gerry Stoker (1988) call 'community government'. Participation is an easier word to use than to implement, as was discovered by the would-be implementers of the 1969 Skeffington Report, and by many idealistic councillors in the 1980s. But to say that it is hard does not make it less desirable, neither does it mean that governments should abandon the attempt. What is clear is that civic or community pride—essential if urban decline is not to turn into urban collapse—and the view of local government as an honourable profession, cannot survive unless the public service which local authorities provide rests on principles of local democracy. Simply handing over powers to local government (or stopping the removal of them) is not enough. But it is the *sine qua non* of progress towards a more sensitive management of urban affairs. Decentralization and local democracy should be the slogans of all who are concerned about the inner city.

CONCLUSION

The essays in this book do not present a monolithic view, and they reflect widely differing perspectives. However, they share common perceptions, as we have already indicated. Though they are neither statist nor paternalist, the authors see a larger role for democratic central and local government in the reduction of urban poverty. They do not—as this administration, despite its early assurances, appears to do—regard urban life as marginal to the issue of economic progress. On the contrary, they place the crisis in the inner cities at the centre of any national programme— of critical importance to this country's future social, economic, and constitutional well-being. They see urban decay not as a peripheral manifestation nor as a growing pain, but as a chronic condition of social polarization that is becoming firmly entrenched in British society. The authors are unconvinced that a reliance on business, left to its own devices or even pump-primed, is sufficient, without full-scale and direct attention to the needs of all residents, those in both the paid and the unpaid workforce, and their dependants.

In the ancient world, during the Middle Ages and Renaissance, even in the twentieth century, the word 'city' was frequently associated with wealth, success, culture, and opportunity. The word 'civilization' itself—and the word 'citizen'—derives from it. It is a bitter indictment of our own time that the phrase 'inner city' should today universally conjure up images of disorder, poverty, fear, vandalism, and alienation. If capitalism can be credited with historic levels of prosperity for many, the inner city is the cockroach at its heart. Homelessness, drug addiction, beggars in the streets give the lie to the assumption that the standardized values and comforts of the suburbs are universally available. This book does not pretend to offer an answer. Its authors seek, rather, by challenging old approaches and re-analysing the problem, both to assert its importance and to suggest new ways of tackling it.

Ben Pimlott wishes to acknowledge the support of the British Academy and Nuffield Foundation for research on unemployment policy.

References

Abel-Smith, B., and Titmuss, K. (eds.) (1987). *The Philosophy of Welfare: Selected Writings of Richard M. Titmuss*, introd. by S. M. Miller (London).

Archbishop of Canterbury's Commission on Urban Priority Areas (1985), *Faith in the City: A Call for Action by Church and Nation* (London).

Audit Commission (1987), *The Management of London's Authorities: Preventing the Breakdown of Services*, Occasional Paper, No. 2 (London).

Beveridge, Sir W. (1942), *The Beveridge Report: Social Insurance and Allied Services*, Cmnd. 6404 (London).

Booth, General W. (1890), *In Darkest England and the Way Out* (London).

Burr, A. (1989), 'An inner city community response to heroin use', in S. MacGregor (ed.), *Drugs and British Society* (London).

CBI (Confederation of British Industry) (1988), *Initiatives Beyond Charity: Report of the CBI Task Force on Business and Urban Regeneration* (London).

Chesshyre, R. (1987), *The Return of a Native Reporter* (London).

Coleman, A., Brown, S., Cottle, L., Marshall, P., Redknap, C., and Sex, R. (1985), *Utopia on Trial* (London).

Davies, H. (1988), 'Local government under siege', *Public Administration*, 66 1, Spring, 91–101.

DoE (Department of the Environment) (1977), *Policy for the Inner Cities*, Cmnd. 6845 (London).

Donnison, D. (1987), 'The new Tory frontier', *Observer*, 20 Sept.

Engels, F. (1845), *The Condition of the Working Class in England*, trans. and ed. W. O. Henderson and W. H. Chaloner (Oxford, 1981).

Harrison, P. (1983), *Inside the Inner City: Life under the Cutting Edge* (Harmondsworth).

Heseltine, M. (1987), *Where There's a Will* (London).
Layard, R., and Nickell, S. (1989), 'The Thatcher miracle', CEPR Discussion Paper (London).
Leech, K., and Amin, K. (1988), 'A new underclass? Race, poverty and the inner city', *Poverty*, 70, 11–14.
MacGregor, S. (1989a), 'The public debate in the 1980s', in S. MacGregor (ed.), *Drugs and British Society* (London).
—— (1990), 'Strategies for the Nineties: The voluntary sector and the State', Greater Manchester Council for Voluntary Services (Manchester).
Parkin, M. (1989), 'Dark days in Deptford', *Weekend Guardian*, 14–15 Jan., 7.
Ridley, N. (1988), *The Local Right, Enabling not Providing*. Centre for Policy Studies, Policy Study No. 92 (London).
Stedman Jones, G. (1971), *Outcast London: A Study of the Relationship between Classes in Victorian Society* (Oxford).
Stewart, J., and Stoker, G. (1988), *From Local Administration to Community Government*, Fabian Research Series, 351 (London).
Townsend, P., and Bosanquet, N. (1972), *Labour and Inequality* (London).
Williams, K. (1981), *From Pauperism to Poverty* (London).
Wilson, W. J. (1987), *The Truly Disadvantaged: The Inner City, the Underclass and Public Policy* (Chicago).

2

Race, Injustice, and Disorder

John Benyon and John Solomos

INTRODUCTION

Civil disorder and unrest were recurring phenomena in many British inner-city areas during the 1980s. In 1980, 1981, and 1985 major riots in Bristol, London, Liverpool, and Birmingham commanded the headlines and became a key theme in policy debates about the future of the inner cities. It is worth stressing that in *each* year since 1980 there have been examples of serious street disorder (Benyon, 1984; Benyon and Solomos, 1987). These outbreaks of disorder have presented a major challenge to the Thatcher Government's image as the guardian of public order. More importantly, however, they have given added urgency to the long-running debate about the future of Britain's inner cities. The sight of violent confrontations on the streets of major cities helped to stimulate yet further the acrimonious political debate about how to regenerate depressed inner-city localities (Robson, 1988).

This chapter explores the political and policy debates surrounding the major outbreaks of urban unrest during 1980–1 and 1985, and the ever-present threat of more violent disorder. After providing a brief overview of the chronology of urban unrest during the 1980s, the chapter concentrates on two main themes. First, the political debates about the origins and causes of the unrest are assessed, and second, the impact of the unrest on the policy agenda is examined. This entails a review of the impact of the Scarman Report, and other important policy documents, on the agenda of both the Government and other political institutions. Finally, the chapter concludes by providing some reflections about the prospects during the decade ahead.[1]

[1] Parts of this chapter draw upon research on the Politics of Urban Unrest in Contemporary Britain funded by the Nuffield Foundation.

THE CONTEXT OF URBAN UNREST: 1981 AND 1985

The first notable instance of urban unrest during the 1980s took place in the St Paul's district of Bristol on 2 April 1980. The immediate reaction to this event was one of shock and surprise, with public and media attention focusing particularly on the interplay between racial and social deprivation in the St Paul's area (Joshua and Wallace, 1983). A year later further serious violence occurred during the weekend of 10–12 April 1981 in the Brixton area of south London; this resulted in many injuries and widespread damage, and it attracted enormous media attention.

Further disturbances took place in many parts of the country in July 1981. On Friday, 3 July a pitched battle occurred in Southall between hundreds of skinheads and local Asian people, and the police quickly became embroiled. On the same night in the Liverpool 8 district of Merseyside, an apparently minor incident sparked off rioting which lasted until Monday, 6 July. The disorder in Liverpool 8 was particularly violent. For the first time ever in Britain, CS gas was fired at rioters by the police. Looting and arson were widespread, and the damage was estimated at some £10 million. On the night of 7–8 July 1981, disorder occurred in Moss Side, Manchester. During the following week disturbances were reported in places such as Handsworth in Birmingham, Sheffield, Nottingham, Hull, Slough, Leeds, Bradford, Leicester, Derby, High Wycombe, and Cirencester.

Disorder again erupted in Brixton on 15 July 1981. At 2.00 a.m. eleven houses in Railton Road were raided by 176 police-officers, with a further 391 held in reserve. The police had warrants to look for evidence of unlawful drinking and to search five houses for petrol bombs, although no evidence of either was found. During the operation the houses sustained very consider-able damage—windows, sinks, toilets, floorboards, furniture, televisions, and personal possessions were smashed. The resultant outcry led to an internal inquiry which exonerated those involved and stated that the police officers had been issued with sledge-hammers and crowbars 'to effect speedy entry'. Compensation of £8,500 for structural damage, and further sums for damage to personal property, were paid by the Metropolitan Police. This raid, and the resultant violence on the streets of Brixton, convinced many people that the way policing is carried out is a vital factor in the context of urban unrest. An inquiry into the Railton Road raid by the Police Complaints Board discovered 'serious lapses from professional standards' and an 'institutional disregard for the niceties of the law' (Benyon and Solomos, 1987).

Disorder was again evident in 1982 and in subsequent years, although on a reduced scale (Benyon and Solomos, 1987). The attention of the news media was firmly focused on the Falklands, and so few accounts of disturbances in British cities were reported. It is clear, though, that urban unrest continued to occur in parts of London and Liverpool, and similar disorder seems to have taken place in 1983. The following year, the Metropolitan Police Commissioner reported that during 1984 there were many mini-riots which had the potential to escalate to Brixton 1981 proportions, and he added: 'London is nowadays a very volatile city.'

A MORI opinion poll in February 1985 reported that 64 per cent of those surveyed expected further riots to occur in British cities, and seven months later their fears were justified. In September and October 1985 serious urban unrest again became the focus of popular attention. The first major eruption occurred on Monday, 9 September 1985 in the Lozells Road area of Handsworth, Birmingham. The riot resulted in the deaths of two Asian men, Kassamali and Amirali Moledina, who suffered asphyxiation in their burning post office. Another 122 people, mainly police, were reported injured and the value of damaged property was put at £7.5 million. Further rioting occurred the next day when Douglas Hurd, the Home Secretary, visited the area. Other disturbances, widely regarded as 'copycat', were reported elsewhere in the West Midlands, for example in Moseley, Wolverhampton, and Coventry, and in the St Paul's district of Bristol.

The Handsworth/Soho/Lozells area, with a population of 56,300, is regarded by Birmingham City Council as the most deprived district in the city. Unemployment is a major affliction, and at the time of the riots 36 per cent of the workforce in Handsworth was out of work, while the figure for people under 24 years was 50 per cent. It is an area in which it was claimed that reasonably good relations existed between young blacks and the police, as a result of the practice of community policing introduced in the late 1970s. However, at the end of 1981 a new superintendent instituted changes which included moving a number of the area's community police-officers to other duties and clamping down on the activities by local youths which had previously been tolerated.

These changes resulted in an increase in tension between youths and the police. In July 1985 two serious disturbances occurred in Handsworth, but both were played down and went unreported in the media. The context within which the eruption on 9 September occurred was thus one of deteriorating relations between young people, especially blacks, and the police, as well as one of widespread unemployment and social disadvantage. The tinder merely required a spark, which was provided when a black youth became involved in an altercation with an officer over a parking ticket. It was alleged that during the incident, at which more police arrived, a black woman was assaulted. Three hours later some forty-five buildings in Lozells Road were ablaze.

Brixton was the scene of the next outbreak of violent disorder, during the weekend 28–9 September 1985. 724 major crimes were reported, 43 members of the public and 10 police-officers were injured, and 230 arrests were made. As in Handsworth, the event which led to the rioting involved police-officers and a black person. At 7.00 a.m. on 28 September armed police entered Mrs Cherry Groce's house in Normandy Road, Brixton, looking for her son. Two shots were fired by an officer, and a bullet damaged Mrs Groce's spine causing permanent paralysis. At 6.00 p.m. the local police station was attacked with petrol bombs, and during the next eight hours large numbers of people, both black and white, took part in burning and looting which caused damage estimated at £3 million. During the riot a freelance photographer sustained injuries from which he died three weeks later.

Two days after Mrs Groce was shot, rioting occurred in Toxteth (Liverpool 8). In this instance, the disturbances were precipitated when four black men were refused bail at Liverpool Magistrates' Court. During the summer there had been reports of rising tension in the area, and on 30 August a crowd demonstrated outside Toxteth Police Station and then attacked police cars and the station itself. A number of assaults on police-officers were also reported. As in Brixton and Handsworth, police relations with youths, and especially with young black people, were a significant factor in the explosive mixture, and in Toxteth, too, the disorder was precipitated by an incident involving police officers and black people.

The most serious of the disorders occurred at the Broadwater Farm Estate, in Tottenham, London. The rioting began about 7.00 p.m. on Sunday, 6 October 1985, and during a night of extraordinary violence Police Constable Keith Blakelock was stabbed to death, 20 members of the public and 223 police-officers were injured, and 47 cars and some buildings were burned. Guns were fired at the police, causing injuries to several officers and reporters, and the forces were issued with CS gas and plastic bullets, although these were not used.

As in Handsworth, Brixton, and Toxteth, the context within which the disturbances occurred in Tottenham was one of deteriorating relations between the police and young people, especially blacks, and the trigger event involved police-officers and black people (Gifford, 1986). The chief superintendent for the area was a firm believer in community policing, and he put as his first priority the prevention of public disorder. However, it is clear that many of his police constables and sergeants did not agree with this approach. During the summer of 1985 there was evidence of increasing tension, and a prominent member of the Hornsey Police Federation was quoted as saying that rank and file officers 'desperately wanted to go in hard and sort out the criminals'. Some serious incidents occurred during this period on the Broadwater Farm Estate, such as an attack on police by youths which resulted in one officer sustaining a bad head wound, and there was also a series of attacks on an Asian-owned supermarket. Senior police-officers appeared to play these incidents down, but black youths complained that on the estate they were increasingly harassed by the police.

The incident which precipitated the riot began when police-officers stopped a car driven by Floyd Jarrett, a 23-year-old black man well known in the area. One of the officers decided to arrest Jarrett for suspected theft of the car, but after an altercation Jarrett was in fact charged with assaulting a police-officer. On 13 December 1985 Jarrett was acquitted of this charge, and was awarded £350 costs against the police. While he was detained at the police station a number of police-officers used a key taken from the arrested man to enter his mother's home. During the police search of the house Mrs Cynthia Jarrett collapsed. The family alleged that her death was caused by a police-officer who pushed her over; the police denied that this had occurred. On 4 December 1985 the inquest returned a verdict of accidental death. Mrs Jarrett was certified dead at 6.35 p.m. on Saturday, 5 October, and news of the tragedy spread quickly around the estate during the evening. The next day, after sporadic incidents, violent disorder erupted at about 7.00 p.m.

Disorder occurred again in 1986. During the spring there were renewed reports of increasing tension in some areas. In Notting Hill, for example, there were allegations of assaults by the police, and the planting of drugs, while in Nottingham a number of forced entries into black people's homes and a series of street searches caused widespread anger. On the Broadwater Farm Estate virtually every black male under 30 was interrogated— over 350 people were arrested although most were released without charge. In July 1986 the Metropolitan Police mounted a huge raid in Brixton, involving nearly 2,000 officers, aimed at selected premises in which cannabis offences were allegedly being committed.

In early September 1986 serious disorder occurred on the streets of the North Prospect Estate in the Devonport constituency of Plymouth. A large crowd of white youths set up burning barricades and smashed windows, doors, and fences on the estate. A few days later the Avon and Somerset Police organized a large raid in the St Paul's district of Bristol. Almost exactly one year after the Handsworth riots, 600 police moved into the area to search several premises in connection with drugs and drinking offences. The reaction was serious rioting and attacks on the police involving petrol bombs, bricks, and stones.

In 1987 disorder occurred in Wolverhampton after a black youth died of asphyxiation while being arrested on 20 February. Later in the year, violent clashes occurred on the streets of

Chapeltown in Leeds, and at Notting Hill in London, both before and during the Carnival. During 1988 there were more warnings of 'race riots' and 'violence in the inner cities' from both within and outside the Government, and there were reports of further sporadic disorder in London, the West Midlands, and Merseyside.

MAKING SENSE OF THE 1981 RIOTS

Reactions to the riots have concentrated on a number of key variables that are said to characterize the localities in which the riots have occurred. Lord Scarman's report on the 1981 disorders highlighted the importance of unemployment, urban deprivation, racial disadvantage, relations between young blacks and the police, the decline of civic consent, and political exclusion as the key issues. Other reactions have concentrated on the issue of the interplay between inner-city decay and racial disadvantage in contemporary Britain. Yet others have argued that the unrest can be seen as a symptom of the breakdown of law and order in British society (Gaffney, 1987; Hall, 1987; Keith, 1987).

The main issues that were prominent in debates during 1980–1 were 'race' and 'law and order'. This was by no means an accident, since throughout the 1970s a powerful body of media, political, and academic opinion had been constructed around the theme of how Britain was drifting into a 'violent society', and how the basis of consent was being shifted by the pressures of immigration and the growth of multi-racial inner city areas.

A glimpse of the impact of the 1980–1 riots at this level can be achieved through two important debates in Parliament. The first took place in the midst of the July 1981 riots, and had as its theme: 'Civil Disturbances'. The tone of the debate was set by Home Secretary William Whitelaw's introductory statement in which he spoke of (*a*) the need to 'remove the scourge of criminal violence from our streets', and (*b*) the urgency of developing 'policies designed to promote the mutual tolerance and under-standing upon which the whole future of a free democratic society depends' (*Hansard*, vol. 8, 16 July 1981: col. 1405). The 'scourge of criminal violence' was, Whitelaw argued, a danger to the whole framework of consent and legality on which the political institutions of British society were based. In reply Roy Hattersley supported the call for the immediate suppression of street violence, but warned that the roots of such riots could not be dealt with until all people felt they had a stake in British society (ibid.: cols. 1407–9).

The second debate took place on 26 November 1981, on the publication of the Scarman Report, and had as its theme: 'Law and Order'. The importance of the riots in pushing the law and order issue, and specifically policing, on to the main political agenda was emphasized by the Liberal leader, David Steel, who argued that 'urgent action' to prevent a drift into lawlessness was necessary from both a moral and a political perspective (*Hansard*, vol. 13, 26 November 1981: cols. 1009–11). A subsequent debate on the same issue in March 1982 was also full of references to the experience of 1981, the impact of street violence, crime, decaying urban conditions, the breakdown of consent between the police and many local communities, and the spectre of 'more violence to come' if changes in both policing tactics and social policy were not swiftly introduced (*Hansard*, vol. 20, 25 March 1982: cols. 1107–81).

The need to support the police was accepted by both the Labour and the Conservative speakers in the parliamentary debate on the riots, and was established as a benchmark for the official response to the riots long before the Scarman Report was published in November 1981. Any substantive disagreement centred around the issue of what role social deprivation and unemployment had in bringing young people to protest violently on the streets.

Intermingled with the discourses about race and law and order were constant references to unemployment, particularly among the young, and various forms of social disadvantage and poverty (Solomos, 1988, pp. 186–90). Throughout 1980 and 1981 debates about the riots in the media, in Parliament, and in various official reports hinged around the interrelationship between racial, law-and-order, and social factors. The importance of this debate can be explained, partly, by the political capital which the Opposition could make from linking the social and economic malaise of the country at large with violent street disturbances. Conversely, throughout this period Government Ministers strenuously denied that unemployment and social deprivation were significant causes of urban unrest.

Although the Scarman Report is often taken to be the central text which argues for a link between 'social conditions' and 'disorder', the terms of the debate were by no means set by Scarman. During both April and July 1981 vigorous exchanges took place in the press and in Parliament about the role that deteriorating social conditions and unemployment may have played in bringing about the riots. During the 16 July parliamentary debate on 'Civil Disturbances', Roy Hattersley's formulation of this linkage provided a useful summary of the 'social conditions' argument. After some preliminary remarks about the Labour party's support for the police, he went on to outline his opposition to the view of the riots as essentially anti-police outbursts:

I repeat that I do not believe that the principal cause of last week's riots was the conduct of the police. It was the conditions of deprivation and despair in the decaying areas of our old cities—areas in which the Brixton and Toxteth riots took place, and areas from which the skinhead invaders of Southall come. (*Hansard*, vol. 8, 16 July 1981: col. 1408)

Much of the subsequent controversy about this analysis centred on the question of youth unemployment. Hattersley had suggested that the riots were a 'direct product' of high levels of youth unemployment, and a furious debate ensued in both Parliament and the media about this assertion.

The final symbolic cue used to make sense of the 1980–1 protests is more difficult to categorize, but its basic meaning can be captured by the term 'political marginality'. While a number of discussions of the roots of urban unrest in the United States have noted the salience of political marginality in determining participation in violent protests (Skolnick, 1969; Fogelson, 1971; Edelman, 1971; Knopf, 1975), this issue has received relatively little attention in Britain. Nevertheless, during the 1980–1 events and their aftermath the political context was discussed from a number of perspectives.

The Scarman Report, for example, located part of the explanation for the riots in the feelings of alienation and powerlessness which were experienced by young blacks living in depressed inner-city areas. A successful policy for tackling the roots of urban disorder was seen as one which sought to involve all the community in dealing with the problems of each area so that they could come to feel that they have a stake in its future (Scarman, 1981, para. 6.42).

Where such arguments did not fit in with the overarching themes of race, violence and disorder, and social deprivation they were either sidelined or pushed into the sub-clauses of official reports. The Scarman Report, for example, contained the following policy proposal: 'I recommend that local communities must be fully and effectively involved in planning, in the provision of local services, and in the management and financing of specific projects' (Scarman, 1981, para. 8.44). Such a move towards greater political integration was seen by Lord Scarman as essential if the gap between inner-city residents and the forces of law and order was to be bridged. But the concern with overcoming political marginality remained on the sidelines of the main public debate because it questioned the perception of the rioters as driven by irrational, uncivilized, and criminal instincts. This did not, however, stop the question of political marginality and the need to reform existing policies from being raised at all, as can be seen subsequently by the attempts after 1981 to introduce both locally and nationally measures which were meant to address some of the grievances of the rioters and to ensure that further disturbances did not occur. Aspects of these measures are considered further on in the chapter.

Perspectives on the 1985 Riots

Despite widespread predictions of further unrest in the aftermath of 1981, the scale and the location of the 1985 riots seem to have surprised even some of the most astute commentators. Handsworth, for example, was presented even shortly before September 1985 as a 'success story' in terms of police–community relations. The outbreak of violence in this area was therefore widely presented as an aberration. Similarly the spread of violence in London to areas such as the Broadwater Farm Estate in Tottenham was seen as a break from previous experience, which had centred on areas such as Brixton.

There are many continuities between 1980–1 and 1985 in relation to the 'common-sense' images used in the press and television to cover the events. But responses in 1985 were different, at least in terms of degree, and probably in relation to the extent to which the riots were seen as a 'race' phenomenon by a wider body of opinion. The ambiguities and sub-clauses to be found in much of the press coverage during 1980–1 had at least acted as a countervailing tendency against the more extreme forms of discourse which blamed the riots completely on black people.

During the 1985 riots and their immediate aftermath, the imagery of 'race' was used by sections of the press without the sense of ambiguity which could still be found in 1980–1. The 'silence over race' was breached in 1980–1, but in 1985 debate about racial issues was taken a step further. Peregrine Worsthorne, for example, used the ferocity of the confrontations in Handsworth, Brixton, and Tottenham to argue that there was a major question mark over the possibility of assimilating the 'coloured population' into mainstream 'British values' (*Sunday Telegraph*, 29 September 1985). To be sure there was still a strong response opposing Enoch Powell's call for repatriation, from all shades of political opinion, but the racialization of public debate about the 1985 riots went much further than 1980–1.

In this context it was the externality of British Afro-Caribbeans and Asians which was highlighted rather than the racist institutions and processes which worked against blacks at all levels of society. The usage of 'race' during the September–October 1985 period took on new meanings, which had little if anything to do with the impact of racism as such, since the emphasis was on the cultural characteristics of the minority communities themselves. After Handsworth part of the press response was to blame the riot on rivalry between West Indians and Asians, and even after the arguments were criticized by local residents and community leaders, they were used to 'explain' what happened. In addition, the question whether the cultures and values of the black communities, their family structures, and their political attitudes 'bred violence' was constantly raised (van Dijk, 1988).

The actual 'facts' of who was arrested during the riots, whether black or white, were hardly debated since it was assumed that they were mostly black and mostly unemployed and involved with crime (Keith, 1987). The imagery of the 'black bomber' used in Handsworth was extended to the notion that there were groups of alienated and criminalized young blacks who saw the riots as a chance to engage in an 'orgy of looting'. The Dear Report on Handsworth captures this image and links it to the social condition of young blacks:

The majority of rioters who took part in these unhappy events were young, black and of Afro-Caribbean origin. Let there be no doubt, these young criminals are not in any way representative of the vast majority of the Afro-Caribbean community whose life has contributed to the life and culture of the West Midlands over many years and whose hopes and aspirations are at one with those of every other law-abiding citizen. We share a common sorrow. It is the duty of us all to ensure that an entire cultural group is not tainted by the actions of a criminal minority. (Dear, 1985, p. 69)

This 'black' criminal minority was constructed not only into the leading force behind the riots, but sometimes as the *only* force. Indeed, throughout September and October 1985, and during the following months, the imagery of race continued to dominate debate about both the causes and the policy outcomes of the riots.

As pointed out earlier, the 'social causes' argument was another major plank of public debate about the 1980–1 riots, particularly in relation to the highly politicized issue of unemployment. During 1985 this issue was raised once again, though by then the extent of mass unemployment and urban de-industrialization and decay was more stark than it had been in 1981. Images of 'urban decay', 'tinderbox cities', and 'ghetto streets' linked up with the images of 'race inequality' and 'black ghettos' to produce an analysis more complex but also more contradictory.

An interesting mixture of the various images was provided by a story in the *Daily Telegraph* under the headline: 'Broadwater Farm: Like the Divis Flats with Reggae' (8 October 1985). The *Mirror* described the estate as 'Living Hell', and quoted one resident as saying that 'You've no idea how awful daily life is' (8 October 1985). Such images were reworkings of arguments already used about Toxteth in 1981 and Brixton in 1981, but they were used more widely than in 1980–1. Even the *Daily Mail*, which deployed the clearest use of 'race' and 'outside agitator' arguments, ran a major story on Broadwater Farm under the headline: 'Burnt-out hulks litter this concrete jungle . . . despair hangs heavy' (8 October 1985). A number of stories using such imagery were run by both the quality and the popular press during this period, but similar arguments are to be found in parliamentary debates (*Hansard*, vol. 84, 21 October 1985, cols. 30–46, 388), and even in official reports produced by the police on the riots in Birmingham and London.

The 'cities of inner despair' were conceived as the breeding ground for disorderly protest, and however hard the Government tried to break the causal link between the two, it was forced to take on board the need to restore order not only through the police but through promises of help for the inner cities. Much as in 1980–1, the 'social causes' argument cannot be seen separately from the broader debate about the future of the British economy and society. The Government's record on unemployment was a heavily politicized issue, and just as in 1981 it vehemently denied any responsibility for the riots through its pursuit of free-market policies. But the Government did find a way of accepting a link between the riots and social problems without bringing its main policies into the debate: namely by linking the growth of violent disorder to crime and drugs.

The emphasis on 'crime' and the 'criminal acts' of the rioters in the official responses to the 1985 riots took a general and a specific form. The general form relied on the argument that the riots were not a form of protest against the insufferable social conditions of inner-city areas or the actions of the police, but a 'criminal act' or a 'cry for loot'. This was an argument put most succinctly by Geoffrey Dear, Chief Constable of the West Midlands (Dear, 1985) and by Douglas Hurd, the Home Secretary, in relation to Handsworth. But it recurred as a theme in official and press responses to the other riots. The specific form was built upon the notion that the outbreak of violence in Handsworth and Brixton, in particular, was brought about by 'drug barons' who saw the police attempting to curb their activities and control 'their territory'. Numerous examples of this line of argument can be found in Dear's report on Handsworth, and in press coverage during the riots.

Taking the specific argument about the role of drugs and 'drug barons' in stimulating the riots, this seems to have served two purposes. First, it distanced the riots from the social, economic, political, and other grievances which had been linked to them by locating the cause outside the 'social problems' of inner-city dwellers and in the 'simple greed' of the drug barons to accumulate 'loot'. Second, just as Dear's image of a few hundred 'young black criminals' was used to explain what happened in Handsworth, the problem of drugs was used to explain what happened at a national level. The issue of drugs provided an everyday image, already a national issue through saturation media coverage and public debate, around which the police, the Home Office, and other institutions could depoliticize the riots.

Responding to the Handsworth events Douglas Hurd was moved to argue forcibly that such events were senseless and reflected more on those who participated in them than on the society in which they took place: 'The sound which law abiding people in Handsworth heard on Monday night, the echoes of which I picked up on Tuesday, was not a cry for help but a cry for loot' (*Financial Times*, 13 September 1985). The Chief Constable for the West Midlands, Geoffrey Dear, took this argument further by pointing out that the day before the riots a successful carnival had taken place, with the support of local community leaders. He drew the conclusion from this that the riot 'came like a bolt out of the blue' (*Guardian*, 21 November 1985). Such language focused attention on the individuals or groups who were 'breaking the law', 'committing criminal acts', and threatening the interests of the law-abiding 'majority'.

SYMBOLIC POLITICS AND POLICY INITIATIVES

The 1980–1 and 1985 riots resulted in a wide variety of responsive measures, emanating from both central and local government, as well as other agencies. The very multiplicity of ideological constructions of the riots is an indication of the complexity of the responses which resulted in policies and programmes of action. There are, however, three analytically distinct and important political and policy responses which need to be examined: (*a*) the Scarman Report; (*b*) policing and law and order (*c*) economic and social policies.

The Scarman Report

In the aftermath of the April 1981 riots in Brixton the Home Secretary, William Whitelaw, used his powers under the 1964 Police Act to appoint Lord Scarman to inquire into the events, produce a report, and make recommendations. This brief was subsequently widened to cover the occurrence of other disturbances during July 1981. Lord Scarman's inquiry was not on the same scale as the famous Kerner Report in 1968 on the US riots, but since the publication of his Report in November 1981 his views and prescriptions have played an important role in fashioning political debate about the riots. It is therefore important to look into the basic analysis which the Scarman Report puts forward in order to understand how the political agenda has developed, in response to the riots, since 1980.

The starting-point of Lord Scarman's explanation of the riots is important. His analysis began by distinguishing between the background factors which had created the potential for urban disorder in areas such as Brixton and the precipitating action or event which sparked off the riots. Scarman identified two views that were commonly held as to the causation of the disorders. The first explained them in terms of oppressive policing, and in particular the harassment of young blacks. The second explained them as a protest against society by deprived people who saw violent attacks upon the forces of law and order as a way of calling attention to their grievances. For Scarman both views were a simplification of a complex reality, or at least 'not the whole truth'. He linked the 'social' and 'policing' aspects of the complex reality of areas like Brixton in an analytic model which emphasized the following issues:

1. the problems which are faced in policing and maintaining order in deprived, inner-city, multi-racial localities;

2. the social, economic, and related problems which are faced
   by all residents of such areas;
3. the social and economic disadvantages which are suffered
   particularly by black residents, especially young blacks.
   (Scarman, 1981, paras. 2.1–2.38)

He saw the existence of all these features in certain deprived areas
as 'creating a predisposition towards violent protest', which
could be sparked off by incidents such as confrontations between
local residents and the police or by rumours about the actions of
the police or other authority figures.

From this account Lord Scarman drew the conclusion that
once the 'predisposition towards violent protest' had taken hold
it was difficult to reverse. Talking about the position of young
blacks, he noted that because they felt neither 'socially nor
economically secure' many of them had drifted into situations
where more or less regular confrontations with the police were
the norm of their daily experience. Noting that despite the
evidence of academic and government reports, which had pointed
to widespread discrimination against young blacks, very little
had been done to remedy the position, Scarman concluded that:
(*a*) many young blacks believed that violence was an effective
means of protest against their conditions; and (*b*) far from the
riots being a meaningless event, they were 'essentially an outburst
of anger and resentment by young black people against the
police' (Scarman, 1981, paras. 3.110 and 2.38). What is important
to note here is that aside from Lord Scarman's condemnation of
the 'criminal acts' committed during the riots, the Report was a
strong argument in favour of a historical and social explanation of
the riots.

Given the close link which the Scarman Report established
between questions of policing and the 'wider social context', the
programme of action which it outlined contained proposals not
only about the reform of the police and the introduction of new
methods of policing and riot control, but about employment
policy, social policy, and policies on racial discrimination. In a
telling phrase Lord Scarman argued: 'The social conditions in
Brixton do not provide an excuse for disorder. But the disorders

cannot be fully understood unless they are seen in the context of complex political, social and economic factors which together create a predisposition towards violent protest' (para. 8.7). Although some of these issues went beyond the main remit of his Inquiry, he drew the conclusion from this basic finding that only a national government-led initiative to deal with problems of policing, unemployment, poor housing, and racial disadvantage could get to the roots of the unrest.

Parliamentary and media responses to the Report varied greatly, although it was widely seen as making an important contribution to the debate about how to respond to the riots and prevent the outbreak of violence in the future. But what became clear after the immediate debate on the Report in late 1981 and early 1982, was that the Government was not going to implement all the recommendations. Some aspects of its proposals for reforming the police and rethinking police tactics were implemented during 1982 and 1983, but evidence of the 'urgent action' which it called for in other areas remained difficult to find.

This returns us to the earlier point about the other major forces which contributed to the development of political responses to the riots: namely the media, Parliament, the political parties, and popular 'common-sense' debate. The Scarman Report formed a part—and a vital one—of this process of political debate, but its role cannot be understood in isolation. This can be seen if we look more closely at the issues of policing and economic and social problems.

Policing and law and order

Indeed, in the aftermath of the Scarman Report's publication, police opinion was divided on the question of whether its proposals for reforming the police and the adoption of new methods of policing could be implemented, or whether such changes could insure against further violence and unrest.

The policy responses after the 1985 riots show some of the same characteristics as those during 1980–1, but as argued earlier, the emphasis on the 'criminality' of the riot participants favoured explanations that linked disorder to the pathological characteristics of inner-city residents which pushed them towards lawlessness and crime. This in turn produced a sharper contrast than in 1980–1 between (*a*) responses which emphasized the need to strengthen and buttress the role of the police, and (*b*) responses which called for greater emphasis on the rejuvenation of the social and economic fabric of the inner cities.

Economic and social policies

In terms of economic and social policies the impact of the 1980–1 riots was equally ambiguous and contradictory. Part of this ambiguity, as outlined above, resulted from the Government's strenuous efforts to deny any link between its policies and the outbreak of violence and disorder. This denial was particularly important, since at the time the Thatcher administration was going through a bad period in terms of popular opinion on issues such as unemployment, social services, and housing. While Lord Scarman was careful not to enter the political dispute between the Government and the Labour party on issues such as unemployment and housing, his call for more direct action to deal with these problems, along with racial disadvantage, posed a challenge to the political legitimacy of the policies which the Government had followed from 1979 onwards. It also posed a delicate problem for the Home Secretary himself, since Lord Scarman had been appointed by him to carry out his Inquiry. Having spent the whole summer denying any link between its policies and the riots, the Government had to tread warily in responding to the economic and social policy proposals of the Scarman Report when it was published in November 1981.

The parliamentary debate on the Report showed the Home Secretary adopting a two-pronged strategy in his response. First, he accepted many of the recommendations of the Report, particularly in relation to the role of the police. Additionally, he accepted the need to tackle racial disadvantage and other social issues. Second, he emphasized the Government's view that, whatever broader measures were taken to deal with racial and social inequalities, the immediate priority was to restore and maintain order on the streets. When the Home Secretary talked of the need for the Government to give a lead in tackling racial disadvantage he therefore saw this as an issue for the longer term. On the other hand, he was much more specific about the reform of the police and the development of new tactics and equipment for the management of urban disorder (*Hansard*, vol. 14, 10 December 1981: cols. 1001–8).

In 1985, however, the Government specifically rejected calls for another inquiry like Lord Scarman's, arguing that since the riots were a 'criminal enterprise' it was useless to search for social explanations or to have yet another report advising it about what to do. Implicitly, the Government was saying that it knew what the problems were, and how they could be tackled.

While some senior policemen, like Metropolitan Police Commissioner Sir Kenneth Newman, wanted to stress the link between the police and other areas of 'social policy' (Metropolitan Police, 1986), the official government response attempted to decontextualize the riots and see them as the actions of a small minority who were either criminalized or influenced by extreme political ideas. The dominant approach of the Government attempted to emphasize two main arguments.

1. that the riots were 'a lust for blood', an 'orgy of thieving', 'a cry for loot and not a cry for help';
2. that the riots did not reflect a failure to carry out the 'urgent programme of action' recommended by Lord Scarman in 1981, but were the outcome of a spiralling wave of crime and disorder in inner-city areas.

The logic of this approach, articulated by Home Secretary Douglas Hurd most clearly, was that the riots were both 'unjustifiable' and a 'criminal activity'. In a widely reported speech to police chiefs at the time of the disorders Hurd made this point clear:

Handsworth needs more jobs and better housing. But riots only destroy. They create nothing except a climate in which necessary development is even more difficult. Poor housing and other social ills provide no kind of reason for riot, arson and killing. One interviewer asked me whether the riot was not a cry for help by the rioters. The sound which law-abiding people heard at Handsworth was not a cry for help but a cry for loot. That is why the first priority, once public order is secure, must be a thorough and relentless investigation into the crimes which were committed. (*Daily Telegraph*, 14 September 1985)

Such arguments resonated through the media and in the various parliamentary debates during September and October 1985. They became part of the symbolic political language through which the riots were understood by policy makers and by popular opinion.

Since the 1985 unrest, and particularly after the 1987 General Election, the Government has announced a number of initiatives on the inner city, and it has presented these as part of an effort to rejuvenate depressed areas on a sound basis. The evidence that has emerged since then, however, points to a major discrepancy between the Government's promises of action and the allocation of resources to implement them (Robson, 1988). It is perhaps too early to reach a conclusion on this point, but a repeat of the period of inaction between 1982 and 1985 seems to be evident, within the current political context. A number of local authorities have attempted to take more positive action to deal with the issues raised by the 1985 riots, but their experience has shown that such local initiatives are often severely limited by the actions of national government, the police, and broader economic and political pressures.

In the years since 1981 the one consistent response to urban unrest has been the provision of more resources, more training, and more equipment to the police. Instead of tackling the causes of urban unrest, the Government has built up force to deal with the manifestation of those root conditions.

Increasingly the most strident political voices are raised in the name of free enterprise and law and order, not for equity and social justice. For the New Right and other influential sectors of political opinion the attempt to achieve racial equality through legal and political means is at best naïve political folly, and at worst a restriction on the workings of the market. The present political climate gives little cause for optimism that a radical change in governmental priorities in this field is likely (Solomos, 1989).

The Government's plan of *Action for Cities* (DoE, 1987), issued after Mrs Thatcher's post-election promise, says very little directly about racial inequality. It remains to be seen whether it will suffer the fate of numerous other initiatives on the inner cities and fade into obscurity. But one thing seems clear: during the past decade the Government has been more intent on reducing the powers of local authorities than on providing for fundamental changes in the social conditions of the inner cities.

Conclusion: Little Room for Optimism

Despite the Government's recently proclaimed intention of re-generating the inner cities, there is little room for optimism. Unless radical action is taken, British cities seem poised to become yet more turbulent, brutalized, and trouble-torn. The excluded black and white citizens in the urban areas seem set to continue to suffer deprivation and disadvantage. The remedy of using tough policing is merely tackling the symptoms of the disorder, and is liable to exacerbate the underlying malaise.

This approach should come as no surprise, however. History shows that the usual response to violent protest and riots was repression. History also shows that this course was normally ineffective and that disorder only diminished when movement was made in the direction of the reforms which were demanded. The auguries for such reforms are not good, and further urban unrest remains in prospect.

References

Benyon, J. (ed.), (1984), *Scarman and After* (Oxford).

—— and Solomos, J. (eds.), (1987), *The Roots of Urban Unrest* (Oxford).

Dear, G. (1985), *Handsworth/Lozells, September 1985: Report of the Chief Constable, West Midlands Police* (Birmingham).

DoE (Department of the Environment) (1987), *Action for Cities* (London).

Edelman, M. (1971), *Politics as Symbolic Action: Mass Arousal and Quiescence* (Chicago).

Fogelson, R. M. (1971), *Violence as Protest: A Study of Riots and Ghettos* (Garden City, New York).

Gaffney, J. (1987), 'Interpretations of violence: The Handsworth riots of 1985', University of Warwick, Centre for Research in Ethnic Relations, Policy Paper No. 10 (Warwick).

Gifford, Lord, Chairman (1986), *The Broadwater Farm Inquiry* (London).

Hall, S. (1987), 'Urban unrest in Britain', in J. Benyon and J. Solomos (eds.), *The Roots of Urban Unrest* (Oxford).

Joshua, H., and Wallace, T. (1983), *To Ride the Storm: The 1980 Bristol 'Riot' and the State* (London).

Keith, M. (1987), ' "Something happened": The problems of explaining the 1980 and 1981 riots in British cities', in P. Jackson (ed.), *Race and Racism* (London).

Knopf, T. A. (1975), *Rumors, Race and Riots* (New Brunswick, NJ).

Metropolitan Police (1986), *Public Order Review—Civil Disturbances 1981–1985*, (London).

Robson, B. (1988), *Those Inner Cities* (Oxford).

Scarman, Lord (1981), *The Brixton Disorders 10–12 April 1981: Report of an Inquiry*, Cmnd. 8427 (London).

Skolnick, R. (1969), *The Politics of Protest* (New York).

Solomos, J. (1988), *Black Youth, Racism and the State* (Cambridge).

—— (1989), *Race and Racism in Contemporary Britain* (London).

van Dijk, T. (1988), *News Analysis: Case Studies of International and National News in the Press* (Princeton).

3

Crime and Policing

Robert Reiner

FULL CIRCLE?

On 13 May 1833 the National Political Union, a body organized to seek the extension of the franchise to the working class, held a meeting in Coldbath Fields, in Clerkenwell, London. This was to become a celebrated and controversial rite of passage for the new Metropolitan Police, then not quite four years old. Fighting broke out between participants and the police, during which a constable, PC Culley, was fatally stabbed. An inquest jury, rapidly assembled in a nearby inn, returned a verdict of 'justifiable homicide'. This was quashed on appeal to the Court of King's Bench, but it symbolized the deep and widespread popular suspicion which attended the birth of Peel's 'New Police'.

For the conventional 'cop-sided' histories of British police development, Coldbath Fields marks the crucial turning-point in their battle to win consent for their very existence. From the middle of the eighteenth century onwards a growing chorus of voices had championed the creation of a professional police. But they were successfully resisted by a rejectionist front which encompassed a variety of social interests and philosophies, ranging from rural Tory gentry to urban working-class radicals. Upper-class objectors worried about traditional civil liberties, central government encroachment on the delicate network of power relations in local parishes, and the expense of a public police. Working-class hostility was roused by the fear of the police being used to control industrial and political organization, and to curb their recreational activities under the guise of maintaining public order in the streets. This alliance of opposition frustrated all attempts to establish a professional police until Peel's 1829 Metropolitan Police Act.

In the conventional view Coldbath Fields was a shock to respectable consciences, and rallied the support of all but the dangerous classes to the Peelers. In fact, however, resistance to the new police continued to be expressed in street violence and riots as 'the plague of blue locusts' spread throughout the country between 1829 and 1856, and in particular as it came to the working-class communities of the North (Storch, 1975, p. 94). Indeed, working-class assent to policing has arguably always been hesitant and brittle (Cohen, 1979; Brogden, 1982).

When PC Keith Blakelock was stabbed to death on 6 October 1985 during the rioting in the Broadwater Farm Estate he was the first Metropolitan policeman to be killed in a riot since PC Culley in 1833. The parallel with Coldbath Fields dramatically symbolizes the way that policing, crime, and public order have turned full circle back to echo early Victorian conditions. The urban disorders of the 1980s are the most explicit index of the deep hostility now felt by many inner-city residents towards the police, and of the problems of policing the inner city.

Nor are the parallels confined to the inner city. Another dramatic instance of historical *déjà vu* came during the miners' strike, when it was reported that an attack had been made on the police station in Malby, South Yorkshire, scene of an anti-police riot a century earlier when the 'new police' first arrived there. More recently a moral panic about 'lager louts' despoiling rural Arcadias has emerged. What has been rudely shattered is the cosy depiction of British history as the progressive 'conquest of violence' (Critchley, 1970) which is celebrated in the conventional accounts of the British police (Reith, 1938, 1943, 1956; Critchley, 1967; Ascoli, 1979; Stead, 1985).

But if the long-term trajectory of 'law and order' in Britain is not the unilinear march of civility which may once have seemed plausible, what is it? And how are we to understand and deal with the contemporary return of the repressed, in terms of spiralling levels of recorded crime and riotous disorder? In this chapter I shall try to locate our present concerns in a pattern of historical development, and seek to excavate from this a prognosis for the viability of current strategies and initiatives.

A Crisis of 'Law and Order': Moral Panic or Reasonable Concern?

In the conventional view, Britain, once a legend throughout the world for its stolid, peaceable, and harmonious character, has experienced in the last decade and a half an alien and shocking advent of unprecedented incivility and disorder. At the visible apex of this trend come the urban disorders of Brixton and Bristol, Toxteth and Tottenham. Underneath lies the more regular procession of smaller-scale crowd disturbances, political, industrial, and recreational. Even less visible except to immediate participants and police is the routine 'slow rioting' of Saturday night street brawling, which (according to the perceptions of all the chiefs constables I have interviewed in a research project over the last year) is assuming more menacing and violent proportions throughout the country. Beneath it all is a growing wave of individual crimes, adding up to a crisis of law and order. This conventional view is summed up by the dominant reactions to the 1981 Brixton disorders. Lord Scarman referred to violence and disorder 'the like of which had not previously been seen in this century in Britain', while one Conservative MP summed up this orthodox reaction in a parliamentary debate (on 13 April 1981) when he spoke of the riots as 'something new and sinister in our long national history'.

The initial response of the Left and liberals to this reaction was to dub the conventional wisdom 'moral panic'. What was new was the growth of a strong state control apparatus, legitimated by the fears generated by manipulation of public anxiety. It was pointed out that contrary to the rose-tinted spectacles view, Britain has a long history of riot and disorder. The conventional perspective is guilty of 'historical amnesia', which has forgotten the turbulent and bloody conflicts of the past (see, for example, Benyon, 1985).

The most thorough-going and influential example of this genre of debunking moral panic is Hooligan by Geoff Pearson (1983). This is a deservedly much-admired, fascinating, and lovingly collected parade of paranoia through the ages. Moving backwards, through four centuries of history, Pearson shows a perennial refrain lamenting a supposedly shocking increase in crime, violence, and public disorder. Each period seems to construct its own mythical golden age 'twenty years ago'. But Pearson assiduously shows how the grandads of that supposed era of tranquillity were themselves bemoaning the sad decline of standards of virtue and discipline since *their* youth. And so on, in a potentially infinite regress of grandadology, wailing and gnashing teeth at the decline of family life, parental irresponsibility, declining national character, and the need for a firm reassertion of authority. 'Street violence and disorder are solidly entrenched features of the social landscape', argues Pearson, at any rate in capitalist societies which necessarily generate a 'residuum', an under-class of the underprivileged and unemployed, unintegrated and potentially threatening to the established and respectable. If this reserve army is always with us, so is social reaction to it: an 'immovable preoccupation' with 'the awesome spectre of crime and violence perpetually spiralling upwards'.

This perspective offers a useful corrective to the ahistorical perception of recent levels of crime and disorder as utterly foreign and novel in British experience. But the critique runs the danger of becoming a facile agnosticism about patterns or trends in crime and disorder. Piecing together a catalogue of recurring laments neither answers nor dismisses the still pertinent question: are things really getting worse, getting better, or remaining the same? It is as if an economic historian, collating woeful *Financial Times* editorials every few years, were to conclude that there really were no business-cycles, let alone longer-term Kondratieff waves of growth and decline.

Furthermore, the litanies of 'respectable fears' and 'moral panics' are only one of the discourses about 'law and order' found in popular, political, or academic discussion over the last century. At the turn of the century, the very time when Pearson documents the coinage of the term 'hooligan' to portray a supposedly new breed of youthful folk-devil, there is found in other sources a mood of contemporary congratulation about the long-term conquest of the problem of order. The Criminal Registrar's Report for 1901 documents a trend for declining levels of crime and violence over more than two decades. The introduction comments: 'We have witnessed a great change in manners: the substitution of words without blows for blows with or without words; an approximation in the manners of different classes; a decline in the spirit of lawlessness.' Nor was this position unique. The latest volume of the magisterial *History of English Criminal Law* (Radzinowicz and Hood, 1986, vol. 5) shows that criminologists at the turn of the century were vexed with explaining the puzzling phenomenon of English success in conquering routine crime and violence. Not that all was well in the sphere of order and crime. On the one hand, there was a variety of political and industrial threats to the order of the established classes. The Fenian menace legitimated the establishment of a specifically political police, which would have been utterly unacceptable in the climate of early nineteenth-century Britain (Porter, 1987). The industrial conflicts of the first quarter of this century stimulated a new level of centralization and sophistication in the state's coercive response to the labour movement (Morgan, 1987). But what differentiates the earlier part of this century from either the present or the early nineteenth century is that these problems did not all coalesce into one disturbing image of a threatening, dangerous, and disorderly criminal class. Various types of criminal—the political, the habitual and the recidivist, the feeble-minded, the inebriate, the juvenile—were all differentiated as separate specimens in the taxonomies of the new science of criminology (Garland, 1985). And with the cognitive optimism of criminology was combined a penological optimism, that the new forms of scientifically grounded interventions would provide a solution to the problems of crime. This penal optimism reigned throughout the first half of this century (Bailey, 1987).

Right down from the last quarter of the nineteenth century to the 1960s one can indeed construct a counter-grandadology to Pearson's 'history of respectable fears'. It is possible to catalogue a chorus of social self-congratulation, as respectable commentators recount the positive achievement of tranquillity since the days of their youth, as the very epitome of social progress. This mood is captured, for example, in Leonard Woolf's autobiography *Sowing* (1960):

I am struck by the immense change from social barbarism to social civilisation which has taken place in London (indeed in Great Britain) during my lifetime. No one but an old Londoner who has been born and bred and has lived for 50 to 60 years in London can have any idea of the extent of the change. It is amazing to walk down Drury Lane or the small streets about 7 Dials today and recall their condition only 50 years ago. Even as late as 1900 it would not have been safe to walk in any of these streets after dark.

This is not intended to supplant Pearson's perennial panic view with a resuscitated Whig theory of progress. The point is only that there *are* long-term trends and patterns in crime, violence, and disorder. There may be a perennial fascination with the crimes which do exist, but more sober analytic or reflective assessments have not always been pessimistic or anguished. It may evoke nostalgia now, or appear quaintly naïve, but there have been periods when crime and disorder seemed soluble, if not yet totally vanished, problems.

Is Crime Increasing?

The statistics on crime, for all the familiar pitfalls in their inter-pretation, should not be dismissed. They can be judiciously appraised, with an open eye for trends which may affect the relation between recorded and unrecorded crime, in combination with broader consideration of historical and theoretical issues which may affect their validity. The major studies of the long-term trends in crime statistics (Gurr, 1976, 1981; Gatrell and Hadden, 1972; Gatrell, 1980) concur in depicting a secular decline in the latter decades of the nineteenth century. This coincided, however, with an increasing prevalence of the conditions and institutions which should lead us to expect the reporting and recording of offences to grow in proportion to the actual occurrence of victimization. As a noted historian of crime recently argued, the decrease in levels of recorded crime 'coincides with increased court activity, with the spread and professionalisation of the new police, and with an apparent increase in public cooperation with both courts and the police. If the radical criminologists' assumptions are correct, then the figures for the second half of the

19th century might probably show the opposite from that which they do' (Emsley, 1988, p. 42).

The secular trend towards declining levels of crime levelled off in the first decade of this century. The recorded rate of crime then remains on a rough plateau until the end of the 1930s. During the late 1930s and early 1940s there is a fairly sharp rise, but then again a rough plateau (albeit with sharp year-by-year fluctuations) in the late 1940s until the mid-1950s, when there begins a sustained and sharp increase, getting ever steeper in the late 1970s and 1980s. From 1975 onwards the rising crime-rate is justifiably referred to as in a stage of 'hyper-crisis' (Kinsey *et al.*, 1986, p. 12). While in the quarter-century from 1950 to 1975 recorded notifiable offences per 100,000 population increased by just over 3,000, from 1,094 to 4,283, it took just the decade from 1976 to 1986 for crimes per 100,000 population to increase another 3,000, from 4,346 to 7,331 (*Criminal Statistics*, 1986, Table 2.2).

In the late nineteenth century the trend to lower levels of recorded crime coincided with developments which, other things being equal, would lead us to expect rising levels of recording. This buttresses confidence that the recorded trend is in the correct direction. But can we be sure that the last three decades of sustained growth in crime are not a recording phenomenon (Bottomley and Pease, 1986)? The plain answer is that we cannot be certain about it. At the same time as recorded levels of crime have increased, so have many other factors which might increase the propensity of the public to report, and the police to record, offences. Police numbers and resources, for example, have increased considerably. The number of police-officers in England and Wales grew from nearly 76,000 in 1961 to nearly 110,00 in 1976, and nearly 122,000 in 1986. Police strength has not, however, kept pace with the increase in recorded crime. In 1961 there were 11 crimes recorded per police-officer, but by 1986 this had grown to 32. Even taking account of the increase in other resources available to augment police-officers, from civilian support staff to more sophisticated technology of all kinds, there is clearly a much greater recorded crime work-load per police-officer.

The only way that we could definitively ascertain the extent of the increase in recorded crime which is due to changes in reporting and/or recording practices would be if there were available victimization data over a long period. Such data is available for the United States since 1973, when the Federal Government initiated an annual series of National Crime Surveys. Overall these indicate that while the rate of victimization recorded in the annual surveys *did* increase in the 1970s and 1980s, this was at a substantially lower rate (1 per cent on average) than the officially recorded crime-rate (3.5–5 per cent average annual increase; cf. Box, 1987, pp. 18–20). Moreover, the global index of either victimization or recorded offences can be misleading, in that it conceals quite large variations in the trends for specific offences. None the less, what the United States data imply is that the upward trend in recorded crime is in the same direction as actual victimization, although at a slower rate. The recorded figures exaggerate the increase in victimization which is occurring, mainly because of a greater public propensity to report certain crimes.

The experience in the United States cannot necessarily be extrapolated to the United Kingdom. In Britain there have been three national crime surveys, in 1982, 1984, and 1988. Overall, between these years, the increase in victimization measured by the survey (30 per cent) roughly matches the increase of police recorded offences (41 per cent). But this cannot be taken as *carte blanche* for assuming that long-term recorded crime trends correspond to victimization. Not only is a comparison between only three years potentially misleading; there are very considerable divergences between trends in victimization and recorded crime for specific offences, which are concealed by the coincidence in the overall direction (Hough and Mayhew, 1985; Dowds *et al.*, 1989).

It is often pointed out that the long-running set of victimization data in Britain, the General Household Survey's regular measurement of the extent of burglary victimization since 1972, indicates that most of the increase in recorded burglary is a reporting phenomenon. Combining the General Household Survey (GHS) and the British Crime Survey (BCS) victimization data reveals that while police-recorded burglaries doubled between 1972 and

1983, the level of victimization went up only by 20 per cent (Hough and Mayhew, 1985, pp. 16–17). Thus the considerable increase in recorded burglary during the 1970s was largely a recording phenomenon. But this may not apply to other offences. Furthermore, the BCS points out (ibid.) that the gap between the trend in recorded burglaries and victimization is much lower in recent years: there has been an appreciable increase in burglary victimization between 1981 and 1983 of 9 per cent, while recorded burglaries increased by 24 per cent. If this gap continues to narrow then the recorded trend of burglaries may be more confidently interpreted as showing the direction of crime.

In conclusion, it seems that we cannot accept without question the dramatic increase in recorded crime as corresponding to a real increase in victimization of the same proportions. But it would be wishful thinking to explain away all, or even most, of the increase as an artefact of recording changes. We can plausibly infer that crime has been increasing in the last two to three decades, presenting a problem for explanation and policy.

CRIME AND INNER CITIES

While crime overall has been increasing, it must be emphasized that both the reality and the fear of victimization are considerably greater in some areas than others. The British Crime Survey found, for example, that (as classified by the ACORN 'Classification of Residential Neighbourhoods' system) there were three types of area which were especially prone to both crime and fear of crime: 'High-status non-family areas' (I), 'Multi-racial areas' (H), and 'Poorest council estates' (G). Whereas the national average frequency of being a 'mugging' victim (robbery/theft from the person) was 1.4 per cent, in these areas it was: I: 3.9 per cent; H: 4.3 per cent; G: 3.3 per cent. In the last two areas, the proportions of people who were 'very worried about mugging' were 32 per cent and 36 per cent, compared to an average of 20 per cent, and (11 per cent in rural areas—these data evidently precede the advent of lager loutishness!). Whereas on average 2.4 per cent of households were victimized by burglary, in the high-risk areas it was 6.3 per cent (Hough and Mayhew, 1985, Table M). These findings are replicated by the recent local crime surveys, notably those in Merseyside and Islington, which have constituted the empirical core of the 'New Left realism' in criminology (Kinsey, 1985; Jones *et al.*, 1986). The Merseyside Crime Survey found, for example, that 44 per cent of interviewees had been victims of crime in the last twelve months, and a quarter had been victimized twice or more. Multiple victimization (two or more experiences) was twice as high in inner-city areas as in affluent suburbs. Fear of crime varied accordingly. Crime was seen as a 'big problem' by 66 per cent in inner-city Liverpool, compared with 13 per cent in wealthier suburbs (Kinsey *et al.*, 1986, p. 4). David Downes (1983) aptly summed up the irony of 'law and order' being seen as a Conservative concern, when he called it 'theft of an issue'.

POLICING, ORDER, AND LEGITIMACY

Rising crime is not an inevitable nor universal problem. It was noted above that for an extended period of our history crime was actually falling. The overall trajectory since the early nineteenth century seems to be a rough U-shape: falling down to the early 1900s, a plateau until the mid-1950s, and a steepening rise since then. It is plausible that disorder follows a similar pattern. It has been shown, for example, that levels of violence during industrial disputes fell in the first three-quarters of this century, but that this trend has been reversed more recently (Geary, 1985).

If crime and disorder follow a U-shape pattern of long-term change, the legitimacy of the police—the extent to which they are broadly accepted as valid in mission and methods—has followed an inverse path: an upside-down U. Starting from the widespread opposition encountered at the birth of the new police, opposition gradually came to be located primarily within the less 'respectable' sections of the working class, as well as in the wider working class during periods of labour conflict. Even here, as the fact of policing came to be established, opposition was not to the police *per se*, but to specific operations or tactics. By the late 1940s and 1950s, the advent of post-war political consensus and social integration was the precondition for the police achieving a pinnacle of widespread popular acceptance. This was symbolized in the

Dixon of Dock Green phenomenon: the only time that a cosy, non-action-man, ordinary uniform bobby has attained heroic stature in a country's folk-lore. But it was confirmed by harder evidence, above all by the national survey conducted for the 1960 Royal Commission on the Police. This found not only a generally high level of support for the police, but that this spread throughout the class structure (indeed was marginally higher in the working class). The very fact that a series of comparatively minor incidents had triggered the establishment of the Royal Commission as the only comprehensive review of the organization of policing in a century, is testimony to the widespread consensus about policing.

Since the 1950s policing has become a highly controversial, politicized issue. More recent poll evidence (e.g. for the British Crime Survey, or the British Social Attitudes Survey by Jowell *et al.*, 1988) continues to show high overall acceptance of the police. But this must be qualified in two crucial ways. First, there is a widespread perception recorded in the surveys of specific types of police malpractice coming to be perceived as problematic, e.g. corruption and racial discrimination. Second, there is a considerable and growing rejection of the overall legitimacy of the police among some sections of the population: youth, the economically marginal, and ethnic minorities especially Afro-Caribbeans. For example, the Policy Studies Institute found that while 29 per cent of Londoners overall thought the police treat particular groups unfairly, this rose to 68 per cent amongst young West Indians (Smith, 1983, pp. 243–6).

How can these recent trends (rising crime and disorder, and falling police legitimacy) be explained?

CRIME, DEPRIVATION, AND MORALITY

Criminologists have scarcely addressed, let alone answered, the broad questions of explaining overall trends in crime. Positivist research has generated much data about specific relationships between individual or social characteristics and the likelihood of conviction. Radical approaches have been characterized more by theoretical or programmatic work than by grounded accounts of changing crime patterns. Even the recent 'New Left realism' does not address the broader questions of causation, though its leading exponent Jock Young (1986) has rightly emphasized the need to return aetiological questions to the foreground. But so far their explanation of rising crime has largely focused on alleged deficiencies in police strategy, in particular on counter-productive militaristic tactics which exacerbate 'public alienation' and therefore impede successful crime control (Kinsey *et al.*, 1986, pp. 40–2). Admittedly the vicious cycle of police militarization and public alienation is seen to be kicked into play by the economic crumbling of the inner city, but thereafter the weight of the explanation is placed on inadequate (or over-heavy) policing. As will be indicated below, I do not feel that much (if any) of the explanation can lie at the door of the police station.

More plausible is the analysis developed in Dahrendorf's Hamlyn Lectures on 'law and order' (Dahrendorf, 1985, 1987). In this the main structural precondition of growing crime is seen as the growth of an underclass. The social prerequisite of the long trend in the late nineteenth and early twentieth centuries towards lower crime and disorder, and greater police acceptance, was the historical process of working–class incorporation. Uneven and limited though this might have been, the gulf between Disraeli's two nations in the early and mid-nineteenth century became blurred and attenuated by the twentieth. The sharp end of routine policing always falls on the economically marginal, those who live out their lives in public places which routine police patrols regulate, and those who are not integrated into the mainstream institutions of economic and political life. Incorporation of the working class reduced the adult part of this residuum to a politically insignificant, atomistic, albeit cyclically fluctuating stratum. The main grist to the mill of policing was working-class youth, but the perennial conflict between youth and the police is one with ever-changing persona and is not the basis of political conflict.

This changed with the re-emergence of long-term structural unemployment, leading to the *de-incorporation* of increasing sections of the working class, 'who are being defined out of the edifice of citizenship' (Dahrendorf, 1985, p. 98). The underclass in Dahrendorf's account is not simply the product of unemployment.

It is the consequence of the apparent structural inevitability of its position: 'The majority class does not need the unemployed to maintain and even increase its standard of living . . . The main point about this category—for lack of a better word we shall call it "under class"—is that its destiny is perceived as hopeless' (Dahrendorf, 1985, pp. 101–7).

Now there are problems with the simple postulation of a link between unemployment, crime, and disorder, as Mrs Thatcher is only too ready to point out. There is an enormous literature of research on the relationship, which the late Steven Box (1987) has usefully summarized and reviewed in his very important last book, *Recession, Crime and Punishment*. Box summarizes some fifty research projects on the relationship between unemployment and crime. Most are aggregate studies, looking at the correlation over time or across space between levels of crime and unemployment. He sums it up:

The relationship between overall unemployment and crime is incon-sistent . . . on balance the weight of existing research supports there being a weak but none the less significant causal relationship. However, properly targeted research on young males, particularly those from disadvantaged ethnic groups, which considers both the *meaning* and *duration* of unemployment . . . has yet to be done'. (pp. 96–7)

Much of this debate has been vitiated by the assumption that if unemployment is causally related to crime, this must be an invariable law: true at all times and places. But it is more plausible to suppose that the meaning of unemployment will vary according to a number of factors, e.g. its duration, social assessments of blame, previous experience of steady employment, perception of future prospects, comparison with other groups, etc. It would be too much, therefore, to expect that there would be a universal and invariant relation. Some support for the link between offending and perceptions of the justice of unemployment is suggested by the research evidence on the connections of *income inequality* and crime. All the fifteen studies of this reviewed by Box suggest a strong association (over time or cross-sectionally) between economic inequality and crime in general (though this is not true of five studies on homicide specifically) (Box, 1987, pp. 86–98). This plausibly supports the view that it is *relative deprivation* which is causally related to crime, and that in conditions where unemployment is perceived as unjust and hopeless by comparison with the lot of other groups, this will act as a precipitant of crime. Two recent studies, one American (Thornberry and Christenson, 1984) and one British (Farrington *et al.*, 1986), have both used a novel methodology to establish that at least in the present climate unemployment *is* linked to crime. They have looked at the commission of offences reported over time by a sample of youths in longitudinal surveys. What is shown is that crime-rates (especially for property offences) were higher during periods of unemployment than of employment. This suggests that holding constant other variables, the same youths commit more crimes while unemployed.

That there should be a link between (*a*) unemployment and (*b*) relative poverty, and crime is hardly surprising. Both exacerbate the incentives to commit offences and erode the social controls which would otherwise encourage conformity (relative fearfulness of sanctions, perception of the justice of the system, involvement in conventional activities and relationships, etc.). So it is clearly right to argue as Dahrendorf does that the emergence of an underclass excluded apparently permanently from dominant economic life is a potent condition of rising crime. This is all grist to the mill of orthodox social democratic analyses of crime.

But it cannot be the whole story. First, there is the problem of rising crime during the so-called period of affluence. It is this indeed which prompted the first 'new realisms' in criminology: the right-wing realism of James Q. Wilson and his associates in the United States (Wilson, 1975); and the 'administrative realism' attributed by Jock Young to our own Home Office Research Unit (Young, 1986). If the rate of crime increases when the adverse social conditions which have been linked to it are becoming ameliorated, the answer must lie elsewhere: either in the failure of the criminal justice system to deliver sanctions with sufficient certainty or positiveness (the 'New Right' analysis), or in changes in the availability of criminal opportunities in the environment (administrative criminology).

Dahrendorf accepts both these as possible contributions, but encompasses them within a much broader idea: the growth of *anomia*, the failure of a social structure to instil adequate commitment to its conventional moral codes, as crystallized into the criminal law. This is more profoundly a matter of the deeper cultural instilling of conformist values than of the effective threat of *post hoc* sanctions by the criminal justice system. The idea of the failure of the agencies of socialization to instil discipline and moral values because of the effects of post-war 'funk' and permissiveness is a favourite stalking-horse of the right-wing populist criminology championed by Norman Tebbit and others (and in a more sophisticated version in Douglas Hurd's Tamworth and other speeches). The Government has eagerly seized on the 'evidence' provided by the new affluent and rural as well as urban 'lager lout' folk-devils to deny any link between inner-city deprivation and crime. Instead, the finger is pointed at a common moral malaise due to over-liberalization and erosion of discipline (Patten, 1988). Because of this pedigree, the opinions of the Left and of liberals have shied away from examination of the issue of morality in relation to crime. This is a great loss, because at root there is an integral relation between the ideas of crime and morality. Older Marxist criminologies (notably Bonger's) saw the link between economic conditions and crime precisely as lying in the culture of egoism which was stimulated by economic advance under capitalism (Bonger, 1916). This is more evident than ever in recent years with the amorally materialistic culture which has been encouraged by the present Government's economic and social policies. (Labour *is* beginning to pick up this theme: *Guardian*, 2 January 1989, p. 3.) But uncomfortable questions must also be raised about the less traditional and disciplinarian approaches to education, to family, and to other social institutions which Left and liberal opinion have championed. What values *do* we want to underpin social relations and criminal law? How can these be instilled? These problems are ones well recognized and analysed, though not answered, by, for example, Durkheim's discussion of anomie (Fenton *et al.*, 1983) and Dahrendorf's of anomia. As both emphasize, moral education cannot proceed effectively in an economically unjust society. This much is social democratic orthodoxy. But *can* less authoritarian forms of moral discipline be effective and if so, how are they to be achieved?

POLICING

Traditional Left analyses have a uniformly negative image of the police as a repressive apparatus of the state. 'New Left realism' specifically challenges this. The nub of its argument is that policing is a necessary function which ideally should control the criminal victimization disproportionately afflicting the most vulnerable members of our society. But it can only be performed well if there is a profound democratization of the structure of accountability. At present the police do not perform their task satisfactorily. Their initial response to the growth of crime, which stemmed from rising unemployment and inequality, was heavy-handed and militaristic. This was counter-productive in alienating those sectors of the community whose co-operation was essential to criminal investigation. Only by restoring the confidence of these sectors can crime control by the police be successful, and the prerequisite of this is democratic accountability to local communities.

There is an unquestioned presumption here, which pervades current thinking about the police from all perspectives: that the effectiveness and quality of policing *have* declined. The evidence presented for this by the 'New Realists' and others is the seemingly inexorable rise of crime and the decline of 'clear-up' rates (Lea *et al.*, 1987). Between 1979 and 1986 the clear-up rate fell from 41 per cent to 32 per cent. But the clear-up rate is a notoriously inadequate measure of police effectiveness, open to manipulation by many factors other than policing skills (Reiner, 1988*a*). To take the most obvious arithmetical point, if the number of crimes per police officer increases, then, other things being equal, the detection rate *must* fall, even if efficiency remains constant. In a recent study Lea and Young recognize this point, and say that the best indicator of police performance in crime investigation is the number of crimes cleared per officer (Lea *et al.*, 1987). What they do *not* say is that on this 'best' measure, police performance has in fact *improved* marginally, not declined (from 7.9 in 1972 to 9.6 in 1986.)

Clearly in the last twenty years there has been growing controversy about fundamental aspects of policing, unprecedented in this century. (Reiner, 1985, charts and tries to explain this.) But, to put it provocatively, the growth of conflict over policing, and evidence of increasing public hostility and questioning, does not itself establish that standards of policing have declined. (When looking at crime trends criminologists are usually hesitant about inferring objective worsening of problems on the basis of moral panics.) There are many reasons to expect *a priori* that standards of policing should have improved. There has, for example, been a progressive improvement in the educational standards of recruits, and in the quantity and quality of police training. Perhaps it is not so much that police behaviour has deteriorated as that public expectations have risen. What, it will be said, about the 'obvious' evidence of brutality and corruption? While there are, of course, many recent *causes célèbres* of police abuse (Reiner, 1985, ch. 2. 2), memoirs of earlier times (e.g. Mark, 1978; Daley, 1986) suggest that there was an enormous extent of subterranean wrong-doing in the cosy days of the traditional bobby on the beat. For obvious reasons the dangers of such malpractice are endemic in policing, and it may be 'respectable fears' about it which fluctuate more than the extent of abuse. In so far as tactics *have* evidently changed (for instance in public order policing: McCabe *et al.*, 1988; Northam, 1988), it is at least as plausible to see these as a reactive response to rising crime and disorder, as the spontaneous *cause* of them.

The 'New Realists' see policing as the key to crime control, and accountability as the key to good policing. Paradoxically, this comes at a time when both the Conservative Government and the police themselves are much more cautious about the potential contribution of policing. Police numbers and resources are no longer seen as a *vade-mecum* by the police or the Government (as Hurd, for example, made clear in his speech to the Police Foundation Conference in Oxford on 11 April 1988)—hardly surprising after nine 'wasted' years. There is in fact a remarkable cross-party congruence on the idea that the effectiveness of criminal justice and policing depends on the 'involvement of the community', though the Government denies that this requires full local democratic control, as opposed to consultation. I am myself sceptical about whether the local democratic control espoused by the 'New Realists' would have the dramatic confidence-building effect claimed. In any case, the extent of central influence over policing has grown remorselessly and may not be reversible (Reiner, 1988b, 1989). This implies that the accountability of central government in relation to policing is the more important problem to address.

CONCLUSION

'New realism', like the old 'law and order' Conservatism, rejects the traditional social democratic analysis that there is no panacea for crime through criminal justice policy, whether of the Left or the Right. But the essential precondition for order is economic justice and welfare, without which moral socialization cannot take root as other than fragile coercion. None the less, in a just and thriving economy, an effective criminal justice system has important functions to perform. It must show that serious offences against the criminal law will be effectively dealt with. But it is not clear that the declining overall effectiveness of the police and of criminal justice is because of internal failings so much as because of the overwhelming growth of work-load due to growing social and economic inequality coupled with moral deregulation.

References

Ascoli, D. (1979), *The Queen's Peace* (London).

Bailey, V. (1987), *Delinquency and Citizenship* (Oxford).

Benyon, J. (1985), 'Going through the motions: The political agenda, the 1981 riots and the Scarman Enquiry', *Parliamentary Affairs*, 38 4, 409–22.

Bonger, W. (1916), *Criminality and Economic Conditions* (Boston, Mass.).

Bottomley, K., and Pease, K. (1986), *Crime and Punishment: Interpreting the Data* (Milton Keynes).

Box, S. (1987), *Recession, Crime and Punishment* (London).

Brogden, M. (1982), *The Police: Autonomy and Control* (London).

Cohen, P. (1979), 'Policing the working class city', in B. Fine *et al.* (eds.), *Capitalism and the Rule of Law* (London).

Critchley, T. A. (1967), *A History of Police in England and Wales* (London).

—— (1970), *The Conquest of Violence* (London).

Dahrendorf, R. (1985), *Law and Order* (London).

—— (1987), 'The erosion of citizenship and its consequences for us all' *New Statesman*, 12 June, 12–15.

Daley, H. (1986), *This Small Cloud* (London).

Downes, D. (1983), *Law and Order: Theft of an Issue* (London).

Emsley, C. (1988), 'Crime in 19th century Britain', *History Today*, Apr. 40–6.

Farrington, D. P., Gallagher, B., Morley, L., St Ledger, R. J., and West, D. J. (1986), 'Unemployment, school-leaving and crime', *British Journal of Criminology*, 26 4, 335–56.

Fenton, S., Hamnett, I., and Reiner, R. (1983), *Durkheim and Modern Sociology* (Cambridge).

Garland, D. (1985), *Punishment and Welfare* (Aldershot).

Gatrell, V. (1980), 'The decline of theft and violence in Victorian and Edwardian England', in V. Gatrell, J. Lenman, and G. Parker (eds.), *Crime and the Law* (London).

—— and Hadden, T. (1972), 'Nineteenth century criminal statistics and their interpretation', in E. Wrigley (ed.), *Nineteenth Century Society* (Cambridge).

Geary, R. (1985), *Policing Industrial Disputes 1893–1985* (Cambridge).

Gurr, T. R. (1976), *Rogues, Rebels and Reformers* (Beverley Hills).

—— (1981), 'Historical trends in violent crime', in M. Tonry and N. Morris (eds.), *Crime and Justice 3* (Chicago).

Hough, M., and Mayhew, P. (1985), *Taking Account of Crime: Key Findings From the Second British Crime Survey* (London).

Jones, T., MacLean, B., and Young, J. (1986), *The Islington Crime Survey: Crime, Victimisation and Policing in Inner City London* (Aldershot).

Jowell, R., Witherspoon, S., and Brook, L. (1988), *British Social Attitudes: The fifth report* (Aldershot).

Kinsey, R. (1985, *Merseyside Crime and Police Surveys: Final Report* (Liverpool).

—— Lea, J., and Young, J. (1986), *Losing the Fight Against Crime* (Oxford).

Lea, J., Matthews, R., and Young, J. (1987), *Law and Order: Five Years On* (Middlesex).

McCabe, S., Wallington, P., Alderson, J., Gostin, L., and Mason, C. (1988), *The Police, Public Order and Civil Liberties* (London).
Mark, R. (1978), *In the Office of Constable* (London).
Mayhew, P., Elliott, D., and Dowds, L. (1989), *The 1988 British Crime Survey* (London).
Morgan, J. (1987), *Conflict and Order* (Oxford).
Northam, G. (1988), *Shooting in the Dark* (London).
Patten, J. (1988), 'Crime: A middle class disease?' *New Society*, May, 12–13.
Pearson, G. (1983), *Hooligan: A History of Respectable Fears* (London).
Porter, B. (1987), *The Origins of the Vigilant State* (London).
Radzinowicz, L. and Hood, R. (1986), *A History of English Criminal Law*, vol. 5 (London).
Reiner, R. (1985), *The Politics of the Police* (Brighton).
—— (1988a), 'Keeping the Home Office happy', *Policing*, Spring, 28–36.
—— 'In the office of Chief Constable', *Current Legal Problems*, 41, 135–68.
—— (1989), 'Where the buck stops: Chief constables' views on accountability', in R. Morgan and D. Smith (eds.), *Coming to Terms with Policing* (London).
Reith, C. (1938), *The Police Idea* (Oxford).
—— (1943), *British Police and the Democratic Ideal* (Oxford).
—— (1956), *A New Study of Police History* (London).
Smith, D. (1983), *Police and People in London* (London).
Stead, P. (1985), *The Police of Britain* (New York).
Storch, R. (1975), 'The plague of blue locusts', *International Review of Social History*, 20, 61–90.
Thornberry, T. P., and Christenson, R. (1984), 'Unemployment and criminal involvement', *American Sociological Review*, 49, 398–411.
Wilson, J. Q. (1975), *Thinking About Crime* (New York).
Young, J. (1986), 'The failure of criminology: The need for a radical realism', in R. Matthews and J. Young (eds.), *Confronting Crime* (London).

4

The Inner-City Battlefield: Politics, Ideology, and Social Relations

Susanne MacGregor

INTRODUCTION

From the moment in 1979 when Mrs Thatcher swept to power on a wave of uncollected garbage following the 'winter of discontent', her radical assault on social democracy and the welfare state was to be a continuing theme of the politics of the 1980s. In her famed speech on election night 1987, as she rallied her party troops on the steps of Party Headquarters not to rest on their laurels but to continue the fight (they were to be allowed one night of 'marvellous partying' but must start back the next day with renewed vigour), she announced that 'we've got a big job to do in some of those inner cities . . . and politically, we've got to get back in there—we want to win those too'. The connection between her public policies and the political arithmetic was precise and clear.

In this chapter, I shall argue that the concept 'inner city' is a fundamentally ideological category. Although it is often presented as a scientific term, relating to features of urban development, its use is better understood as part of an ideological set which has been borrowed from the United States. The use of the very term is therefore questionable. As used in politics and social policy in contemporary Britain, the concept 'inner city' is part of a move to a more conservative and punitive set of social practices and attitudes.

THE 'INNER CITY'

The 'inner city' is a representation which serves as a focus for politics and policy. It is a public issue which represents a constellation of social worries, to do with urban poverty, squalor, ill-health, deprivation, decay, crime, social disintegration, and social polarization. The core issue is that of *urban poverty*.

Poverty has been a continuing problem in post-war Britain. Its size and shape have varied and the names used to describe it have varied. What we have seen in the 1980s is a process by which poverty has been redefined as to do with the 'inner city'. This involves an association of poverty with crime and violence, and with decay and backwardness.

The redefinition of poverty as urban poverty and as a problem of the inner city reflects also a change in perceptions of appropriate policy responses. Specifically, the concentration on the spatial dimension, the grounded location of poverty in certain areas, arose when attempts were being made to restrict the scope of public policy and the extent of public expenditure, to limit its focus to targeted areas. However, reality intrudes on such constructions, as indicated by the gradual widening of the category 'inner city' to refer also to 'outer estates' and then to whole cities, like Bradford; in some cases it is even used as a code for whole regions of deprivation in conjunction with that other metaphor, the North–South divide.

The battle of ideas is about the very categories to be used in policy debate. Those who prefer limited, selective superficial policies exert pressure to restrict the scope of the categories. Those arguing for more fundamental change, tackling the *causes* rather than merely the *symptoms* of social distress, utilize categories embracing wider sections of society, extending from the still limited concept of the 'bottom third' to wider notions of the 'public' and 'citizens'.

This chapter has a double focus. It aims to show that closely related to the objective of resurrecting conservative social policies is a political method which involves an attempt to change Britain's political landscape. Mrs Thatcher's expressed aim was to rid the country of socialism forever, and part of this involved destroying the Labour party's local government base. In the 1980s, Labour local authorities had emerged as defenders of the poor and of public services. The third term reforms to local government, the 'inner-city' policies, were much less about doing good for the poor and arresting decline and decay than about undermining Labour's power bases. The flagship reform, the poll tax, and the related flotilla of changes affecting privatization and contracting-out, education, housing and social services, as well as specific 'inner-city initiatives', were designed to change the political structure and quite precisely to replace local democracy by the 'market'.

The explicitly anti-democratic nature of the radical Right project was put succinctly in an Institute of Economic Affairs pamphlet:

it is clear that the machinery of representative parliamentary democracy has so far proved unsuitable as the mechanism for translating personal preferences into day-to-day practice. Profoundly disturbing questions must be raised about the imperfections or obstacles in the representative political process that frustrate the wishes of the sovereign populace it is ostensibly designed to represent. (Harris and Seldon, 1987, p. 64)

Rather than propose ways in which representative democracy could be strengthened and improved, these authors concluded: 'the weight of the evidence is that a vote is much less effective than purchasing power . . . the market is potentially more democratic than the state' (p. 65).

DIVIDED BRITAIN: THE ASSAULT ON THE WELFARE STATE

Britain has become an increasingly divided kingdom under Mrs Thatcher: the years 1979–87 witnessed major changes in Britain's electoral geography, reflecting growing socio-economic polarization—the divide between the relatively prosperous and the relatively deprived areas widened (Walker and Walker, 1987).[1]

[1] Johnston and his colleagues (1988) have demonstrated that polarization is manifested in class cleavage (occupational class origins and local contexts), which remains the single most important influence on the development of political attitudes and the identification of voters with particular political parties. There is in addition a geography of class cleavage, reflecting the dominance of different parties and ideologies in different local milieux. Yet, in spite of party identification, an increasingly large proportion of the British electorate is not willing to give that party its support habitually and unconditionally. Instead they evaluate its record, policies, and leaders relative to those of other parties. The extent of 'economic optimism' is the major reason for shifts in voting in recent years.

Johnston and his colleagues (1988, pp. 325–7) have argued that

this polarisation of the country and its potential political consequences was recognised by the Conservative Government almost certainly well before the results of the 1987 general election were known . . . the development of policies to tackle the economic run-down and social deprivation of inner city areas was identified as a major thrust for the new government and many new initiatives were conceived in the first weeks of the new Parliament. To a large extent, these continued and crystallised earlier attempts to tackle similar problems . . . The nature of those policies with their emphases on private sector developments, home ownership and small businesses, suggests that in part at least the Government is seeking to produce electoral change by introducing traditional Conservative supporters to areas where the party has been very weak—as, for example, in many of the residential developments in London's Docklands.

Mrs Thatcher's identification of the 'inner cities' as the focus of her third term's agenda was not therefore a new conversion to the need to do something about urban poverty, squalor, and alienation. Rather it was one more step in the *step by step* approach to the reform of both local government and the politics and values of British society, which has been followed through consistently and vigorously throughout the 1980s. For the third term, the key policy areas, which would tackle the 'really big job' of the 'inner cities', were named as the policies for local government, education, and housing.

Much of the right-wing discussion of policies for inner cities has been framed as though the attack was solely on two forms of 'extremists': one, the 'Loony Left' and the other, disorderly, criminal elements fomenting riots and social disorder. But the Thatcherite counter-revolution is much more all-encompassing: it is an assault on social democracy and all that that term entails, just as much if not more so than on simply 'taking out' pockets of resistance in specific local areas.

Key state agencies in the social democratic arrangements identified for attack were local authorities.[2]

[2] That local authorities and the universities were singled out as bases of opposition to the Thatcherite project was made clear by Mrs Thatcher herself in an interview in April 1989: ' "Q. To what extent has your government succeeded

Tackling the Town Halls

The programme of reforms to local government, to reduce the
power and status of local authorities, is part of a planned programme which, it is intended, will stretch into the 1990s. Because
some reforms are hidden from public view over the horizon does
not mean that they have not been thought out and designed. As
we move along the road, they will come into sight. Mrs Thatcher
herself supported this reading: 'I'm here because I believe in
things—because I'm always thinking forward' (speaking on
Panorama, 25 January 1988).

The Bradford model represents Thatcherism in action in the
'inner city'. (Bradford as a whole was frequently described as an
'inner city' in news broadcasts in 1988, demonstrating clearly that
the term signified 'poverty and decline' rather than a specific area
in a city.) Shortly after the Tories won control of the council in
September 1988, almost £6 million of cuts in local authority
expenditure were announced. The Leader of the Council, Eric
Pickles, speaking at the Tory Conference in 1988, had promised
that these reforms would place the customer first and that Labour
would be swept from control of the cities and Town Halls.

In this constellation, the Right identifies housing as of particular
significance. The long period of domination by municipal socialism
is said to have produced a dependence on the local authority,
especially through provision of council housing. Low rents are
seen as a form of bribery of the electorate. And this special culture
is thought to be found in a particularly acute and virulent form in
Scotland and in some parts of the North of England.

Michael Heseltine was the main spokesman of the Conservative
approach to the inner cities until his ministerial career was

in permanently turning the British away from socialism?" "A. The people have
truly moved away from it. But perhaps not yet permanently, because some have
a vested interest in it. Let me say this: socialism did not come from the people. It
is a doctrine of intellectuals who had the arrogance to believe they could better
plan everyone's life. You will see it in our left-wing Labour authorities (in local
government) and in some university groups." ' (*A Conversation with the Prime
Minister*: an advertisement by *Reader's Digest* which appeared in the *New York
Times*, Wednesday, 19 Apr. 1989, pp. A14–A15.)

abruptly interrupted by the Westland affair in 1986. He has remarked on the apparent fact that the 'Loony Left' were 'increasingly to be found in the more deprived and distressed parts of our country' (Heseltine, 1987, p. 131). The Government had, he said, four choices.

They could let conditions worsen; or they could move power back to national government; or they could re-organise the electoral boundaries so that the irresponsible Left loses its tight inner urban constituencies; or they could push power out beyond local government and into the hands of the people whom it is elected to serve. (p. 132).

In practice, all four of these options have been pursued by the Thatcher administrations. But it was the fourth option which the Tories emphasized in their rhetoric. Local authorities would be encouraged to see themselves primarily as 'service-providers'. Once this was conceded, the next step would be to move to their becoming semi-independent public bodies (much the same might happen to hospitals and other public services), with the 'freedom to manage' without regard to political pressure from local electors or 'vested interests' (trade unions and professionals) and the freedom to cut labour costs (the main item in service budgets) by paying people only what it was necessary to pay them in that local market. National pay settlements and negotiating arrangements which hinder that process which would be improved, they argue, by 'flexibility' in wage-rates and local pay bargaining. The *economics* of the enterprise culture and the shape of *service provision* are thus integrally related, two sides of the same coin. And such changes mark a decisive shift away from local democracy.

INSTITUTIONAL REFORM AND SOCIAL ENGINEERING

Two developments—opposition to central government policies by Labour local councils, and urban riots—forced the Government to develop policies for the 'inner cities' (Heseltine, 1987). That riots and local socialism were both found in the most acutely stressed parts of the country is no accident. Each was a form of opposition to the direction and effects of government policy and protest at economic changes. Hence the Tory Government's need to try to destroy such opposition. This could be done by beating down, as in the assertion of dominance over local author-ities. Or it could be done through fragmentation.

Fragmentation takes place where blocks of low-income poor housing and their associated populations are broken up and dispersed, either through deliberate slum clearance and dispersal of population, as in the late nineteenth century (Stedman Jones, 1971); or by the decentralizing effects of the policies of earlier post-war years, overspill outer estates and new towns; or through the later processes of 'gentrification' (Glass, 1964)—a term first used by Ruth Glass but popularized in the late 1970s—i.e. the emergence of new wealthy areas as in Islington or Docklands and the displacement of the poorer local population, likely to be further encouraged by the impact of the poll tax.

Both the assertion of central authority and the fragmentation of local social structures and economies are integral to the overall desire to use power to restructure social arrangements in such a way that certain interests are favoured over others, to reward supporters, *and* to maintain these arrangements by using social institutions to entrench an alternative set of ideas, those of the 'enterprise culture'.

The Thatcherite counter-revolution should be seen, then, as consisting of a number of interrelated policies designed to re-structure taxation, restructure public expenditure, reshape the welfare services, and curb the power of professionals, trade unions, and local authorities. These are closely interrelated and the Government's plans for the 'inner cities' cannot be understood unless seen as part of this overall enterprise.

Thatcherism's social engineering—just as much social engin-eering as that of the Fabians or the very different local socialists they oppose—aims to 'temper expectations'. The post-war boom's revolution of rising expectations is said to have fostered an in-satiable appetite for more, without concern for the question of 'who pays?' Thatcherism is the revolt of the haves against the demands of the have nots. Mrs Thatcher, speaking on *Panorama* (25 January 1988), said that her constituency is that of those who are working 'for an increased standard of living for their own families' (not, we should note, for others). She receives more complaints, she said, from those who are *in work* but feel they would be as well off on supplementary benefit; her aim is to increase the gap between those who are working and the non-working.

An interesting aspect of any 'counter-revolution' is that it takes the terms of the 'revolution' and turns them to its own purposes. As Arno Mayer (1971, p. 45) commented, 'As if by reflex, the counter-revolution borrows its central ideas, objectives, styles and methods from the revolution'. Thus ideas and principles are taken over, redefined, and reapplied in order to structure and manage discontent and political rebellion. Key words such as self-help, accountability, responsibility, hard work, thrift—many central to the tradition of the English working classes and trade unions—have been appropriated and presented as specifically Conservative and in some way under threat from socialism and collective action.

So the Thatcherite counter-revolution has redefined the idea of justice. John Redwood, Head of the Prime Minister's Policy Unit in 1983–5, now a Conservative MP, sees two different kinds of justice: protection for the poor; and that all who enjoy services should pay (speaking on *Weekend World*, 11 October 1987). The poll tax, he said, is central to change and to improving the inner cities. Enterprise has been driven away by high business rates and high domestic rates. Enterprising people, in Thatcherism's view, are those who create new jobs. These are the highly successful, who must be encouraged to stay and to do well for they are the motor that pulls the rest up; they create prosperity and employ other people. Part of the drive to improve inner cities is deliberately to reward success, increase the gap between the working and the non-working, retain business and talented and successful people in these areas, and charge those who use services the economic cost of these services, so that if they don't like the price they will be encouraged to move out to areas where 'the price is right'. This is called 'consumer choice' and it also opens up the possibility of charging for more services. The effect on the demography of the inner cities could be dramatic, as migration into and out of inner cities is in any case already high. Since housing is also crucial to mobility, the break-up of local authority control of low-income estates is also part of the package of reforms.

Reports that the numbers registering on the electoral rolls are falling (*Weekend World*, 11 October 1987; the *Independent*, 23 February 1988, p. 6) indicate that the political arithmetic will also play its part. If some of those who resist and resent the imposition, opt out of the electoral system (and the calculation is that these will be those who are thought, either now or in the future, likely to benefit from the present array of public services), while others are more inclined to vote at local elections for a party which offers to cut and reorganize services, the electoral outcome would be dramatic. Michael Howard, then a Minister at the Department of the Environment, reported an opinion poll as having found that one-quarter of people who had not previously voted in local elections intended to vote in future as a result of the community charge (interview on *This Week, Next Week*, 21 February 1988). Quite how they will choose to vote is less certain, however, as the poll tax becomes labelled 'a Tory tax' and as environmental issues and collapsing public services assume a higher priority.

Another concept which has been taken over and reinterpreted is that of 'decentralization'. One argument against the Government's third term agenda for local government and the public services has been that, by undermining local authorities, they are increasingly centralizing decision-taking. On the contrary, argue the Thatcherites, we are 'putting power further away', for example to parents through the education reforms. With the opting-out opportunity, schools will have greater responsibility and liberty than under local authorities. In addition, capital is said to have been spread among the people.

FROM ENTITLEMENT TO OBLIGATION

The new enlightenment's assault on social democracy has focused particularly on the concept of 'dependency'. Dependence on bureaucracies (local authorities, the NHS, the social security system) is said to present people with a lack of control over their own lives, to damage the spirit of independence. The sole supporters of the 'social democratic' welfare state are, so the argument goes, the publicly employed educated classes, whose careers are linked to the state. Removing the supports of these state agencies—

the welfare net, subsidized public services—would face people with a 'reality test': that if you don't sweep floors eight hours a day, you won't have any money to live on. Young people are thought to have imbibed this dependency culture to an extent not found in their parents and grandparents—a product of the high rates of social expenditure of the 1960s and 70s.

To effect a new social discipline, a new relationship is being established between the state and its subjects: society, that is the government, plays the role of the strict disciplinarian father; the people are their children who have to be taught to mend their ways. John Moore, then Social Services Secretary, set this out explicitly in a key speech in autumn 1987, when he argued the need to move from social protection towards attacking dependency. In doing this, he said, 'we are following the oldest pattern of behaviour known to man: the way parents raise their children. The aim of all parents is to teach their child to become an independent, self-reliant adult, able to participate in life and gain satisfaction. This should be society's aim for all its citizens too.' A clearer statement of the top-down direction of the people by government would be hard to find. It demonstrates the emphasis on moral regulation and discipline which distinguishes the conservative from the liberal phases of Thatcherism.

The American writer Charles Murray, one of Mr Moore's mentors, has justified moves away from the language of entitlement to the language of obligation by reference to something he calls 'popular wisdom'. This he defines as characterized by 'hostility towards welfare (it makes people lazy), toward lenient judges (they encourage crime), and toward socially conscious schools . . . The popular wisdom disapproves of favoritism for blacks and of too many written-in rights for minorities of all sorts' (Murray, 1984, p. 146). John Moore continued his 'assault on dependency' in 1989 by arguing that real poverty has already been abolished in modern Britain. Very few are really poor any more. To make this case, he defined poverty in 'the old absolute sense of hunger and want' or as 'starving children and squalid slums'. By defining poverty as starvation and destitution, he was able to claim that not many people in Britain are poor and that those who argue the case for improvements to welfare provision, 'the poverty lobby and the media', are really intent on furthering their socialist aims through calling Western material capitalism a failure. Where others might see a more complex situation with a conceptual continuum between starvation, hunger, destitution, poverty (want), and inequality, Moore abolishes poverty by dividing it up between the two extremes of the continuum, also at the same time neatly side-stepping discussion of the visible increase in begging, destitution, and homelessness in major British cities.

The sub-text, or hidden message, of Moore's attack on the poverty lobby is an attack on the poor themselves, part of the move to a harsher, conservative approach to social policy. The poor are in reality simply experiencing the effects of inequality and can indeed be blamed for their condition. 'It is hard to believe that poverty stalks the land when even the poorest fifth of families with children spend nearly a tenth of their income on alcohol and tobacco', was Mr Moore's dismissive conclusion.

Such new social engineering is based on a specific form of behaviourist psychology—rewards and punishments directed at *individuals* teach them that actions have consequences, that failures or mistakes are punished and not rewarded, so that behaviour changes. This stress on merely *individual* responsibility ignores the reality of the interrelatedness of human life. No consideration is given to the fact that actually *society is everything*—that one person's effort may bring reward to someone else; that one person's mistake can bring disaster to another.

The aim of the Thatcherite reforms to the public services is said to be to give consumers the power to go elsewhere if they are not satisfied. This policy is limited, however, in two crucial ways: first, that such 'choice' in effect reduces to the ability to pay, and ability to pay has been profoundly affected by other policies which have increased the differences among groups with regard to income and wealth; and secondly, that many public services must be provided in the local area if they are to be of real value and if other costs, not only financial, are not to be incurred, for instance, in travelling or moving residence in order to receive them. For example, proposals such as those to base service provision on charges or vouchers are impractical and tend only to increase the differences between the services available in different areas and to shift the costs from the more visible budgets of the services to the less visible ones of the individual, relatively powerless consumer: either their pockets or their time and energy will be hit.

As we have seen, the language of this welfare revolution is American, much of it popularized by writers like Charles Murray (1984). The aim to move away from the language of *entitlement* to the language of *obligation* is very different from the language of freedom and liberty which dominated the earlier phases of Thatcherism. As the terms 'accountability' and 'democracy' were redefined in the poll tax debates, so the concepts of 'justice' and 'active citizenship' have been redefined in the debates about public services.

The Thatcherite assault on the welfare state involves two key aspects: lowering expectations and imposing work discipline. The object of the 'training schemes' being promoted as part of the inner-city package is to drive down wages, for without reducing wages there will be no job creation. The creation of the enterprise culture in deprived areas of the North and the 'inner cities' is fundamentally about the creation of jobs at lower wages than were previously viewed as acceptable *and* reducing entitlement to benefit and levels of benefit in order to increase the incentive to take on these jobs.

The end of entitlement is perhaps best demonstrated by the introduction of the Social Fund in the social security reforms of 1988. The Social Fund replaced the previous system of additional and urgent needs allowances and grants, which had been an area of supplementary benefit responsive to demand and welfare rights pressure. The solution to the complexities of the system and the growing complexity of case law adjudication was to abolish the notion of additional allowances completely, replacing them with loans from a limited budget and no right to independent appeal. This signified a 'campaign against the benefit culture'. Benefits would go only to those in 'genuine need' so as not to 'featherbed' the rest. A distinction would be made between the deserving and the undeserving poor. The main aim of these reforms was *not* to meet need precisely and in a neat, targeted form. Rather it was precisely to change attitudes, to stress individual responsibility—you're on your own, don't expect any help from us—and to reduce the state's obligations.

THE BATTLE OF IDEAS

'The welfare state is at once Britain's proudest achievement and the biggest man-made disaster', Sir John Hoskyns has written. (He is another former Head of the Prime Minister's Policy Unit and a key figure in the Institute of Directors.) In a series of articles in *The Times* to celebrate Mrs Thatcher's ten years as leader (11, 12, and 13 February 1985) he wrote that she had inherited 'forty years of muddled policy'. The first stage of the attack on the 'muddled policy' involved reducing the power of the trade unions, especially the public sector unions, who were thought to dominate the welfare state itself. Having cowed the trade unions, we can see that the next step was to take on the local authorities and the poor. Next in line for the 1990s are child benefit, pensions, and the NHS. By the year 2000, little will remain of the 1940s social legislation, assumed by Beveridge.

Beveridge's Report was based on three guiding principles: the second of these was that:

the organisation of social insurance should be treated as *one part of a comprehensive policy of social progress*. Social insurance fully developed may provide income security: it is an attack upon Want. But Want is one only of five giants on the road of reconstruction and in some ways the easiest to attack. The others are Disease, Ignorance, Squalor and Idleness'. (Beveridge, 1942, para. 8, my emphasis)

Thus Beveridge had assumed that the elimination of poverty was integrally linked to policies for health, education, housing and town planning, and full employment. Under Thatcherism, full employment commitments, family allowances, the NHS, town planning, council housing, education, social security, all will have been radically reformed.

The battle of politics and ideas which focuses on the inner city represents a conflict between sets of interests and values which have a long history, dating at least from the 1830s and the New Poor Law of 1834. These are conflicts between democratic and anti-democratic, socialist and anti-socialist, egalitarian and anti-egalitarian ideas. The ideas of the radical Right are not new. They go back a long way. They are old ideas stated in new form, in new language. In all the post-war years, both currents have been present. What changed was the party political situation: the seizure of power by the radical Right in the Conservative party and thence in government.

For example, Ian Macleod and Enoch Powell (1952) had argued:

Given that redistribution is a characteristic of the social services, the general presumption must be that they will be rendered only on evidence of need, i.e. of financial inability to provide each particular service out of one's own or one's family's resources. Otherwise the process is a wasteful and purposeless collection and issue of resources, which leaves people in the enjoyment of the same facilities as before.

And Geoffrey Howe (1961) argued that 'over the whole field of social policy, the firm aim should be a reduction in the role of the state'. These ideas were given a great push forward by the increasing impact of American thinking on British social policy from the late 1960s onward. The collapse of thinking about social policy in Britain, a result largely of the failure of the Labour party to develop new policies and not to defend adequately basic principles and institutions, created a vacuum into which right-wing ideas flooded.

It was easier for the Thatcherites to attack the welfare state successfully because its principles and institutions had not been adequately defended, as Dorothy Wedderburn and others were warning as early as 1964 (Wedderburn, 1965). The slippage of support for universalism, equality, and public services was illustrated in comments made by Roy Jenkins. Writing in 1959, and with reference to Peter Townsend's calculation that a fifth of the population had not shared in the general improvement in living standards since the war, Roy Jenkins argued:

Any believer in social justice, or indeed any believer in a civilised society, must surely give a high priority to providing such an improvement. Some, including Mr Townsend himself, would give it an absolute priority. They would deny the right of those whose standard of living is already at or above the average to any further improvement until the submerged fifth had been given more or less equivalent benefits. *I would not accept this extreme position.* Neither the economic policy of a nation nor the political programme of a party is likely to achieve a successful dynamism if it is based solely upon the assistance of lame ducks. (Jenkins, 1959, pp. 56–7, my emphasis)

Thus even in 1959 advocacy of equality was cast as extremism. The need for incentives was accepted if economic growth was to be attained. And any chance of winning an election on proposals for social justice was 'realistically' denied.

It is important to stress that while there is within right-wing attacks on the welfare state a concentration on shifting culture and attitudes, with the increasing emphasis on 'business' and 'enterprise', on managing tight budgets and devolving responsibility for effecting cuts to lower levels, the intentions are determinedly economic. Ideology provides the justification and politics the means for shifts in economic outcomes—redistribution of income and wealth away from some sectors and groups towards others. This shift requires crucially a lowering of labour-costs and restructuring of the labour market. Social discipline is wanted not just for itself but for these ends.

Much of what happened with the ascendency of the radical Right in British politics was predicted in at least one prescient article (Leonard, 1979). What is interesting, however, is that it has taken over ten years to bring about the changes Leonard anticipated. This is important and tells us two things. First, that the radical Right's assault has been carefully managed; the step by step approach was brilliantly conceived and managed by diligent and unerring control from the centre; secondly, that the speed of its success has varied in different areas of public provision, which tells us much about the role of resistances, resistances built on organized opposition within the public services. In the areas most closely concerned with the inner city, opposition from local authorities has been crucial.

RECENT POLICIES ON THE INNER CITIES

Conservative policy on the inner cities has diverged in some ways from the earlier policies of the 1970s, especially in shifting away from social and environmental programmes towards an emphasis on economic and enterprise-generating ones. In other ways, however, there is a continuity in these policies, especially in so far as inner-city and urban initiatives specifically target defined spatial areas and direct resources deliberately towards them through special schemes. The assumptions lying behind such targeted programmes are that the 'problem' is a bounded one, concerned with 'pockets of poverty or deprivation', restricted areas of decay, which can be remedied through relatively limited expenditure and precise targeting of funds and activities to 'special', different, difficult problems, limited problems which remain to be rooted out, while the rest of the system is assumed to be functioning well and on course for prosperity and harmony. That is, inner cities are perceived as 'deviant communities', areas which need to be turned around and brought back into the mainstream, a mainstream that requires little or no restructuring or reform.

This shift in policy from universalism towards selectivism and area targeting was criticized as early as 1976 by Peter Townsend, who was quick to note its implications:

The perception that the ills of society are relatively more prevalent in some areas than others has innocent and fairly obvious origins . . . But then material and environmental deficiencies become heavily associated in the public mind with other socially perceived problems. For social reasons, both the degree of concentration of certain acknowledged problems and the extent to which they can be explained by internal processes of self-generation rather than externally imposed processes may be grossly exaggerated. (Townsend, 1976, p. 168)

He foresaw the dangerous drift in urban policy, which began under a Labour government, towards beliefs in contamination, self-generation of problems, individualistic explanations for poverty, pathologizing of areas and their populations. These perceptions were encouraged by policies which assumed that problems of urban deprivation had their origins in the characteristics of local populations and that these could be resolved simply by better co-ordination of the social services and encouragement of citizen involvement and community self-help.

The 'Urban Underclass'

A key feature of this situation is the extent to which public policy itself acts to create an 'underclass' of excluded poor, who are compressed into densely populated, poorly served physical spaces, crowded estates, and 'inner cities'. This also implies, as recognized by the community development activists of the 1970s and their inheritors the 'local socialists', that poverty is a political condition as much if not more than a social or economic one. The power-lessness of the poor, their inability to influence the distribution of life-chances and rewards, helps to explain their poverty (Miliband, 1974; MacGregor, 1981). Some political activists concluded from this that what was needed was to 'empower the poor', encourage their civic and political participation as a way to redress the balance, give them the strength to organize in such a way as to make effective claims on society, to receive those citizen's rights to which they were said to be entitled. Much welfare rights activity and anti-poverty campaigns of local authorities, as well as anti-racist, anti-sexist equal opportunities policies, were based on this analysis.

Once again, the counter-revolution has taken over the key concepts of this approach and turned them on their head. The 'enabling state' and the concept of empowering people have been interpreted as encouraging more individual consumer choice and limited, voluntary self-help welfare activity and 'community care' (Thatcher, 1985; Ridley, 1988).

The perceptions of the 'inner city' and of the 'underclass' which inform government circles today are drawn from the United States, whose cities offer a terrifying picture of our future if we continue to move down the road to a residual, extremely selectivist welfare system. These perceptions emphasize the pathology of the victims themselves and the pathological influences found in certain areas. Fear about a drugs epidemic fuelled this alarm (MacGregor, 1989). 'We have seen the future and it is frightening', said Robin Corbett MP returning from a visit to New York's Lower East Side with the Home Affairs Select Committee in 1985. The picture was sketched by John Banham (1988, p. 23),

Director-General of the CBI, describing Lawndale on the south side of Chicago. This, he said,

represents a future to be avoided at almost any cost. There, a combination of poor housing and education, high crime rates, much of it drug-related, large-scale immigration and associated racial tensions, an exodus of jobs and the more well-off to the suburbs, high youth unemployment and welfare dependency and the break-up of traditional family structures have served to create what some commentators in the United States have described as an 'urban underclass'.

John Banham's understanding of the term 'underclass' derives from his days as a Director-General at the Audit Commission. It reiterates an orthodoxy whose source can be traced to one specific article (Lemann, 1986). This perception found expression also in an important Audit Commission Occasional Paper (Audit Commission, 1987) from which Banham's statement quotes and which is itself a direct repetition of Lemann's views.

The paper set out in diagrammatic form a view of the factors causing an urban underclass (see Figure 4.1). At the centre of the conception is high youth unemployment which, it is assumed, in the case of males leads to crime and trouble with the police; in the case of females it leads to single-parent families. Single-parent families, that is *mothers*, are blamed for continuing this process, producing a culture of dependency and poverty in that their children are said to grow up with poor interpersonal skills, low educational achievement, and lack of marketable skills. Recent US research and policy have focused on '*dependent* mothers'. Welfare is seen as a drug of *addiction* but studies of long-term welfare recipients have found that only one in five daughters of dependent mothers themselves become dependent. Furthermore, half of all mothers on welfare come off it within two years (Daly, 1989). However, superficial reading of research findings, combined with prejudice, has led to a growing stress on workfare in the United States where mothers, whose children may be as young as six months in some States, could be forced to accept training or low-paid work even where the child care support services are inadequate. The harshly punitive impact of the new

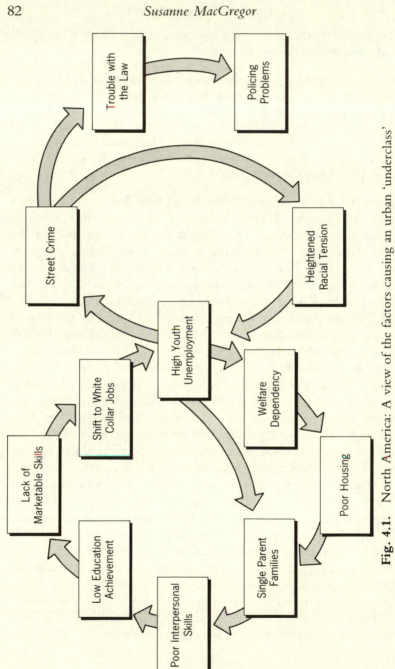

Fig. 4.1. North America: A view of the factors causing an urban 'underclass'

social conservatism on these women and their children contrasts with right-wing rhetoric expressing concern for the family. These views are being borrowed by right-wingers in Britain (Redwood, 1989).

The social historian John Macnicol (1988) has criticized the 'pursuit of the underclass' which characterized the 1970s and 1980s. He pinpoints the beginnings of the contemporary resurgence of this theme as Sir Keith Joseph's speech to the Pre-School Playgroups Association on 29 June 1972, when he was Secretary of State for Social Services. Macnicol shows that the roots of these views lie deeper and can be found in the social debates of the past one hundred years. Investigations of a hereditary or hard-core social problem group have always been crucial in conservative social reformist strategies. Joseph had mused: 'perhaps there is at work here a process, apparent in many situations but imperfectly understood, by which problems reproduced themselves from generation to generation' (Joseph, 1972). The focus on the pattern of births among the very poor, a feature of the American concept of the underclass, one which prioritizes 'single-parent female headed households' as major issues (blaming the mothers), appeared explicitly in Joseph's 1974 Birmingham speech when he maintained that, because an excess of births was apparently occurring in mothers of social class V, 'the balance of our population, our human stock, is threatened'. Birth control might help to prevent the excess production of 'problem children, the future unmarried mothers, delinquents, denizens of our Borstals, subnormal educational establishments, prisons, hostels for drifters'.

Extensive research failed to support the cycle of deprivation thesis but the stereotype lived on, and grew to more prominence with the dominance of the right wing in the Conservative party and thence in British society and politics: Keith Joseph was of course an early leading figure in this faction within the party.

The apparent existence of an economically unproductive residuum of social outcasts has been traced as a feature of social investigation and social policy by, among others, Stedman Jones (1971) and John Macnicol (1988). The words used—the labels— have varied over time: residuum; social problem group; hard-core; problem families; the culture of poverty; alienation; hereditary poverty; the inadequate poor; the urban underclass. The search for personal inadequacy and behavioural defects has been the key focus of such research and policy. Macnicol argues that 'in its periodic reconstruction, the underclass concept has tended to consist of five elements':

1. an artificial 'administrative definition relating to contacts with particular institutions of the state and welfare agencies, social workers, the police etc.';
2. the separate question of inter-generational transmission, through either heredity or socialization;
3. identification of particular behavioural traits as antisocial, ignoring others;
4. stress on resource allocation issues, emphasizing high demand for services by defined categories of users; and
5. 'it tends to be supported by those who wish to constrain the redistributive potential of state welfare and thus it has always been part of a broader conservative view of the aetiology of social problems and their correct solutions' (Macnicol, 1988, p. 316).

The centrality of the 'family' in these conservative perceptions, and the double-edged nature of the disciplines advocated to deal with the problem, were illustrated in an editorial in the *Wall Street Journal* (Europe) of 17 January 1989. Entitled *Today's America*, this explained the split between the successful, socially mobile blacks and the rest thus:

the key to the difference . . . lies in the family—a truth Daniel Patrick Moynihan was pilloried for stating a few years before Martin Luther King's assassination. In the past week, it happens, we have heard intelligent and well-meaning whites talking in apocalyptic terms about the problem of the black underclass—that it can only be solved by draconian measures of enshrining abortion or taking children away from mothers.

Rather than this, argued the *Wall Street Journal*:

the solution to the underclass lies in stricter enforcement of the criminal laws, in giving tenants a stake and a say in public housing, in educational innovation opposed by teachers' unions, in changing welfare laws so that a baby is not a ticket for an apartment separate from mom's. Much of the problem of the underclass, we continue to believe, arises from perverse incentives rooted in misguided paternalism.

This explanation of urban poverty in terms of 'perverse incentives' is being picked up by the right wing in Britain and used as the basis for proposals for new policies and regulations regarding unemployment benefit, income support, and housing entitlement as they apply to lone mothers.

In the same week in which the *Wall Street Journal* editorial appeared, it was announced in Britain that an extensive study of lone parents' reliance on social security would be carried out after comments from Ministers that the state is having to foot the bill for the so-called dependency culture (*Guardian*, 18 January 1989, p. 3). Mr John Moore, then Social Security Secretary, had spoken of a young woman in his constituency who obtained special benefit and a council flat by becoming pregnant. He had said that the Government needed to be 'wary of providing incentives to obtain a particular benefit which can erode a sense of personal responsibility and adversely affect behaviour'. Similarly, discussions are developing on how to limit the housing provided for single mothers and their children to very low standard institutional care, 'to discourage the others'.

BLAMING AND EXPELLING THE VICTIM

While disputing the definition of an underclass composed of recalcitrant or wayward pathological individuals, it should be noted that current developments in public policy, especially the poll tax registration and payment procedures, are encouraging the formation of an 'underclass' in the sense of a section of society which does not participate even formally in society, let alone participate fully as citizens. Townsend's most important definition of poverty[3] which emphasizes that lack of money leads to an

---

[3] 'Poverty can be defined objectively and applied consistently only in terms of the concept of relative deprivation . . . individuals, families and groups in the population can be said to be in poverty when they lack the resources to obtain the type of diet, participate in the activities and have the living conditions and amenities which are customary or at least widely encouraged or approved in the

inability to join in fully in social life, producing an exclusion of individuals and social groups from ordinary life, focuses crucially on the role of lack of participation and powerlessness in the social construction of the 'poor'. Some features of public policy may add to this informal exclusion and outcast status by encouraging people to opt out completely even from formal status as a citizen, thus losing all civic rights. The poll tax is crucial here (MacGregor, 1988). The pressures to evade the tax—a new imposition bearing particularly hard on poor people in deprived, 'high spending' areas—will encourage some people to disappear from all public record and perhaps to keep on the move to avoid detection. Recent changes in social security regulations add to this. Shelter estimated that 25,000 to 40,000 young people slept out in the open in Central London in 1987. Others say the numbers increased in 1988. The census of 1991 may be affected by these processes and since the census returns will form the basis of some resource-allocation calculations, severe underestimation of the needs of some areas may be the result. In the United States cities already have to argue for a notional amount to compensate for such under-recording: the same will probably have to happen in Britain.

THE DEBATE IN THE UNITED STATES: SOCIAL DEMOCRACY'S ALTERNATIVE

In his book *The Truly Disadvantaged*, William Julius Wilson avoided the simplistic banalities of writers like Murray and Lemann (Wilson, 1987). He confronted the evidence on inner cities and, being a black social democratic scholar, dared to observe the clustering in 'ghetto' neighbourhoods of 'socially isolated' blacks and Hispanics. This is due, he argued, to decreasing employment opportunities with the shift from goods-producing to service-producing activities and the loss of 7 million unskilled jobs, and the undesirable concentration effects of this. But this situation was not, he claimed, the result of personal inadequacy;

societies to which they belong. Their resources are so seriously below those commanded by the average individual or family that they are, in effect, excluded from ordinary living patterns, customs and activities.' (Townsend, 1979, p. 31.)

it resulted from wider impersonal economic and demographic forces. The loss of employment opportunities led to a loss of 'marriageable men' in inner-city areas. A key factor in the process, Wilson argued, was the collapse of *institutions* in these neighbourhoods, a direct result of poverty and social isolation, which produces a continuing social disorganization.

Wilson's work has been lauded by the centre-left in the United States and is an important reminder that not all Americans are Reaganites. But this brave attempt to 'face facts' contains problems. The concept of social disorganization, for example, which has a long history in sociology, assumes its contrast to be with a 'community', a harmoniously well-organized and integrated society. What we see, however, are *different* forms of organization, *alternative* institutional arrangements. We may prefer arrangements based on institutions like the church and the shop but gangs and parties are also forms of social institution, not perhaps quite so easy to break down and displace as 'disorganization' would imply.

We may agree with much of Wilson's emphasis on the need for public policy that promotes *universal* programmes and increases employment and training opportunities *open on the same basis to all people*. However, his analysis has been criticized as 'abominably sexist not to mention atavistic' (Reed, 1988). The tangle of behaviours Wilson discusses consists of crime rates, teenage pregnancy, female heads of families, welfare dependency, and out of wedlock births. Clearly four of these are overlapping categories and focus on women specifically. To condemn this analysis as sexist is not however exact. Young men and underclass men in general are also portrayed in disparaging terms in the book, even though the explanation for their behaviour (criminality, violence, drugs, hanging round pool halls, lack of responsibility for offspring) is placed at the door of external forces. Rather, the analysis is pro-nuclear family and implicitly pro-patriarchy and favours a clear set of moral rules and values, which perhaps are ones of which many respectable working-class people, both black and white, Afro-American, European-American, and others, might approve. But by focusing on a particular selection of empirical evidence, the book seems to shift the blame from the poor and the underclass to women and to their lack of available, acceptable marriage partners. The implicit solution is a resurgence of the 'normal' nuclear family. Whatever the support or not for these values, the book fails to recognize the wider changes that have gone on in the family and in gender relations, changes which may be quite separate in origin from the question of poverty, although they add to the poverty of women and children. Remedies for the poverty of single mothers and their families in an economy where the two-income family sets the norm in both the production and consumption systems would need to be more far reaching than those proposed by Wilson. It is quite clear that the lone parent is greatly disadvantaged in terms of available resources, money especially, but also time and energy, compared to the two-parent or three-generation family, and she and her children suffer because of this. But other factors cross-cut and a given lone-parent family may still be better off than if they were in a two-parent household characterized by vindictiveness, meanness, or violence (Pahl, 1985).

Importantly, the politics behind the 'impersonal' economic and demographic forces at work in British and American cities need to be brought out.

The transformation of postwar industrial cities was driven not by some abstract historical force but by a combination of private investment decision and state action. This impetus was centred around an urban renewal policy that—along with explicitly segregationist policies in federal public housing—cut off minority communities, displaced large sections of these communities and concentrated them between expressways, office complexes, stadiums and civic centers. There lies the source of Wilson's 'social isolation'. (Reed, 1988, p. 169)

Wilson in the end fails to escape from 'the nexus of moralistic ideology and patriarchal vision dressed up as social science' (ibid.), much as the writers reviewed by Macnicol failed to do. However, his conception of the 'underclass', its causation and policy remedies, differs markedly from those of the far Right whose views have been so easily absorbed into British government and establishment thinking.

Conclusion

The single point that emerges from a close reading of the literature on the underclass and the inner city is that there is no valid need to identify the poor by their putative behaviour at all. Many of the indicators chosen are suspect, as Macnicol has shown for earlier periods, in that they simply count contact with state agencies, and it is a commonplace observation that the poor are more likely to be in contact with social workers because they are poor (Becker, 1988); young drug-takers in inner cities are more visible than wealthy socialites but drug-taking and drinking stretch across social groups (O'Bryan, 1989; Plant, 1989); desertion of women by husbands and the choice to remain unmarried are not restricted to the poor; and so on and so on. All these 'signs' of 'inadequacy' are nothing of the kind but are indicators of poverty and powerlessness. Only measures of material social conditions, unemployment, income, housing conditions, density of population, can usefully serve to characterize the deprivation encountered by those forced to live in these circumstances. The 'underclass' is what the working poor become when they are not employed. Once jobs arise and if they are paid for their labour, they become the workers again; sometimes they are just as poor but their class position has changed. However, long-term un-employment and disconnection from the social relations of work and employment are bound to produce different patterns of social life, norms, and values and possibly despair and hopelessness. It may lead to a gap between the values of those most closely tied to the institutions of the labour movement and the unwaged. But this problem too is not confined to the gap between the 'workers' and the unemployed. It affects the gap between unionized and non-unionized sectors, between men-dominated and women-dominated work-situations and areas of social life. These varieties are complex and changeable: at times of rapid social restructuring such changes are also more rapid. What is clear is that public policies that come from outside and are imposed on inner-city populations are often based on prejudice and ignorance. What is needed is a change in the processes of decision-making so that policies are informed from below by the people involved, who are the only ones who really know what life there is like and what people really want and are able to do.

In the dominant conceptions of inner-city public policy, breaking the cycle focuses on the issues of 'welfare dependency' and 'youth unemployment': it does not include far-reaching and fundamental reorganization of social and economic life and the redistribution of income, wealth, and life-chances.

Hugh Stretton (1978) has provided four metaphors to characterize the city: the city as machine; as community; as a market place; and as a battle-ground. In this chapter I have concentrated on the image of the inner city as a battle-ground—a battle-ground on which opposing forces, ideas, and values can be identified. The argument has been that the geography of poverty and the geography of voting are interconnected and thus party politics and public policies are interconnected too. Attitudes to social problems and public policy and electoral strategies are closely intertwined, most effectively by the Thatcherites in their overall strategy of social engineering. Their opponents have not been able to make the connections as effectively, either through working out a coherent ideology or through practice and organization. Only municipal socialism offered any coherent alternative, but this was limited by its restriction to the local level; the balance of power went against it and it has now been thrown back.

Dominant perceptions of poverty in divided Britain as characterized by urban poverty, decay, and concentration in areas defined as 'inner cities' and inhabited by an 'underclass' call forth increasingly punitive and extremely tight-fisted selectivist policy responses. An alternative view sees the shape of poverty as reflecting the shape and condition of the wider society and requires more wide-ranging policy responses, especially those founded on universalist principles.

In a critical article written several years ago, Townsend concluded by reminding his readers what Tawney had written in 1913. *Plus ça change*: in the 1990s these words (apart from their dated gender references) remain as relevant and as enlightening as in the 1970s and at the beginning of the century: the problem of poverty is the condition of the normal man [and woman] in normal circumstances, neither better nor worse off than his [or her] neighbours, not of those whose failings qualify them to be the text for the moralist, and who are no more common in the manual working-classes than in other sections of the society. It is in short the question of the economic status and opportunities of those who make up seven-eighths of the community, not of any submerged residuum . . . The problem of poverty with which the student is concerned is primarily an industrial one,—and only secondly in its manifestations,—[found] in the mill, in the mine or at the docks,—not in casual wards or on the embankment. (Townsend, 1976, p. 171)

References

Audit Commission (1987), *The Management of London's Authorities: Preventing the Breakdown of Services*, Occasional Paper No. 2 (London).

Banham, J. (1988), 'Urban renewal and ethnic minorities: The challenge to the private sector', *New Community*, 15/1, 23–9.

Becker, S. (1988), 'Debt, poverty and social services', Conference on Women and Poverty (Thomas Coram Research Unit), 11 Nov.

Beveridge, Sir W. (1942), *The Beveridge Report: Social Insurance and Allied Services*, Cmnd. 6404 (London).

Daly, S. (1989), 'A view from the USA', Keynote speech to Child Poverty Action Group Conference: A Fairer Future for Children, 15 Apr.

Glass, R. (1964), *Aspects of Change* (London).

Harris, R., and Seldon, A. (1987), *Welfare without the State: A quarter century of suppressed public choice*, Institute of Economic Affairs (London).

Heseltine, M. (1987), *Where There's a Will* (London).

Howe, G. (1961), 'Reform of the social services', *Principles in Practice*, Conservative Political Centre (London).

Jenkins, R. (1959), *The Labour Case* (Harmondsworth).

Johnston, R. J., Pattie, C. J., and Allsopp, J. G. (1988), *A Nation Dividing? The Electoral Map of Great Britain 1979–1987* (London).

Joseph, Sir K. (1972), 'The cycle of deprivation', Speech given at conference organized by the Pre-School Playgroups Association, 29 June.

Lemann, N. (1986), 'The origins of the underclass', *Atlantic Monthly*, June, 31–61

Leonard, P. (1979), 'Restructuring the welfare state', *Marxism Today*, Dec., 7–13.

MacGregor, S. (1981), *The Politics of Poverty* (London).

—— (1988), *The Poll Tax and the Enterprise Culture* (Manchester).

—— (1989), 'The public debate in the 1980s', S. MacGregor (ed.), *Drugs and British Society* (London).

Macleod, I., and Powell, E. (1952), *The Social Services: Needs and Means,* Conservative Political Centre (London).

Macnicol, J. (1988), 'The pursuit of the underclass', *Journal of Social Policy*, 16/3, 293–318.

Mayer, A. (1971), *Dynamics of Counter-Revolution in Europe* (New York).

Miliband, R. (1974), 'Politics and poverty', in D. Wedderburn (ed.), *Poverty, Inequality and Class Structure* (Cambridge).

Murray, C. (1984), *Losing Ground: American Social Policy 1950–1980* (New York).

O'Bryan, L. (1989), 'Young people and drugs', in S. MacGregor (ed.), *Drugs and British Society* (London).

Pahl, J. (1985), *Private Violence and Public Policy: The Needs of Battered Women and the Response of the Public Services* (London).

Plant, M. (1989), 'The epidemiology of drug misuse', in S. MacGregor (ed.), *Drugs and British Society* (London).

Redwood, J. (1989), 'Whose family life is it anyway?', *Guardian Tomorrow*, 19 Apr., 25.

Reed, A. jun. (1988), Book review of Wilson, 1987, in *The Nation*, 6 Feb.

Ridley, N. (1988), *The Local Right, Enabling not Providing*, Centre for Policy Studies, Policy Study No. 92 (London).

Stedman Jones, G. (1971), *Outcast London: A Study of the Relationship between Classes in Victorian Society* (Oxford).

Stretton, H. (1978), *Urban Planning in Rich and Poor Countries* (Oxford).

Thatcher, M. (1985), 'Facing the new challenge', in C. Ungerson (ed.), *Women and Social Policy* (London).

Townsend, P. (1976), 'Area deprivation policies', *New Statesman*, 6 Aug., 168–71.

—— (1979), *Poverty in the United Kingdom: A Survey of Household Resources and Standards of Living* (Harmondsworth).

Walker, A., and Walker, C. (eds.) (1987), *The Growing Divide: A Social Audit 1979–1987*, CPAG, (London).

Wedderburn, D. (1965), 'Facts and theories of the Welfare State', *Socialist Register* (London).

Wilson, W. J. (1987), *The Truly Disadvantaged: The Inner City, the Underclass and Public Policy* (Chicago).

5

Living Standards and Health in the Inner Cities

Peter Townsend

The inner city has been a recurrent preoccupation of my working career. In the 1950s I interviewed extensively in the metropolitan areas of Lancashire, Bethnal Green, and Stepney. At the end of the 1960s I helped direct an ambitious social survey of poverty and living standards throughout the United Kingdom. Among the fifty constituencies in the sample were all the metropolitan areas; and special follow-up surveys were carried out in the poorest districts of Glasgow, Belfast, Salford, and South Wales. In the 1980s I have investigated, or joined with others in investigating, the relationship between ill-health and deprivation in the poorest districts of Bristol, Liverpool, Manchester, and North Tyneside. I have also taken part in a major survey of living standards in Greater London.

The object of the national study of poverty at the end of the 1960s was not just to try to identify the worst urban problems in the United Kingdom, but to put them into measured perspective by studying prosperous and middle-income areas too, where there were many of the same problems, though smaller percentages of the local populations were affected. The result was to recommend giving priority to national, not area-based, policies, though the latter clearly had to play an important supplementary role (see, for example, Townsend, 1976, 1979, ch. 15). Even twenty years ago the tendency of those in administration, the professions, politics, and the media was to misrepresent national problems as area problems, with the effect of minimizing their extent, and scapegoating whole communities. Another effect was to divert attention from central political, market, and institutional responsibility for social ills to the vagaries and lesser importance of local administration and local social relationships. Indeed, the term 'the inner city', which came into widespread use in the 1970s (DoE, 1975, 1977; Jones, 1979; Lawless, 1981; Hall, 1981; Harrison, 1983), has to be qualified and deployed as just one concept among a set of structural concepts that have to be used in explaining a national disorder, or it will end up reinforcing the self-same tendency.

In the 1980s my research has concentrated on two themes: the contemporary measurement of, and trends in, poverty, in other countries as well as Britain; and the relationship between ill-health and deprivation. There are two claims which might be made for this research, as it affects the discussion of problems in the centres of our cities. One is that both the difference *and* the social ramifications of those differences between the populations of small areas can be defined more precisely. On the basis of work going on in sociology, political science, urban and social geo-graphy, and epidemiology the mapping of inequality has become something of a major industry. It has become quite sophisticated (Centre for Urban Studies, 1964; Donnison and Eversley, 1973; Abrams and Brown, 1984; Jarman, 1984, 1987; Thrift *et al.*, 1987). It is only by the punctilious exposure and scientific meas-urement of social structure that we can properly pose the questions which have to be answered—politically no less than scientifically.

The second claim for the research is that it is identifying trends which can be explained scientifically only if conventional theor-etical perspectives and ideologies are abandoned. We have to find better theories to account for what is taking place as the basis for the strategies which deserve to be adopted. I mean theories of urban development and of the management of the economy in particular. Thus, multinational corporations and international agencies are currently having a big impact on the labour market and the housing market which, in turn, are having a big effect on the overall structure of jobs and settlement in many local areas.

INNER-CITY AREAS IN THE STRUCTURE OF INEQUALITY

It is important to map prosperity as much as deprivation, because that helps to reveal common causation. On the basis of Census indicators of material deprivation quite elaborate maps can be constructed, showing the geographical concentrations at either extreme of a measured continuum. There are many examples in recent literature. In elaborating the theme of the poor living standards of the inner city this means providing evidence not only of low average disposable income or purchasing power of individuals and families, but of increased risk of experiencing a range of material disadvantage. This is the first distinctive feature of the work I shall illustrate in this chapter.

My recent research with Paul Corrigan and Ute Kowarzik involved interviewing a cross-section of adults in the London population, and subsequently two further cross-sections of adults in the two boroughs at either extreme of a continuum of boroughs placed on a number of criteria from prosperity to deprivation, namely Bromley and Hackney. This was on the basis of Census indicators. As a third step employers in these two boroughs were also consulted and their information analysed.

The results of this research in London provide a more comprehensive picture than the necessarily superficial sweep provided by the Census. Of course, degrees of material deprivation are by no means uniform either in boroughs or in the smaller wards into which they can be divided—with a mode of between 8,000 and 10,000 population. Just as there are pockets of deprivation in prosperous areas, like Bromley, so there are pockets of prosperity, and more commonly individual households enjoying substantial relative prosperity dotted about in areas marked overall by their hardship. Social scientists have been reporting such paradoxes for generations, though they seem to be recording them more frequently in today's conditions, with quite dramatic examples. Some of this is obviously due to the recent history of the housing market and of housing finance in particular, though the contributory causes will be discussed later.

In the London survey of 1985–6, 30 wards were selected systematically from a total list of 755 in Greater London, ranked according to their material deprivation, on the basis of 1981 Census indicators of unemployment, overcrowding, and absence of car ownership and home ownership. Figure 5.1 shows the result. Choosing 30 representative areas meant we could carry

Fig. 5.1. Wards in Greater London

25 most deprived wards

25 least deprived wards

out representative interviewing at smallest financial and administrative cost but it also meant that we were able to divide the selected wards into three groups of 10 to undertake a more specialized analysis of the correlates of deprivation.

Our object was to investigate and measure different dimensions of deprivation, first to check whether Census data could be regarded as representative indicators of more widespread social conditions, and second, to explore whether or not those conditions may be said to possess 'structural regularity'. It will be appreciated that in selecting 30 from 755 wards each group of 10 represents a wide range of conditions. Of the 10 most deprived wards only two (Greenwich Nightingale and Brent Manor) are in outer London, while of the 10 least deprived wards only one (Lewisham St Andrew) is not in outer London. Table 5.1 shows first that the two sets of wards at either end of the continuum are quite distinct in their ratings according to the four Census indicators of deprivation (unemployment, overcrowding, and absence of car and home ownership).

In the second and third columns of Table 5.1 average scores are given of both material and social deprivation in the three sets of London wards. Our questions covered the following forms of

Table 5.1. *London wards according to different measures of deprivation (1985–1986)*

Wards ranked by 4 Census indicators of deprivation	Mean score of deprivation		
	4 from 1981 Census (z-score)	50 indicators 1985–6 survey (material)	27 indicators 1985–6 survey (social)
Most deprived third	3.6	15.0	7.0
Middle third	0.1	11.0	4.5
Least deprived third	−5.1	7.0	3.0

Note: A full list of the indicators used in the 1985–6 London survey will be found in Townsend, with Corrigan and Kowarzik, 1987, pp. 90–4. The same source also provides a detailed list of the 755 Greater London wards with information about their levels of deprivation or prosperity.

material deprivation: dietary; clothing; housing; home facilities; environment; location; and work; and also covered the following forms of social deprivation: lack of employment rights; deprivation of family activity; lack of integration in community; lack of formal participation in social institutions; and recreational and educational deprivation (for a full list of individual items see Townsend, with Corrigan and Kowarzik, 1987, pp. 90–4). It can be seen that the correlation between the summary and more complex measures is high. Perhaps more important, the difference between the most deprived and least deprived third of London's wards is very striking when a substantial range of both physical and social criteria are brought into the reckoning.

The evidence of deprivation needs to be weighed carefully to find the severity but also the degree of geographical concentration of the worst problems. This will assist theory no less than the formulation of new policies. Table 5.2 portrays the distribution of experience of deprivation in inner and outer London. As many as 37 per cent of the adult residents of the most deprived group of wards, principally in inner London, but only 9 per cent in the least deprived group of wards, principally in outer London, experience severe material deprivation. Only 11 per cent of the former experience little or no deprivation, compared with 35 per cent of the latter. While therefore it is true that even in the richest

Table 5.2 *Severity of material deprivation in different groups of London wards (1985–1986)*

Severity of deprivation (50 indicators of material deprivation)	Wards on 4 Census indicators		
	Most deprived (%)	Middle group (%)	Least deprived (%)
Little or none (under 6)	11.3	16.1	34.9
Some (6–10)	25.0	29.6	35.1
Fairly severe (11–15)	26.9	30.6	21.1
Very severe (16+)	36.9	23.6	8.8
Total number in sample	869	854	980

wards people can be found who are experiencing material deprivation of a severe kind, their numbers are relatively few.

Table 5.3 provides estimates of the concentration of material deprivation. More than half the problem is concentrated in the poorest third of London wards. As many as 657,000 people in these wards experience severe deprivation. Another 415,000 in the next third of London wards experience severe deprivation but only 179,000 do so in the most prosperous groups of wards.

Table 5.3. *Estimated adult population of Greater London; according to severity of deprivation (1985–1986)*

Degree of severity of deprivation	Estimated population (000s)		
	All wards	Most depr. third of wards	Least depr. third of wards
Little or none	1,187	201	702
Some	1,671	446	706
Fairly severe	1,441	480	425
Very severe	1,250	657	179
TOTAL	5,549	1,784	2,012

These generalized measures take on fresh meaning when they are broken down into their constituent parts. For the great majority of individual items comprising the indices of both material and social deprivation there was a linear relationship between deprivation and the ranked groups of wards. Table 5.4 provides a large number of examples. For housing, household facilities, home possessions, and clothing the differences make a fairly regular pattern. The same applies to some environmental and locational amenities, but not all. Thus, nearly one in 3 of those interviewed in the poorest group of wards but as few as one in 25 in the most prosperous wards did not have access to a garden. The difference was much smaller for access to a surgery or hospital. Substantial minorities in the prosperous wards expressed concern about litter in the streets and the risk of street accidents, though the largest percentages continued to be found in the poorest wards.

Another feature of Table 5.4 is the much smaller difference that can be discerned between the three groups of wards according to different criteria of deprivation at work. A very high percentage of employed adults claimed to experience at least three of the nine possible disadvantages of the work environment recommended for investigation by the Organization for Economic Co-operation and Development (OECD) (1985). These nine include dust, polluted air, damp, noise, vibration, heavy lifting, high temperature, low temperature, and bad lighting. It can also be seen that large percentages of employed adults in the prosperous wards and not only in the poorest wards worked unsocial hours and spent at least three-quarters of each working day on their feet. Again, however, the highest percentage was to be found in the poorest group of wards.

Table 5.4 *Experience of different forms of deprivation in different groups of London wards (1985–1986)*

	Wards on 4 Census indicators		
	Most deprived (%)	Middle group (%)	Least deprived (%)
Form of material deprivation			
Inadequate footwear	10.6	8.0	3.9
Inad. protection rain	20.8	12.7	9.0
Housing overcrowded	13.4	9.1	3.8
Some rooms not heated winter	37.1	36.4	26.5
External structural defects	31.5	26.6	13.9
Internal structural defects	15.0	14.1	6.9
Housing infested	11.2	8.6	5.1
No car	50.9	40.3	20.8
No washing machine	32.6	28.5	10.5
No central heating	37.8	36.6	22.0
No telephone	18.3	11.9	3.2
No radio	6.2	3.0	1.5
No television	2.6	3.0	1.4

No garden	29.8	26.4	4.4
No play facilities nearby for under-fives	43.9	44.4	26.0
No play facilities nearby for children 5–10	37.9	40.9	28.1
Industrial and air pollution	7.3	7.7	4.5
Other forms of pollution	13.4	13.4	7.2
No surgery/hosp. 10 mins.	11.3	7.3	6.8
Risk of road accidents	36.5	33.1	25.1
Street litter problem	44.4	39.0	24.9
3+ poor conditions at work	50.2	47.1	40.9
Works unsocial hours	56.8	54.0	47.1
Stands ¾ths of day	45.8	32.7	37.6
Form of social deprivation			
No summer holiday	37.7	27.4	21.7
Child no holiday 12 months	52.4	34.5	21.5
Child no outing last month	34.4	27.1	29.6
Moved house 3+ times in 5 yrs	29.1	27.6	16.1
Health problem in family	47.0	41.6	40.2
Alone and reports isolation	10.9	8.6	6.9
Unsafe in surrounding streets	15.2	7.8	4.6
Not voted last election	27.6	24.2	19.0
Less than 10 years education	14.9	6.7	5.4
No educational qualifications	40.1	28.5	26.7

Note: Total numbers are around 2,700 except in the case of employment-related questions, when the number is approximately 1,550, and children-related questions, when the number is approximately 820.

Different forms of social and material deprivation are more closely correlated than might be supposed. Examples of individual indicators are given in the lower half of Table 5.4. Some forms of social deprivation are more obviously related to underlying material resources than others. For example, holidays of both adults and children plainly depend on a minimum of available resources. Few would question the connection. But other indicators invite more reflective explanation. An example is the frequency of moving house. That people may not know others in a neighbourhood is in fact related to this frequency in the local population. Those living on low incomes are less secure than those living on high or middle incomes. They move house more frequently. The outward mobility of neighbours also affects middle-aged and older people with small incomes, who may have protected tenancies and who do not have resources to move elsewhere. Younger members of their families and neighbours move away to get work or for other reasons. From each of these perspectives potential social networks are truncated or diminished.

The themes of disability, alienation, educational deprivation, and racial discrimination are also themes which, in their different ways can be said to illustrate non-participation in inner-city areas and hence social deprivation. Each is related to shortage of material resources.

In measuring material and social deprivation our intention was that the result would be 'objective'—even if, for convenience and at smaller cost, we came to rely on subjective reports of objective states and conditions instead of collecting independent observations on every dimension of deprivation. But we were also anxious to describe subjective attitudes and feelings about the situations in which people were placed. Subjective attitudes do of course shed light on the relation between material and social deprivation and help us to understand their impact and importance. Despite exceptions many people recognize their condition and reflect lack of both resources and social integration in their demeanour and feelings. Table 5.5 shows the attitude towards their living standards of people in the three groups of wards. While a significantly higher proportion of people in poor than in prosperous wards said they were worse off than the national average, the picture changed when they were invited to make the same comparison with neighbours in their locality. There were no significant differences in numbers in the three groups of wards saying they felt themselves to be worse off than other people locally.

Detailed information about income was collected. Informants were then invited to give their definitions of poverty and to say how much they thought was needed to keep a household like their own out of poverty. There proved to be remarkably close agreement on average between poor and prosperous families

Table 5.5. *Subjective attitudes towards own living standards in London wards (1985–1986)*

Selected criteria	Wards on 4 Census indicators		
	Most deprived (%)	Middle group (%)	Least deprived (%)
Worse-off than relatives	41.5	36.9	25.6
Worse-off than locals	13.3	18.5	15.7
Worse-off than nat. average	22.9	13.8	9.0
Worse-off than previously	21.4	14.2	11.0
Judgement of income to be below own defined poverty line	35.2	20.5	12.7

about these amounts (Townsend and Gordon, 1989). Plainly, however, substantially more of the population living in the poorest than in the most prosperous group of wards considered themselves to be below their own defined poverty line, being 35 per cent, compared with 13 per cent, as Table 5.5 shows.

Finally, Table 5.6 vividly portrays the scale of subjective deprivation in the inner-city areas. Towards the end of our interviews we said to informants: 'Here are some of the problems people have told us they face. Which, if any, of these are major problems faced by you or your immediate family in the last 12 months?' The table sums up the replies in relation to the three groups of wards. They have been ranked in order of frequency. Except for matters of health and employment the difference between the groups of wards is large. Important to remember is that the first column represents a third of the population of Greater London, or nearly 2 million people. Had smaller areas within the inner city been singled out for attention, the percentages in the first column would have been higher still.

There are respects in which these statistics tell a familiar story. The disadvantages of the inner city have been widely documented (Robson, 1969; Pahl, 1970; Rex and Tomlinson, 1979; Scarman,

Table 5.6. *Extent of subjective deprivation in different groups of London wards (1985–1986)*

Form of deprivation	Wards on 4 Census Indicators		
	Most deprived (%)	Middle group (%)	Least deprived (%)
Health of someone in family	33.8	30.9	29.1
Not enough money to make ends meet	32.5	19.7	11.3
Vandalism/theft	30.3	23.1	14.5
Paying for fuel and light	28.3	16.8	10.5
Employment prospects own children	22.8	18.2	17.5
Own health	21.5	14.8	14.0
Fear of unemployment	21.4	14.3	11.3
Poor public transport	20.4	17.5	11.2
Unemployment	20.1	11.2	6.7
Owing money at present time	18.8	10.8	8.5
Street/estate violence	17.7	7.5	4.6
Poor housing	16.4	7.2	1.3
Being alone and isolated	12.1	9.5	6.9
Fear of eviction	10.1	5.6	4.3
Poor local schools	8.2	5.4	3.0
Conflict at home	7.1	5.5	4.5
Racial harrassment	7.0	2.6	1.4

Notes: The total numbers range only between 2,681 and 2,690. Complaints for example about racial harrassment are applied to the whole population and not for racial minorities only.

1981; Higgins *et al.*, 1983; Halsey, 1986). But they go beyond the familiar. The London survey shows that the disadvantages of people living in the inner city are more pervasive than many suppose. Some of the old adages about 'poor but happy' do not apply. While there is a fine dividing-line between the conditions which people report and what they feel about these conditions, a depressing picture about both emerges from the poorest wards. On the very large number of criteria which have been used that picture is also one which is unrelieved.

Thus, a very high proportion of the local population express anxieties about having enough money to make ends meet and pay for fuel and light; many have worrying debts; many are un-employed or fear unemployment or are concerned about their children's prospects of becoming unemployed; many fear eviction, are concerned about their isolation, experience racial harrassment, and experience conflict at home.

I did not expect the pattern of subjective deprivation to follow as consistently as it does the pattern of objective material and social deprivation. A third of those in the worst third of London's wards picked out vandalism and theft as a problem they felt keenly about and as many as 18 per cent picked out street and estate violence. These percentages are high, by any standards. More than any others, these indicators reveal the scale of the inner-city problem. We can begin to appreciate the full implications for the quality of ordinary life of the deprivation people experience in these inner areas. As I have said, this account may not be new but the assembled evidence has an indisputable and irresistible power and coherence which demands to be confronted by rational administration.

PATTERNS OF ILL-HEALTH

Perhaps the single most important set of evidence to emerge from recent studies of the inner city demonstrates the causal link between deprivation and premature death and ill-health. This could be said to be a rediscovery rather than a discovery. Chadwick (1842), John Snow, William Farr (1885), Sir John Simon (1987), and Charles Booth (1892–7) were among those, especially in London, and Engels one of those, especially in Manchester, who played a big part in the mid- and late nineteenth century in establishing the connection between deprivation and premature death, urging government action and not only adding to scientific knowledge. Such people helped to lay the basis for the public health measures and the wide range of public social services introduced in the latter part of the nineteenth century and early twentieth century.

When Frederick Engels went to Manchester in 1842 to work in his father's factory, he put together *The Condition of the Working*

Class in England, completed in 1845 but not published in Britain until 1892 (Engels, 1845). In this he made considerable play with the high rates of mortality in working-class areas and quoted an 1844 report by a Royal Commission:

> When we find the rate of mortality four times as high in some streets as in others, and twice as high in whole classes of streets as in other classes, and further find it is all but invariably high in those streets which are in bad condition, and almost invariably low in those whose condition is good, we cannot resist the conclusion that multitudes of our fellow creatures, *hundreds of our immediate neighbours*, are annually destroyed for want of the most evident precautions. (Report of Commission of Inquiry into the State of Large Towns and Populous Districts, 1844)

By contrast, the scientific correlation between the same two phenomena now being established at the end of the twentieth century seems to be being treated much less seriously than by mid-Victorians, and even being ignored, by the present Government. The reception given to the reports by Black (1980), Whitehead (1987), the BMA (1987), and Smith and Jacobson (1988) could all be cited to justify that conclusion.

Here it is necessary simply to emphasize the strength of the correlation between deprivation and poor health and to call attention to a variety of recent scientific testimony. We can begin at the level of the metropolitan borough. Among the boroughs of Greater London the differences in expectation of life correlate highly with combined as well as specific measures of deprivation. Thus, when the boroughs are ranked on a combined index of deprivation those ranked highest are found to have the lowest average expected years of life. Life tables covering the period 1979–82 show the metropolitan borough of Tower Hamlets, for example, having an estimated expectation of life for males of 68.2 years, compared with 73.0 years in a borough such as Harrow. For females the difference is less sharp, the figures being 75.4 and 78.7 years respectively.

Survey data on ill-health bear out the data on mortality. In a series of studies in Greater London in the mid- and late 1980s I undertook with colleagues two local surveys in Bromley and in Hackney. These boroughs had been chosen because, according to the indicators from the Census of 1981, one was the least deprived and the other the most deprived borough in the city. Information bearing this out was collected from 407 adults in the former and 381 adults in the latter.

In Hackney far more were registered unemployed; had gone short of food in the last twelve months to help meet the needs of someone in their family; had not had a summer holiday; had children who had nowhere safe to play; lived in poor housing; complained about serious levels of air pollution, accidents, noise, street litter, and lack of safety walking in the neighbourhood of their homes; and said they were living in poverty. Less predictably, more said that local services were less than adequate; that they felt lonely; and that they had neither relatives nor friends in the neighbourhood upon whom they could depend in illness or for other needs in the home. Fewer felt they played a part in the life of the local community. This research provided a more rounded picture than some of the available statistical snapshots of the ravages of social as well as material deprivation in the inner city.

There was more ill-health in Hackney too than in Bromley. As many as 36 per cent, compared with 23 per cent, said their health was poor or only fair. Significantly more said that problems with health had been the worst of their problems in the previous twelve months. And significantly more reported that they had problems with nervous depression.

ILL-HEALTH IN SMALL AREAS

A next step is to consider health in areas much smaller than that of boroughs—of which there are 33 in the Greater London region. Table 5.7 sets out two groups of wards from among the 755 which could be analysed in relation both to mortality and to deprivation indicators of the early 1980s. The table compares the 25 most deprived with the 25 least deprived wards in Greater London. Four indicators of deprivation were combined to rank all the wards in London. For those at the top and bottom of the ranking, mortality rates for different age groups could then be compared. The mortality rates for the middle-aged (over 45 and under pensionable age) afford the most reliable comparison. The

Table 5.7. *Deprivation and mortality for most and least deprived wards in Greater London (1981–1986)*

Measure of deprivation Z-score 1981	Ward Name	Age specific death rates			Standard mortality ratio	
		0–14	15–44	45–59/64	All ages	Under 65
Most deprived						
9.80	Spitalfields (Tower Hamlets)	1.46	1.03	12.27	130.1	143.9
7.80	St Mary's (Tower Hamlets)	1.21	1.96	18.81	135.7	197.8
7.40	Carlton (Brent)	1.05	1.38	10.34	115.9	123.2
7.20	Golborne (Kensington and Chelsea)	1.13	1.38	9.62	119.2	132.5
7.10	Haggerston (Hackney)	0.78	1.08	10.19	96.7	113.2
7.10	Shadwell (Tower Hamlets)	1.52	1.49	13.91	136.8	156.5
7.00	Blackwall (Tower Hamlets)	0.93	1.02	10.99	118.4	118.3
6.90	St Katherine's (Tower Hamlets)	1.76	1.14	12.19	119.2	143.5
6.80	King's Park (Hackney)	1.46	0.78	12.62	124.3	140.9
6.70	White City and Shepherd's Bush (Hammersmith and Fulham)	1.12	1.40	12.22	114.7	144.1
6.70	Ordnance (Newham)	1.33	1.32	15.01	133.7	159.9
6.60	Angell (Lambeth)	1.33	1.69	13.32	122.0	156.6
6.50	St Dunstan's (Tower Hamlets)	1.36	0.83	11.97	114.2	125.5
6.50	Liddle (Southwark)	1.02	0.92	9.87	117.1	113.9
6.30	Harrow Road (Westminster)	1.06	1.01	10.24	104.5	128.5
6.30	Westdown (Hackney)	1.32	1.21	11.01	124.9	137.1
6.30	Queen's Park (Westminster)	1.12	1.48	9.49	108.4	129.2
6.30	Weavers (Tower Hamlets)	1.37	1.50	11.81	111.6	137.6
6.20	Eastdown (Hackney)	1.40	1.11	11.77	99.4	138.0
6.10	Westbourne (Westminster)	1.66	1.83	11.93	120.3	121.0
6.10	Avondale (Kensington and Chelsea)	1.47	1.15	8.92	96.0	118.5
6.10	Vassall (Lambeth)	1.15	1.34	9.36	126.7	117.5
6.00	Bromley (Tower Hamlets)	1.60	1.14	12.91	124.4	144.2
6.00	Larkhall (Lambeth)	1.65	1.03	9.51	111.5	121.8
6.00	Stonebridge (Brent)	1.67	1.23	11.55	110.5	141.6
	Average	1.32	1.26	11.67	117.5	136.2
Least deprived						
−8.90	Selsdon (Croydon)	0.61	0.68	6.18	83.1	74.1
−8.70	Cheam South (Sutton)	0.45	0.80	6.37	127.7	72.7
−8.30	Cranham West (Havering)	0.28	0.45	6.27	93.4	72.3
−8.10	West Wickham North (Bromley)	0.30	0.65	5.71	75.1	65.3
−7.70	Farnborough (Bromley)	0.67	0.80	6.11	94.4	76.6
−7.70	Crofton (Bromley)	0.93	0.61	6.91	89.8	78.6
−7.60	Woodcote (Sutton)	1.05	0.75	5.19	73.5	67.2
−7.60	Grange (Enfield)	0.48	0.39	3.34	73.4	39.1
−7.50	Malden Manor (Kingston)	0.00	0.00	6.66	93.6	59.8
−7.40	Biggin Hill (Bromley)	0.33	0.44	6.69	88.1	70.1
−7.40	West Wickham South (Bromley)	0.57	0.83	5.67	76.2	69.1
−7.40	Trent (Enfield)	1.37	0.38	6.08	80.4	69.3
−7.40	Petts Wood and Knoll (Bromley)	0.46	0.64	5.95	80.4	68.6
−7.30	Ickenham (Hillingdon)	0.29	0.70	6.45	81.9	72.6

−7.10	Shortlands (Bromley)	0.33	0.58	5.27	90.6	59.6
−7.00	Upminster (Havering)	0.56	0.76	6.76	81.7	76.9
−7.00	Emerson Park (Havering)	0.30	0.77	6.34	86.5	76.3
−6.90	Pinner West (Harrow)	0.19	0.47	5.52	72.3	60.1
−6.90	Woodcote and Coulsdon (Croydon)	0.86	0.91	8.57	136.7	101.3
−6.80	Monkhams (Redbridge)	0.31	0.85	5.78	79.6	68.9
−6.70	Worcester Park South (Sutton)	0.30	0.40	7.05	74.6	73.0
−6.60	Merryhills (Enfield)	0.15	0.52	5.54	93.1	60.4
−6.50	Bickley (Bromley)	0.36	0.78	6.09	85.4	70.6
−6.50	Headstone North (Harrow)	0.74	0.62	5.05	70.0	62.2
−6.40	Tolworth East (Kingston)	0.32	0.65	7.26	79.8	79.9
	Average	0.49	0.62	6.11	85.5	69.8

mortality rate in the most deprived wards, including places like Spitalfields, St Mary's, Blackwall, and St Katharine's in Tower Hamlets; Haggerston, King's Park, and Westdown in Hackney; Carlton in Brent; and Golborne in Kensington and Chelsea, was on average nearly double that in the least deprived wards. The rate for people under 45 was more than double that in the least deprived wards, and even among those aged 60+ or 65+ there continued to be a statistically significant excess of deaths in the most deprived wards. In short, small area analysis confirms, and in many respects heightens, the inequalities in social conditions and health broadly apparent in the case of boroughs.

For the purposes of comparing wards, Standardized Mortality Ratios (SMRs) for people under 65 years of age as well as for people of all ages were calculated for the period 1981–6 for all wards in London. The 25 wards adjudged most deprived on 1981 criteria had an average SMR of 136.2, compared with only 69.8 for the 25 wards adjudged least deprived, as Table 5.7 shows. More sophisticated statistical treatment of measures of poor health and deprivation confirmed the close link between the two (Congdon, 1987, 1988). In a number of studies different indicators of deprivation have been combined into a 'z-score' and this more generalized measure compared with SMRs. When deprivation, measured according to Census data for 1981, was compared with SMRs for 1981–6, 'the correlation between ward level standard mortality under 65 and the z-scores, controlling for the proportion of professional and managerial workers, is 0.67 . . .' (Congdon, 1988, p. 456). Figure 5.2 illustrates the big difference between inner and outer London.

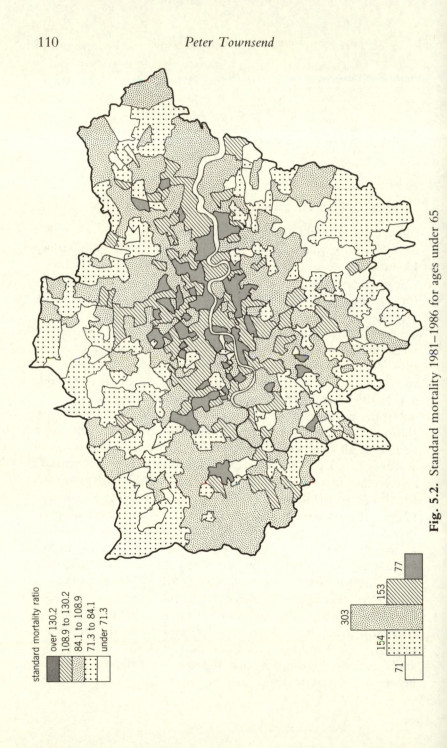

Fig. 5.2. Standard mortality 1981–1986 for ages under 65

standard mortality ratio

over 130.2
108.9 to 130.2
84.1 to 108.9
71.3 to 84.1
under 71.3

77
153
303
154
71

The same pattern has been found in all the other metropolitan regions of the United Kingdom. For example, one major study of the distribution of health in the 678 wards of the Northern Region of England, covering a number of densely populated urban areas including Tyneside and Teesside, demonstrated the high correlation between material deprivation and ill-health in their different forms. In addition to standardized mortality, area measures of disablement and low·birthweight were developed. This allowed a more robust test to be made of the links between ill-health and deprivation. A regression analysis revealed that 65 per cent of the variance in health, as measured by the three combined indicators of mortality, disablement, and low birth-weight, was 'explained' by the operational definition of material deprivation, based on the same four indicators as in the London study illustrated in Table 5.7 (Townsend, Phillimore, and Beattie, 1987).

A special analysis of all 216 wards in the Greater Manchester conurbation also allowed those who experienced the severest deprivation to be distinguished from those who experienced the least deprivation. Table 5.8 sets out the results for 25 wards at the head of the ranking on deprivation and the 25 at the foot of that ranking. Again, the difference between the two groups at either end of the continuum is striking. There are wards in the poorest areas of Manchester and Salford which as long ago as 1981 had unemployment rates of 30 per cent or more; there were very few owner-occupiers, and possessions were so scarce that only one in five or six households had a car. Such impoverishment relative to majority national experience is not new. In his fine account of Salford life in the first quarter of the century, which of course then applied to a more compact city, Robert Roberts (1973) described the differences in living standards within the working class but, nevertheless, the huge numbers with few possessions. 'The tragedy was that in the most opulent country in the world so many possessed so little' (p. 41).

The wards found to have the poorest health are the same wards as were found to be the most deprived. Wards in Manchester like Hulme, Ardwick, Beswick, and Moss Side, and in Salford like Regent, Ordsall Park, experienced relatively high rates of mortality

Table 5.8. *Deprivation and mortality in most and least deprived wards in Greater Manchester (1981–1983)*

Measure of deprivation Z-score		(% of households)				Measure of health	
		un emp	no car	not own-occ	over crowd	SMR	Excess deaths
Most deprived							
3.69	Trafford Clifford	19	59	53	7	160	52
4.04	Oldham St James	18	63	64	6	143	41
4.05	Oldham St Marys	17	68	48	8	131	29
4.18	Manchester Bradford	18	68	60	6	157	59
4.19	Manchester Newton Heath	18	67	69	5	163	65
4.27	Oldham Hollinwood	19	67	68	5	134	28
4.39	Oldham Coldhurst	17	70	58	7	152	41
4.42	Oldham Alexandra	17	65	60	8	162	61
4.72	Manchester Woodhouse Park	18	58	93	5	136	47
4.74	Rochdale Central and Falinge	20	67	56	8	162	51
4.75	Rochdale Middleton Central	17	62	77	7	153	48
4.93	Manchester Cheetham	20	65	53	10	183	95
4.97	Wigan Norley	19	63	81	6	135	34
4.97	Stockport Brinnington	20	68	79	5	173	72
5.29	Rochdale Smallbridge and Wardleworth	22	64	53	11	146	38
5.46	Manchester Longsight	23	65	53	11	159	65
5.86	Bolton Central	22	74	60	9	182	74
6.27	Bolton Derby	23	71	51	14	141	41
6.58	Manchester Harpurhey	24	77	84	6	127	26
7.30	Rochdale Middleton West	21	69	91	11	174	65
8.07	Manchester Beswick	29	81	94	7	169	70
8.52	Manchester Ardwick	28	80	96	9	183	90
8.89	Manchester Hulme	34	84	99	7	211	90
8.98	Salford Regent, Ordsall Park	30	79	99	10	148	48
9.24	Manchester Moss Side	30	80	88	14	148	54
	Average					153.5	
Least deprived							
−8.37	Stockport East Bramhall	4	11	4	1	75	−30
−7.63	Stockport West Bramhall	4	15	14	1	72	−35
−7.47	Stockport Cheadle Hulme South	4	16	16	1	84	−17
−7.47	Rochdale Norden and Bamford	5	15	8	1	69	−25
−6.99	Stockport Heald Green	5	18	14	1	90	−11
−6.89	Trafford Hale	5	18	16	1	96	−4
−6.61	Salford Park and Worsley	6	20	11	1	79	−18
−6.45	Trafford Brooklands	5	24	17	1	71	−22
−6.18	Stockport South Marple	6	23	16	1	100	0
−6.10	Trafford Mersey St Marys	6	25	15	1	84	−16
−5.97	Stockport Cheadle	5	27	23	1	87	−14
−5.87	Bury Tottington	5	23	11	2	95	−4
−5.81	Trafford Timperley	6	30	14	1	83	−14
−5.73	Trafford Bowdon	6	22	27	1	85	−13
−5.52	Oldham Saddleworth East	6	28	23	1	84	−14
−5.39	Bury Unsworth	6	21	16	2	98	−2
−5.01	Stockport Hazel Grove	6	26	17	2	97	−4
−4.90	Wigan Langtree	7	22	18	2	93	−7
−4.79	Trafford Flixton	5	33	20	2	100	0
−4.79	Wigan Winstanley	7	23	19	2	77	−21
−4.75	Bury Church	6	30	17	2	75	−20
−4.73	Stockport North Marple	6	26	23	2	76	−22
−4.60	Bolton Hulton Park	7	28	16	2	105	5
−4.58	Trafford Davyhulme East	6	29	22	2	102	1
−4.45	Oldham Saddleworth West	6	31	22	2	98	−2
	Average					87	

Note: In the case of least deprived wards a number of wards have not been included because change in boundaries during the early 1980s makes impossible a direct comparison between mortality and deprivation.

Source: Townsend, 1988.

as well as high levels of material deprivation. The table shows the contrast in standardized mortality ratios and also provides an estimate of the number of excess deaths during the period 1981–3. Evidence about disability was also combined with evidence about low birthweight. Unfortunately these data could not be amalgamated with mortality data because some wards have had their boundaries altered since 1981. Altogether, the coefficient of correlation between deprivation and poor health (as measured in this context by prevalence of disability and low birthweight), when calculated for all 216 wards in Greater Manchester, was found to be 0.74 (Townsend, 1988, p. 23).

There are three District Health Authorities of the city of Manchester, each with three or four sub-areas. One sub-area of Central Manchester District Health Authority is made up of the wards of Moss Side, Hulme, and Ardwick, all three of which are listed in Table 5.8 among the five most deprived wards. This sub-area of the city turns out to have the highest proportion of premature deaths in the city (with an SMR of 178), the highest post-perinatal mortality rate (11.5 per 1,000 live births compared with 2.5 in a prosperous sub-area of South Manchester District Health Authority), and the highest proportion of low-weight babies (12.5 per cent, compared with 7.1 per cent in another prosperous sub-area of South Manchester District Health Authority). On a range of comparisons, covering deaths by major causes, the group of three wards in the central part of the city features as one of the worst areas or the worst area (Manchester Joint Consultative Committee, 1987: and see also Manchester City Council, 1986).

The table also brings out the immense variation between wards in death rates, with around three times as many deaths in the wards at one extreme, compared with the other. This has been expressed in the table also as the number of deaths exceeding the number expected if national rates had applied to those local populations. It can be seen that there were 1,384 'excess' deaths in the 25 wards with most severe levels of deprivation, and 309 fewer deaths than expected in the wards with least deprivation.

The geography of death has been mapped in a number of reports on different regions, cities, and boroughs in Britain in recent years, and they provide confirmation of what I have described for Greater London and Greater Manchester. For example, the six wards in Birmingham ranked as having the worst socio-economic deprivation—Sparkbrook, Soho, Nechells, Handsworth, Aston, and Washwood Heath—were found to have the worst overall health in the city (Appleby, 1986, pp. 15 and 53). Five of the seven wards ranked as having the worst deprivation in Liverpool—Everton, Vauxhall, Abercromby, Granby, and Gillmoss—were the five ranked worst in overall health, and the other two wards were not far behind (Liverpool City Planning Department, 1987 and see also Ashton, 1984: for an interesting complementary account of the 23 wards in the neighbouring borough of Sefton, see Marsden, 1989). Finally, while experiencing smaller variation than the cities quoted, a similar link between deprivation and both mortality and morbidity was emphasized in a report on the 29 wards of Sheffield (Sheffield Health Authority, 1987; Thunhurst, 1985). The most comprehensive contribution to the evidence of the link between area deprivation and area ill-health (though varying the concept of 'deprivation' to that of 'underprivilege') has been made by Brian Jarman (1983, 1984).

The material which I have described carried a powerful and largely consistent message. There is the consistency of the material and social deprivation indicators, despite expected individual variations. There is too the consistency of different indicators of poor health, when analysed by wards. This has sometimes been disputed in recent years, largely as a consequence of the recommendations of the Resource Allocation Working Party, which argued that a mortality formula should be used in redistributing resources from the South to the North. Critics, many of them with a vested interest in recipient authorities in the South, argued against mortality and in favour of morbidity-based criteria. Unfortunately they overlooked the incomplete and highly debatable nature of morbidity criteria and failed to appreciate that when the more reliable as well as measurable aspects of morbidity were examined closely, there was a large degree of agreement with mortality patterns. Some critics also pointed out that there were areas of the South with exceptionally large representation of lone parents, black minorities, and pensioners living alone, as well as of shared housing. This was argued to intensify certain morbidity problems and increase the workload of general practitioners. However, representatives of the North have responded by emphasizing the social problems which have been peculiarly intensive there—such as the collapse of manufacturing industry, high rates of very long-term unemployment, and high rates of disablement. The debate is important and can only be resolved when a larger range of health and deprivation measures than are available administratively and from the Census are introduced for large national samples of the population.

In the Greater London survey we asked a lot of questions about disability, the restrictions of activity because of chronic sickness or disablement, perceptions of health, including subjective indicators of stress and nervous depression, whether a recent illness had been experienced, and frequency of contact with general practitioners. We found a largely consistent correlation (although different in degree of variation) between poor health and material and social deprivation. However, the pattern was not consistent by age or condition and was inconclusive at the advanced ages. Table 5.9 shows how many in the three groups of wards said they had only fair or poor health. At the oldest and youngest ages, numbers are too few to draw reliable conclusions but in each age group between the ages of 20 and 70 a higher percentage of adults in the more deprived than in the less deprived or middling wards reported poor or only fair health. This difference also applies to the smaller group included in the figures who declare that they have poor health.

The difference between the populations in perceptions of health are especially marked in middle age. Thus as many as 19.0 per cent of those in the more deprived wards said they had poor health, compared with 9.1 per cent in the middle group of wards and 5.7 per cent in the less deprived wards. This feature of life-cycle inequality corresponds with that shown by the data on mortality.

Table 5.9 also summarizes information about recent illness. The disadvantage of the most deprived wards remains statistically significant but is less pronounced than in the case of perceptions

Table 5.9. *Inequalities in patterns of health among three groups of London wards (1985–1986)*

Category of ill-health	Wards on 4 Census indicators		
	Most deprived (%)	Middle group (%)	Least deprived (%)
Health perceived as poor or fair			
aged 20–9	30.9	19.3	19.5
30–9	22.0	17.2	16.9
40–9	34.8	28.7	21.5
50–9	53.2	32.5	24.1
60–9	47.9	33.3	29.5
70–9	(33.3)	39.7	32.0
80+	(57.9)	(44.4)	(51.7)
All ages	35.9	27.0	24.6
Reports being ill or unwell in last 2 weeks	29.5	26.3	25.1
Ditto—and being obliged to take time off work	15.1	12.2	11.2
Seen doctor in last 2 weeks	19.7	16.4	19.1
No. seeing doctor in last 2 weeks, as % of no. saying they were ill during that period	66.2	61.8	76.0
Mean score disability index	1.79	1.51	1.50
Total number in sample	863	852	978

Notes: The figures provide the raw results: they have not been standardized by age or sex. Percentages are placed in brackets when total number is less than 50.

of poor health, 29.5 per cent reporting illness in the previous two weeks, compared with 26 per cent and 25 per cent among the other two groups. This difference is not explained by age variations in the structure of the populations. Indeed, because relatively fewer adults interviewed in the deprived wards were elderly than elsewhere, the difference would have been larger had the figures been 'age-standardized'. Neither does the difference appear to be explained by any variation in the reporting of minor ailments. We asked a follow-up question to find how many people had been obliged to take time off work, college, family care, or housework because of their illness. In fact, as the table shows, more in the more deprived than in the less deprived wards had done so.

The data about contacts with doctors correlate, though not so closely, with this pattern of perceived ill-health and illness. More of the population living in the more deprived than in the middling or less deprived wards reported seeing a doctor in the previous two weeks. However, the excess is smaller than the figures of 'need' would seem to suggest. This seems to be partly because people in the more prosperous areas are readier, or are more often encouraged, to see a doctor than in the deprived areas (as the table shows).

Close scrutiny of our data suggested that more serious under-utilization of doctors' services in inner-city areas by adults under retirement age is masked by the large number of instances where it is necessary to obtain a doctor's note for an employer because of absence from work, but also by the relatively frequent contacts with doctors which a few very infirm elderly people have. Frequent visits by or to a few isolated elderly people can have a quite substantial effect on total consultations.

Partly because of its relevance to small areas the strength of the evidence on the link between deprivation and ill-health is re-cognized in many parts of the country, where meetings and conferences are being arranged, follow-up studies organized, and information channelled to politicians, health-care professionals, and the media. Local authorities and local communities have found great interest in being able to compare local wards and pick out those which are severely deprived and which therefore demand priority in any action that can be offered. Their efforts have also been reinforced by the Healthy Cities Project of the World Health Organization, which was initiated in 1985–6. This has resulted already in a large number of enthusiastic meetings and publications containing ambitious programmes in Britain and elsewhere in Europe (for example, Ashton and Knight, 1988; and Kaasjager, van der Maesen, and Nijhuis, 1989. See also WHO, 1985). Despite the fact that central government has far greater power than local and delegated authorities to apply resources, this does not mean that action has not been taken. Both health and local authorities have already concentrated resources on a number of the most problematical wards—though the scale and balance of their commitment has often remained in dispute. (For a review of the new public health movement see Scott-Samuel, 1989; and also Betts, 1990.)

SOCIAL POLARIZATION

The gap in material and social conditions in British cities has been growing. This is illustrated by trends in unemployment and trends in other forms of material and social deprivation. There are a number of available statistical indicators. They show some areas experiencing a greater concentration of certain problems at the same time as other areas are becoming relieved of them. The pattern is by no means consistent but examples for Manchester, for instance, are overcrowding, poor housing facilities, frequent moves of house, and lack of assets or income, as measured by non-ownership of a car and by rough measures of cash income. More unequal living standards also correspond with new relationships with the economy. Jobs for women have expanded in some local labour markets and have contracted in others. And although regions like Greater Manchester or Greater London allow people to travel long distances to work, the deterioration of local economic opportunities and social amenities forces people who can afford it to move away from the area and imprisons others in conditions from which there is little or no means of escape. Certain minorities become more prominent in these areas with worsening economic conditions because their incomes and opportunities of getting paid work are low, their dependencies are often restrictive, and their need to counter discrimination and not merely maintain cultural practices familiar to them draws them together. They are obliged to resort to places where they can get a home and a modicum of social support at least cost. Some areas therefore become backwaters of the city's economy. While this is not a new process it is becoming very marked in inner cities at the start of the 1990s.

For different metropolitan regions there are indicators of growing inequality. Thus, for Greater London rates of change in the richest and poorest boroughs have been traced, according to Census information for the period between 1971 and 1981 (Elliott, in Abrams and Brown, 1984; Townsend, with Corrigan and Kowarzik, 1987). The changes on a range of indicators are not consistent but in both richest and poorest boroughs there has been a tendency to depart further from average conditions and circumstances. Higher than average growth in unemployment has driven more people to work outside the borough, and the numbers of women working have fallen particularly sharply. In inner London boroughs with large increases in unemployment, such as Hackney, Tower Hamlets, and Newham, the number of women in paid employment grew much less than expected in the 1970s. By contrast, in outer London boroughs with small increases in unemployment, like Hillingdon, Sutton, and Bromley, the number grew much more than expected. Areas with high rates of unemployment tend also to be areas with below-average numbers of households with two or more wage-earners and with disproportionately large numbers with low earnings. This helps to explain why the trends in unemployment represent a more general polarization of economic and social conditions.

For Greater Manchester the trend can be illustrated for unemployment between 1971 and 1987. Although changes in the boundaries of some wards do not allow the rates to be compared reliably, the increase in unemployment in the least deprived wards was smaller proportionately as well as absolutely than in the most deprived wards during the decade 1971–81. By May 1987 the unemployment rate in Manchester Hulme had reached 46 per cent and in seven other deprived wards was over 30 per cent. Increases in unemployment in some of these wards was three, four, five, and even sixfold between 1971 and 1987. For the 10 wards among the 25 least deprived wards which can be followed from 1971, on the other hand, unemployment increased less than 2½ times to May 1987. This increase was of course from a very low base (Townsend 1988, pp. 25–6).

There has also been a growth in the number of people who are black or in one-parent families in some metropolitan areas with relatively worsening conditions. In 1981 slightly more than 10 per cent of the City of Manchester's children lived in one-parent families and the highest proportion, 18 per cent, were in Moss Side, Hulme, and Ardwick wards. At the other extreme a group of wards in the southern part of the city had only 7 per cent. By 1985 the total percentage of the City's children in such families had grown to 18 per cent, as recorded by the Council's population survey. Another example is provided by a statistical report prepared for the former Greater London Council (GLC). This concluded that there was 'a widening gap between boroughs containing few deprived groups and those containing many' (Congdon, 1984, p. 24). During the 1970s there were dispro- portionately large increases in ethnic minorities living in London boroughs like Tower Hamlets, Newham, and Southwark. In Hammersmith and Fulham and in Islington the increases were less than expected, partly because of a marked 'gentrification' of housing in the former borough and a marked expansion of new council housing (to which access was sometimes difficult) in the latter. Boroughs with above average numbers of Asians in 1971 (Newham, Tower Hamlets, Brent, and Ealing) had numbers even more above average in 1981, while boroughs with below average numbers in 1971 were even further below average ten years later (Bexley, Bromley, and Sutton).

CONCLUSION

This chapter has documented the material and social deprivation of inner-city areas and has demonstrated the connection with ill- health and premature mortality. One of the themes has been the structural basis of widening social and geographical inequality. This requires a lot more study. Some people like to assume that widening inequality applies only to the years of the Thatcher Government. There is evidence, however, from trends in income distribution (Townsend, 1979, ch. 4) and from trends in inequality of mortality (Wilkinson, 1989) that this is not the case. There has been a longer process going on of what might be described as a 'restoration' of social inequalities after the narrowing processes of the war and immediate post-war years. Power has been mobilized on behalf of middle- and upper-class interests by means of a reconstruction of the benefits of the public welfare state, the growth of private welfare associated with market employment, and the inequalities of indirect welfare derived from the handling of fiscal policy and especially tax allowances by the Treasury. Underlying these developments, of course, have been the structural changes taking place in industry and the labour market.

This conclusion depends on being more critical of the evolution of the so-called welfare state during the 1960s and 1970s than most observers and historians have been inclined to be hitherto. Partly it depends on judgements which have to be made about the impact of employer fringe benefits and new forms of wealth on the distribution of real living standards, as distinct from trends in the distribution of measured disposable incomes. There has been a gradual shift in taxation from progressive to regressive, a diminution of the proportion of income subject to tax (less than half total gross household income is actually taxed), and the professionalization of tax avoidance. The growth in numbers of students in accountancy has been faster than in any other subject in Britain in the mid-1980s. Accountants protect companies but also middle- and upper-class private customers from progressive taxation—or any taxation. Over a very long period we have been witnessing a gradual move away from the presumed redistributive character of the welfare state—in terms of revenue (which has often been neglected in analysis) as well as benefits. This reinforcement of inequalities has been masked in part by inflation but also by structural changes in the balance of personal resources commanded by individuals, which have not been reflected and measured in official statistics and administrative categories.

Mortality data are in fact very revealing about trends in living standards. The divide in health between occupational classes has grown unambiguously wider in the last 30 to 40 years (see, for example, the Black Report, 1980; Koskinen, 1985; Hart, 1986; Wilkinson, 1986; Marmot, 1987; Whitehead, 1987; Fox, 1989;

Wilkinson, 1989). The work of relating trends in patterns of health in this century to trends in incomes, taxation, housing, and employment is still in its early stages (see, for example, Wilkinson, 1989). The most prosperous quarter of the population (usually in the managerial, senior administrative, and professional occupations) continues to achieve considerable improvements in health every ten years. This can be extracted with difficulty from the microfiche issued with the decennial mortality reports (OPCS, 1978, 1986). By contrast, the poorest quarter of the population, including people in partly skilled as well as unskilled occupations and those who are long-term unemployed, has experienced only slight improvements. There is doubt whether some groups have experienced any improvements at all; some may even have slipped back, according to certain absolute standards. Thus the mortality experience of unskilled manual workers during the 1970s and early 1980s remains to be properly disentangled and explained (Townsend, Phillimore, and Beattie, 1987, ch. 9).

The locational problems of inner cities have to be traced back repeatedly to differences nationally between the social classes and especially to the social distribution of incomes and other resources. I have concentrated in this chapter on the poorest groups. In understanding developments, however, changes which apply to the most prosperous groups are a necessary and complementary ingredient of the analysis. Improvements in working conditions have applied especially to administrative and professional jobs. Industrial and technological changes have increased the inequality of gross wages or salaries. Young and middle-aged couples with two good salaries coming into the home and no or few dependants are a common feature of many communities. They are often heavily subsidized by tax allowances on mortgage interest. High levels of prosperity are also reached because child-rearing is completed in early middle age, and couples have had only one or two dependent children. Changes in the structure of employment have also underpinned the emergence of a highly prosperous quarter of the population. The number of jobs in banking, insurance, and finance in Greater London is now half as many again as in all of manufacturing industry put together. The most prosperous quarter of the population has gained substantially during the Thatcher years.

The problems of the inner city, therefore, have to be traced to the distributions of employment, industry, wages, rented and owner-occupied housing, public transport, and the rest. These problems are deepened or alleviated, in different mixes, by government policies. We have seen that urban aid and special area policies have been small in total resources and effect, and have attracted smaller real investment in the 1980s. While it would be wrong to dismiss them as cosmetic only, it would be difficult to claim that they have been developed as either substantial or really serious measures. Far more important has been the variety of national economic and social policies controlled by Government—its employment, investment, fiscal, public expenditure, and social security policies—all of which stem from its particular management of the economy, as guided by choice of economic theory. In the early pages of this chapter the connections between different economic theories and the policy packages as well as ideologies of those theories were briefly explained, and there is little doubt that the extreme forms of inner-city problems in recent years have been due to the consequences of the Government's adherence to neo-monetarist economic and social doctrine.

But this brief résumé of the analysis of inner-city deprivation in Greater London would not be complete without acknowledging the larger role being played by multinational forces—especially multinational corporations and the international agencies which largely serve their interests. The market is increasingly being internationalized and internal economic and social developments are increasingly being determined by external market forces outside the control if not the influence of solitary national governments. In following its neo-monetarist policies the British Government is, at least in part, only playing its part in the restructuring of an international market which as yet has few of the restraints which came to be imposed on national markets at the end of the nineteenth century and in the twentieth century by 'Welfare State' policy developments. One of the frustrations of national life and politics is that problems like those of the inner city are no longer so susceptible to national remedial action.

References

Abrams, P., and Brown, R. (eds.) (1984), *UK Society: Work, Urbanism and Inequality* (London).

Appleby, J. (1986), *Social Inequality and Public Health in Birmingham* (Birmingham).

Ashton, J. (1984), *Health in Mersey: A Review* (Liverpool).

—— and Knight, L. (1988), 'The UK Healthy Cities Conference', University of Liverpool Conference Papers.

Betts, G. (1990), 'Inequalities in health and the development of local authority strategies', Ph.D. thesis (Bristol).

Black, Sir D. (1980), *Inequalities in Health: Report of a Research Working Group* (London).

BMA (British Medical Association) (1987), *Deprivation and Ill-Health* (London).

Booth, C. (1892–7), *Life and Labour of People in London*, 9 vols. and book of maps (London).

Centre for Urban Studies (1964), *London: Aspects of Change* (London).

Chadwick, Sir E. (1842), *Report on the Sanitary Condition of the Labouring Population* (London).

Congdon, P. (1984), *Social Structure in the London Boroughs: Evidence from the 1981 Census and Changes since 1971* (London).

—— (1987), 'Ward level population monitoring and forecasting in Greater London', Population Geography Group of the IBG, Oxford University Paper (London).

—— (1988), 'Deprivation in London wards: Mortality and unemployment trends in the 1980s', *The Statistician*, 37, 451–72.

DoE (Department of the Environment) (1975), *Study of the Inner Areas of Connurbations* (London).

—— (1977), *Policy for the Inner Cities*, Cmnd. 6845 (London).

Donnison, D., and Eversley, D. (eds.) (1973), *London: Urban Patterns, Problems and Policies* (London).

Engels, F. (1845), *The Condition of the Working Class in England*, trans. and ed. W. O. Henderson and W. H. Chaloner (Oxford, 1981).

Farr, W. (1885), *Vital Statistics: A Memorial Volume of Selections from the Reports and Writings of William Farr*, ed. for the Sanitary Institute of Great Britain by N. Humphreys (London).

Fox, J. (ed.) (1989), *Health Inequalities in Europe* (London).

Hall, P. (1981), *The Inner City in Context* (London).

Halsey, A. H. (1986), *Change in British Society* (Oxford).

Harrison, P. (1983), *Inside the Inner City: Life Under the Cutting Edge* (Harmondsworth).

Hart, N. (1986), 'Inequalities in health: The individual versus the environment', *Journal of the Royal Statistical Society*, Ser. A, 149/3, 228–46.

Higgins, J., Deakin, N., Edwards, J., and Wicks, M. (1983), *Government and Urban Poverty* (London).

Jarman, B. (1983), 'Identification of under-privileged areas', *British Medical Journal*, 286, 1705–9.

—— (1984), 'Under-privileged areas: Validation and distribution of scores', *British Medical Journal*, 289, 1587–92.

—— (1987), *Primary Care in Inner Cities* (London).

Jones, C. (ed.) (1979), *Urban Deprivation and the Inner City* (London).

Kaasjager, D. C., van der Maesen, L. J. G., and Nijhuis, H. G. J. (eds.) (1989), *The New Public Health in an Urban Context*, WHO Healthy City Papers, No. 4 (Copenhagen).

Koskinen, S. (1985), 'Time-trends in cause-specific mortality by social class in England and Wales', *International Union for the Scientific Study of Population Conference* (Florence).

Lawless, P. (1981), *Britain's Inner Cities* (London).

Liverpool City Planning Department (1987), *Health Inequalities in Liverpool* (Liverpool).

Manchester City Council (1986), *Poverty in Manchester* (Manchester).

Manchester Joint Consultative Committee (1987), *Health Inequalities and Manchester* (Manchester).

Marmot, M. G. (1987), 'Social inequalities in mortality: The social environment', in R. G. Wilkinson (ed.), *Class and Health: Research and Longitudinal Data* (London).

Marsden, J. (1989), 'Health and deprivation: Inequalities in Sefton', BA dissertation (Liverpool).

OECD (Organization for Economic Co-operation and Development) (1985), *Social Expenditure: 1960–1990: Problems of Growth and Control* (Paris).

OPCS (Office of Population Censuses and Surveys) (1978), *Registrar-General's Decennial Supplement on Occupational Mortality 1970–1972* (London).

—— (1986), *Registrar-General's Decennial Supplement on Occupational Mortality 1979–1982* (London).

Pahl, R. (1970), *Whose City?* (London).

Rex, J., and Tomlinson, S. (1979), *Colonial Immigrants in a British City: A Class Analysis* (London).

Roberts, R. (1973), *The Classic Slum: Salford Life in the First Quarter of the Century* (Harmondsworth).

Robson, B. T. (1969), *Urban Analysis: A Study of City Structure, with Special Reference to Sunderland* (Cambridge).

Scarman, Lord (1981), *The Brixton Disorders 10–12 April 1981: Report of an Inquiry*, Cmnd. 8427 (London).

Scott-Samuel, A. (1989), 'Building the new public health: A public health alliance and a new social epidemiology', in C. J. Martin, and D. V. McQueen, (eds.), *Readings for a New Public Health* (Edinburgh).

Sheffield Health Authority (1987), *A Profile of Health Care and Disease in Sheffield* (Sheffield).

Simon, Sir J. (1987), *English Sanitary Institutions: Review in their Course of Development and in Some of their Political and Social Relations* (2nd edn., London).

Smith, A., and Jacobson, B. (1988), *The Nation's Health: A Strategy for the 1990s* (London).

Thrift, N., Leyshon, A., and Daniels, P. (1987), ' "Sexy greedy": The new international financial system, the City of London and the South East of England', Working Papers on Producer Services, No. 8 (Bristol).

Thunhurst, C. (1985), *Poverty and Health in the City of Sheffield* (Sheffield).

Townsend, P. (1976), *The Difficulties of Policies Based on the Concept of Area Deprivation*, Barnett Shine Foundation Lecture (London).

—— (1979), *Poverty in the United Kingdom: A Survey of Household Resources and Standards of Living*, (Harmondsworth).

—— (1988), *Inner City Deprivation and Premature Death in Greater Manchester* (Ashton-under-Lyne and Bristol).

——Phillimore P., and Beattie, A. (1987), *Health and Deprivation Inequality and the North* (London).

—— with Corrigan, P., and Kowarzik, U. (1987), *Poverty and Labour in London*, Interim Report of a Centenary Survey (London).

—— and Gordon, D. (1989), *What is Enough? New Evidence on Poverty Allowing the Definition of a Minimum Benefit*. House of Commons, Social Services Committee, *Minimum Income*, 579 (London).

Whitehead, M. (1987), *The Health Divide: Inequalities in Health in the 1980s* (London).

WHO (World Health Organisation) (1985), *Targets for Health for All— 2000* (Copenhagen).

Wilkinson, R. G. (ed.) (1986), *Class and Health: Research and Longitudinal Data* (London).

Wilkinson, R. G. (1989), 'Class mortality differentials, income distribution and trends in poverty, 1921–81', *Journal of Social Policy*, 18/3, 307–35.

6

Family Life in Inner Cities

Hilary Land

INTRODUCTION

In 1945 the Conservative party manifesto stated: 'The children must always come first. The Education Act, school meals, family allowances, all show that Parliament is realising it.' Although the Conservative party today still claims to be 'the Party of the family', the dominant strand in their ideology is now very different. Looking at how social policies have developed in the 1980s, it is quite clear that children have *not* been given priority and neither have their mothers. Instead the rights of children, along with the rights of women, to some share in the resources of the community as its citizens, are being subordinated to certain beliefs about the economy: first, that wages are too high; and second, that public expenditure on social welfare stifles initiative and enterprise because it both requires high levels of taxation and creates 'a culture of dependency'. Thus benefits for women and children, as well as benefits for men, are being restructured in an attempt to impose greater industrial discipline on low-paid workers so that they will accept, or remain on, low wages. The first part of this chapter will examine some of the ways in which this is being done.

The second part will look at the ways in which women's rights to benefits arising from their *unpaid* work in the home are also being eroded. These were not part of the post-war social security reforms. While William Beveridge acknowledged that as wives and mothers, women were doing 'vital, but unpaid work in the home', he and the other policy-makers of the time believed it more appropriate to give them, in return, claim to support from their husbands who could claim on their behalf additional dependants' allowance. It was not until the 1980s that women began to have claims to support from the state in their own right arising from the *caring* they were doing, and then married women's claims were far weaker than those of single women. However, even these modest steps are being eroded, as policies for 'community care' become based even more firmly on the assumption that most of this care must take place within the family and remain unpaid. As the Department of Health and Social Security (DHSS) admitted in their review of research studies of community care services at the end of the 1980s, 'The cost-effectiveness of these packages often depends on *not* putting a financial value on the contribution of the informal carer' (quoted in Tinker, 1981, my emphasis). Meanwhile, however, in the name of equality, the claims women have on their husbands have been reduced. Without stronger claims on the state to benefits in their own right and on improved access to better jobs and pay in the labour market, women and those who depend on them are being trapped in a vicious triangle of inadequate support from the family, from the state, and from wages. That can only spell more poverty, particularly in inner-city areas which are characterized by disproportionate levels of unemployment, badly paid jobs, and a high incidence of lone parents and dependent elderly people.

LOW WAGE EARNERS: FAMILY MEN, WOMEN, AND YOUNG PEOPLE

The 1986 Social Security Act was based on a review of social security, the principles of which revealed the Government's intention to use the social security system to impose greater discipline on the male workforce and to give this greater priority than meeting the needs of mothers and children. The changes proposed in the benefits designed to support families with children show this very clearly.

Ideally the Government would like to abolish child benefit (formerly family allowances) which are not means-tested and are paid, usually to the mother, on behalf of every child under 16 years or in full-time education. Because they do not depend on employment or marital status of the parent(s), child benefits do not trap parent(s) in particular household or employment situations. To the Government's surprise (and to some extent the poverty lobby's too) child benefits are popular among others in *all* income groups and public opinion polls show that most people believe them to be important. So far, instead of abolishing them, the real value of child benefits is being allowed to fall and more emphasis placed on means-tested support for low wage-earner families. The means-tested Family Income Supplement (FIS) has been replaced by Family Credit. This is clearly an instrument to reduce demands for higher wages among low-paid men.

First, because Family Credit is based on net rather than gross income, the Government asserts the poverty trap is alleviated. Those in receipt of Family Credit, unlike recipients of FIS, do not get other benefits such as free school meals and welfare foods: these are now restricted to those on the new means-tested Income Support (Supplementary Benefit's successor). The proposals therefore 'will prevent families in nearly all circumstances from facing a position in which there is little or no financial benefit to be gained from *continuing in lower paid jobs*' (my emphasis) (DHSS, 1985, vol. 2, para. 4.53). It does mean however that cuts in income tax are of little benefit to those families, for by increasing *net* income, their benefit is cut.

Second, the Secretary of State for the Department of Health and Social Security (since September 1988 split into the Department of Social Security (DSS) and Department of Health (DH)) had learned during the health workers' strike two years earlier that the existence of child benefit did not diminish demands for a *family wage*, because it did not show up in the man's wage packet. So although FIS or child benefit was being paid by order book usually to the mother, it was proposed that the Family Credit would be paid by the employer to the *man*'s wage packet. This, the Green Paper stated, will 'offer significant advantages for employers in ensuring that employees perceive more clearly the total net remuneration they receive rather than earnings net of tax and national insurance alone' (DHSS, 1985, vol. 2, para. 4.50). The added advantage of this would be that Family Credit could be withheld when the father was on strike. Fortunately the combined poverty and women's lobbies were supported by the Federation of Small Businesses and the National Farmers' Union who did not want the trouble and expense of administering the scheme, and, during the final stages of the bill, the Government had to agree to administer family credit in the same way as FIS.

This was an important battle to have won, although the future of child benefits is by no means assured. However, the take-up rate for Family Credit is even lower than predicted by the Government (30 per cent instead of 60 per cent) and at the time of writing a big advertising campaign is being launched. Meanwhile the 1989 Employment Bill currently before the House will remove what statutory protection there is for the low-paid worker.

In 1986 the Government abolished the jurisdiction of Wages Councils over workers under 21 years of age and limited their job to setting minimum basic hourly and overtime rates. This, together with substantial reductions in the entitlement of un-employed young people to social security benefits, paying them instead a weekly allowance of £25 provided they accept a place on a youth training scheme, the Government believes has encouraged 'more realistic levels of youth pay' (Department of Employment, 1988, p. 27). Indeed, the gap between the earnings of young workers and adults has widened: in 1979 18–20-year-olds earned 60 per cent of average adult pay. By 1986 this had fallen to 54 per cent (Low Pay Unit, 1988, p. 6). In addition to repealing the restrictions on hours of work for 16–18-year-olds, the 1989 Employment Bill contains proposals to abolish Wages Councils altogether. This will particularly affect married women, for two-thirds of the 2.5 million workers covered by Wages Councils (which include trades such as retailing, clothing, and catering) are part-time employees. Between 1983 and 1987 two-thirds of the growth in the labour force was made up by married women and between now and 1995 women will account for four-fifths of the growth in the labour force. (In contrast there will be 1.2 million fewer under-25-year-olds in the labour market by 1995.) It is therefore increasingly important that their pay is 'realistic'. Moreover, many of these jobs will be in the service sector, for it is predicted that by 1995 services will account for 70 per cent of employment, compared with two-thirds in 1987 and half twenty years ago (Department of Employment, 1988, p. 11). The Government justify the abolition of these 80-year-old Wages Councils on the grounds that 'the system predates the modern social security structure, let alone the existence of substantial in-work benefits' (Department of Employment, 1988, p. 27). This is nonsense: part-time workers in Britain have very few rights to either state or occupational benefits. Sir John Hoskyns, the Director-General of the Institute of Directors, and former adviser to the Prime Minister, was more direct in admitting their likely impact on wages when he said that 'anyone whose pay dropped because of their abolition could rely on the Family Credit welfare system' (*Guardian*, 30 January 1989). However, only workers who have children and are in *full-time* employment (i.e. working at least 24 hours a week) are eligible to claim Family Credit, and few two-earner couples qualify, so the majority will have to accept a lower income. In addition, under the 1988 Local Government Act, a whole range of existing local authority services will have to compete on price and quality with outside contractors. This, the Government claims, 'will give a significant impetus to the setting of realistic pay within local government' (Department of Employment, 1988, p. 35). For 'realistic' read 'lower', for the Treasury blames the continued increase in local government expenditure on 'unnecessarily high pay awards and increases in manpower' (Treasury, 1989, p. 63). (The figures show that the numbers employed by local authorities have increased very little in the last three years).

In the 1986 Social Security Act the needs of the unemployed received scant attention, in spite of the Government's claim that this was the most fundamental review of social security since that of Beveridge. This Act did however give the Secretary of State the power to vary the annual uprating of unemployment benefit 'if he considers it appropriate, having regard to the national economic situation and any other matters which he considers relevant' (Matthewman and Calvert, 1987, p. 103). The 1980 Social Security Act which abolished the earnings-related supplement and made unemployment benefit taxable had already changed the base for annually uprating pensions from the higher of movements in earnings or prices to the lower of the two. The value of the single person's unemployment benefit indexed by earnings fell by 20 per cent between 1978 and 1987. The unemployed person with dependent children was also worse off because in 1984 he (or she) lost the additions to benefit for children, which had begun to be phased out as a result of the 1980 Act. Those with incomplete contribution records were disqualified altogether as a result of the 1986 Act for they could no longer qualify for *any* benefit. Since the 1946 National Insurance Act those who did not have a full contribution record had been able to qualify for half or three-quarters rate of benefit. This change has affected even larger numbers of unemployed since October 1988 because as a result of the 1988 Social Security Act entitlement to benefit depends on the contribution record for the previous *two* tax years instead of one tax year. The contribution condition has to be satisfied for *each* tax year: deficiencies in one year cannot be made up by contributions over the minimum acquired in the other year. Moreover, these contributions must be *paid*, not credited. In other words, those with erratic earnings are particularly affected. In addition, full-time carers in receipt of Invalid Care Allowance (ICA) no longer have their rights to short-term benefits protected.

In addition to reducing the *value* of unemployment benefit, changes in the administrative rules defining availability for work have made it harder to establish eligibility for benefit. Since the beginning of 1987 would-be claimants have to show that if they have children or other dependants requiring care, they are able to make arrangements for substitute care *within 24 hours*. (The official will expect the claimant to name a child-minder (not a relative) and he or she will check that arrangements can indeed be made.) There are also tougher questions concerning willingness to travel and the type of job being sought. In 1987 107,000 people (compared with 53,000 in 1985) were disqualified from claiming unemployment benefit because they were deemed not to be available for work. The 1989 Social Security Bill currently before Parliament will tighten these rules still further by disqualifying claimants who do not appear to be active enough in seeking work and who refuse to accept a job because it does not match up to the skill level and pay of their previous job or indeed the level of benefit currently being received. Clause 9 of the bill will restrict the period during which a claimant can refuse to accept a job for these reasons. As John Moore told the House of Commons during the second-reading debate in January 1989, the unemployed 'must not delude themselves about the wages they can command'. The Government had intended to disqualify claimants refusing to take part-time work, even though they must be available for *full-time* work in order to claim benefit. This was defeated in the Committee stage of the bill.

Those who leave a job voluntarily or who are dismissed for misconduct have always been disqualified from claiming benefit for a certain period. In 1911 when the first National Insurance Act was passed, the period stipulated was six weeks and this remained unchanged until the 1986 Social Security Act. From October 1986 the disqualification period was extended to 13 weeks and in April 1988 it was further extended to 26 weeks. The 1988 Act also gave the Secretary of State power to count this disqualification period against the total period for which unemployment benefit is paid. (Unemployment insurance benefit can be paid only for a maximum of 52 weeks.) Those disqualified have recourse to means-tested assistance (Income Support, formerly called Supplementary Benefit) but this will be paid at only 40 per cent of the normal rate. In 1987. 420,000 received a reduced means-tested benefit because they had left their jobs 'voluntarily'.

This series of decisions is only a sample of nearly forty measures affecting the unemployed person's rights to benefit; some are quite small in themselves but their cumulative effect has been seriously to erode the national insurance scheme for the unemployed. Only a minority of unemployed people rely on the contributory unemployment benefit system, more and more being forced on to the means-tested system (see Table 6.1) so that in November 1987, nearly 2 million unemployed claimants had recourse to a means-tested benefit. The value of the benefit received by those who do qualify has been seriously eroded. Recent estimates indicate that a return to the 1978/9 national insurance benefit system would have increased the income of those unemployed in 1988 by over £500 million, i.e. a third more than they actually received in contributory benefits (Atkinson

Table 6.1. *Social Security benefits received by the unemployed (1961–1986)*
(%)

	1961	1971	1981	1986
Male				
Unemployment benefit only	47.2	40.9	30.0	20.2
Unemployment ben. & supplementary ben.	9.4	13.6	10.9	7.5
Supplementary benefit	21.9	27.1	46.0	59.3
No benefit	21.6	18.4	14.4	13.0
TOTAL unemployed male claimants (000s)	283	721	1076	2086
Female				
Unemployment benefit only	39.7	41.0	38.9	32.5
Unemployment ben. & supplementary ben.	2.5	6.7	3.8	2.7
Supplementary benefit	12.2	20.5	37.4	40.8
No benefit	45.5	31.8	20.0	23.0
TOTAL unemployed female claimants (000s)	101	138	709	955

Source: CSO, 1989, p. 92.

and Micklewright, 1988, p. 29). In contrast, while benefits have been declining, the standard contribution has increased, although changes in the last Budget have modified their regressive nature by introducing lower rates for those on lower incomes. The national insurance fund into which employers, employees, and the Exchequer notionally pay contributions has been in surplus throughout the whole post-war period although with high unemployment rates this surplus fell substantially during the 1980s. In the 1989 Social Security Bill it is proposed that the national insurance scheme for the first time in its history will be funded *entirely* by employers' and employees' contributions, thus saving the Exchequer from 1990 £2.4 billion annually. In 1979 Exchequer contributions represented 18 per cent of the fund's income. The scope for using the national insurance scheme as a vehicle for redistribution has thus been diminished.

IMMIGRANT WORKERS

Other workers particularly affected by further restriction of social security entitlement, in combination with changes in other areas of law, are members of ethnic minority groups. The 1985 social security review means that immigrants, or those believed to be immigrants, are facing increased difficulties in getting the benefits they need. There is already evidence that black claimants may have to produce additional information such as a passport to confirm their citizenship. There is also liaison between the DSS and the Home Office if there is any doubt about their status.

In addition, the rights of some immigrants, although lawfully settled here, are limited by the system of sponsorship. The 1986 Social Security Act confirms and increases these limitations. Children, elderly parents, and other relatives may be sponsored by a relative already living here. The sponsor is liable to maintain and accommodate them if they have entered either under the terms of the 1971 Immigration Act, or after May 1980. The Act makes it very clear that the sponsor will continue to be liable to maintain them, *sets no time limit* on that liability, and excludes them from eligibility to claim Income Support, and probably Family Credit too.

The immigration rules introduced in August 1985 specified the 'public funds' on which sponsored immigrants should make no demands and these explicitly included Supplementary Benefit. The scope of the sponsorship system was also extended. Foreign fiancé(e)s and spouses are admitted to the UK on condition that they make no claims on public funds either before the marriage or for a period of twelve months. In effect the fiancé(e) or spouse is their sponsor. After a stay of twelve months they are usually given indefinite leave to say, but each remains liable to support the other and their dependants. In other words, although lawfully living here those who originally came under the sponsorship system will be treated differently from the rest of the settled population and the more benefits become means-tested and discretionary, the greater the difference will be. Britain is developing, in effect, a system of guest workers.

The Government has thus used the social security system as a key component in a package of policies designed not only to save public expenditure, but to reduce the wages and rights of certain groups of workers. The insurance principle has almost been abandoned as far as the unemployed are concerned, and as

Atkinson and Micklewright (1988, p. 29) argue, 'the contribution conditions for social insurance provide an incentive for labour force participation and for people to take "regular" as opposed to "marginal" employment'. This is how the social insurance scheme was used in the early days before the First World War, and how William Beveridge intended it to be used after the Second World War, although avoiding 'voluntary' unemployment and maintaining incentives for men to take up full-time paid employment have always been of concern, as indeed they are in any social security system. The aim of government policies in the 1980s and 1990s is the opposite: to tighten the boundaries of the formal labour market and push more and more workers into its margins or what is officially called the 'flexible' labour market. In this labour market women outnumber men by almost two to one.

PUBLIC SUPPORT FOR AND PROVISION OF CARE

While the British social security system has always been constrained by the need to maintain work incentives, 'work' has been defined differently for men and for women. For men it has meant *paid* work in the labour market, and in future that will mean at whatever wage is offered. For women it has meant *unpaid* work in the home, caring for children, sick or elderly people, and husbands. This, as the discussion above shows, does not mean that women are not expected to be in the labour market, but that they must never forget their domestic responsibilities. Britain has never adopted a comprehensive policy of public provision for children, except in a modest way during the Second World War. There was neither the ideological commitment nor the need to do so. In the post-war years women with children joined the labour market anyway and have continued to do so. It was possible to do this without child care services because many of the jobs they took were part time and they relied on relatives to provide child care. In the Department of Employment's words, 'part-time work is popular with both employers and workers. It enables employers to adapt the size of their workforce to match workflows and employees to combine paid employment with domestic responsibilities and leisure' (Department of Employment, 1988,

p. 12). In 1951 part-time workers accounted for only 5 per cent of the labour force; by 1981 they accounted for over 25 per cent. Eight out of ten of the 5 million part-time workers today are women, most of them married. Women with children are the most likely to take part-time employment (three-fifths of part-time employees have children) and as Table 6.2 shows the majority of women with pre-school children do not have paid employment at all.

Table 6.2. *Proportion of mothers in full-time and part-time employment by age of child and marital status of mother (1976–1986)*

	1976–8		1980–2		1984–6	
	lone	married	lone	married	lone	married
Ch. under 5						
Full-time	15	5	11	6	9	7
Part-time	13	21	13	20	9	24
TOTAL	28	26	24	26	18	31
Ch. 5+						
Full-time	27	22	27	20	22	22
Part-time	28	44	30	45	31	44
TOTAL	55	66	57	65	53	66

Source: OPCS, 1989.

This is hardly surprising given the lack of day-care facilities. The education system provides free education for those who are in their fourth year. In 1987 just over 47 per cent of children aged 3 or 4 years old were in public sector schools, just over half of them attending full time (9 a.m. to 3.30 p.m.). This compares with 34 per cent of the age group in schools in 1976 and 20 per cent in 1971. However, as most of the increase is accounted for by those attending only part of the day, the extension of this provision has not occurred in response to the needs of mothers in employment, but rather in response to the believed educational and social needs of children.

Local authority social service departments provide some day nurseries. In 1987 there were 33,000 places, only 1,000 more than in 1981. (This is 11 places/1,000 children under 5 years old.) These places are taken almost entirely by children who are considered by social workers to be 'deprived' or 'at risk'. The direct cost to parents is small because although fees are charged they are means-tested. The care provided is, however, full time. The more common form of child care provision, which is only *regulated* by social services departments, is by child-minders. In 1987 there were 150,600 places with registered child-minders (i.e. 50 places/1,000 children under 5 years old), nearly twice as many as ten years earlier. Children are looked after in the child-minder's home and each child-minder is limited to three children; i.e. it is a form of care which most closely resembles family care. Child-minder's fees are not subsidized at all.

Employers' nurseries, which are few and far between, charge fees which may or may not contain an element of subsidy. If they *are* subsidized, then since 1984 the employee is taxed on it as a fringe benefit if she (or he) earns more than £8,500 per annum. (Fringe benefits have been taxable since the introduction of pay-as-you-earn after the Second World War but then the income threshold was much higher. If the threshold had been maintained at its real value it would be about £23,000, thus excluding all but a minority of employed mothers.) The Department of Employment is looking to employers to make more child care provision but it places a greater faith in flexible hours. After all, employers 'will need women employees, and must recognise both their career ambitions and domestic responsibilities. This will involve broadening company training policies, much more flexibility of work and hours and job-sharing, to facilitate the employment of women with families and help adapt to their needs' (Department of Employment, 1988, p. 8). Mrs Thatcher dismisses the idea of any state responsibility for child care to enable women to take paid work much more directly. In an interview published in a women's magazine this year, when asked about tax allowances for working mothers, she said:

No, there would be the most terrible abuses. Women make their own arrangements now and they can carry on doing so. Where women are going out and earning money while their children are still young they have some basic fundamental decisions to make. Can they in fact go out at all at that stage in their children's development or should several women get together and arrange that one looks after the children while the rest go out part-time? (*She*, Feb. 1989, p. 54)

These remarks should be put in the context of a British government who, alone in the EEC, is opposing a draft Directive on part-time workers which would give them, on a pro rata basis, the same occupational and state benefits as full-time workers.

In Britain, then, state policies with respect to child care derived from a residual welfare model. State maternity benefits have been cut and maternity grants, once universal, have been means-tested since 1988; even the poorest mothers will get a grant worth only *half* its value twenty years ago. Only a minority of mothers qualify for unpaid, let alone paid, maternity leave. For the immediate future women are going to have to continue to rely on their families, unless they are one of a minority of workers with scarce skills for whom employers are willing to provide nurseries or sufficiently high wages to purchase child care in the private sector.

The Department of Employment's study of women's employment in 1980 showed how important relatives were in providing child care (Martin and Roberts, 1984). Altogether, of mothers with pre-school children, half of those who had full-time employment and a third of those in part-time employment relied on a relative, usually a grandmother. Among those with school children over a third relied on a relative and half on their husbands. There is very little after-school provision and this also poses problems for working parents: the structure of the school day and week for young children assumes the availability of parents at home. The present Government is not even prepared to continue to *regulate* child care provisions for the over-fives, let alone *make* provision. In the 1989 Children's Bill currently going through Parliament, the Government introduced an amendment removing these provisions from the 1948 Nurseries and Childminder Regulations Act.

Another change in government policy with respect to the cost of child care has made it harder for those dependent on social security to earn a little money to supplement their benefit. Prior to the 1986 Social Security Act, child care and travel expenses could be offset against gross earnings for the purpose of calculating the earnings disregarded for the means-tested Supplementary Benefit. Lone parents could earn £12 a week *net* of expenses before their benefit was affected. Since April 1988 claimants can earn only £15 a week *gross*, thus not making it worth while for lone parents in particular to earn. Such a move is likely to sustain the *downward* trend in economic activity rates among lone mothers (see Table 6.2). In other words, the social security system is trapping increasing numbers of claimants into dependence on state benefits—the opposite of John Moore's stated objectives as discussed in Chapter 4, above.

Indeed, the position of lone mothers is causing the Government some concern. Their numbers are growing: in 1986 14 per cent of all families with dependent children were headed by a lone parent, compared with 9 per cent ten years earlier. In 1979 322,000 lone parents were receiving means-tested Supplementary Benefit on behalf of themselves and half a million children; by 1987 this had increased to 664,000 lone parents with over one million children. Of those in paid employment, 90,000 were receiving the means-tested Family Income Supplement. In other words, the majority of lone parents and their one and a half million children depend partially or wholly on the state. (Altogether in 1987 there were 2.1 million (19 per cent) children in households depending on Supplementary Benefit compared with under one million (7 per cent) in 1979.) In 1988 this was estimated to be costing £4.5 billion—the same as the cost of child benefits—and the Government announced earlier this year that they were considering measures to reduce this cost. Making men more responsible for their children, providing more child care facilities, reducing lone mothers' access to state benefits and services such as housing are all under consideration. In 1988 three-quarters of lone mothers receiving income support received *no* maintenance from their children's fathers (Treasury, 1989, p. 14). However, getting fathers to pay more will do nothing to improve the living standards of lone mothers and their children because maintenance is offset against benefit entitlements pound for pound. It would of course save the DSS money. In the current climate, with a residual model of welfare informing policy development, it seems unlikely that more public child care will be forthcoming. Instead the economic circumstances and lives of lone mothers and their children are going to get even harsher, whether they be claimants or workers. Already between 1979 and 1984, the average gross income of lone parent families fell from 51 per cent of a two-parent family with two children to 40 per cent (Kahn and Kammerman, 1987, p. 143). Listening to the recent speeches of John Moore and other ministers, it would seem that the Government is more concerned to find disincentives against women embarking on lone parenthood than to meet the welfare needs of lone mothers and their children. After all, there is currently no concern about the birth-rate, and increased numbers of women are not needed in the labour market full time. The fact that it is difficult to support a family on only one full-time wage, especially if it is a woman's wage (women's full-time earnings are 66 per cent of those of men), and near impossible on a part-time wage (women's hourly earnings in part-time work are 58 per cent of men's hourly earnings in full-time work), is seen as a private problem and not a public responsibility.

COMMUNITY CARE

Women's—and some men's—opportunities to take up paid employment are also affected by their responsibilities for caring for sick, handicapped, or infirm relatives. In Britain for the last thirty years 'community care' has been promoted as the desirable policy to pursue in developing services for adult dependants. The meaning of that policy has changed. Initially it was an understandable reaction against large, remote institutions which provided low standards of impersonal care. Community care in contrast meant care *in* the community. By the end of the 1970s this had shifted to mean care both *in* the community and *by* the community. Thus in their White Paper, *Growing Older*, the Government in 1981 stated:

Whatever level of public expenditure proves practicable and however it is distributed, the primary sources of support and care for elderly people are informal and voluntary. These spring from personal ties of kinship, friendship and neighbourhood. They are irreplaceable. It is the role of public authorities to sustain and where necessary develop—but never to displace—such support and care. Care *in* the community must increasingly mean care *by* the community. (DHSS, 1981, p. 3).

Of course, state social services have never *replaced* informal care. Instead families, and women in particular, have been subject to more professional advice and quality control over their caring, but it is they who had to do the work of caring, including time spent mobilizing the resources public authorities do provide.

The amount of care provided by the family is substantial and has recently been documented in the General Household Survey (GHS). In a report published in September 1988, based on an analysis of the 18,500 adults living in private households included in the sample for the annual General Household Survey, it is estimated that one adult in seven is providing informal care and that one household in five contains a carer. Altogether there are 6 million carers in Britain, 3.5 million women (15 per cent of adult women) and 2.5 million men (12 per cent of adult men). Four out of five were caring for a relative, one in five was caring for more than one person, and nearly one in four was spending at least 20 hours a week in caring.

Middle age (45 to 64 years) is the peak age for caring: nearly a quarter of all women of this age and 16 per cent of men were carers. Interestingly, caring affected the employment status of men of working age far less than that of women. Of those in this age group providing at least 20 hours of care a week, 45 per cent of men were working full-time compared with 16 per cent of women. In contrast only 3 per cent of men worked part time compared with 25 per cent of women. These figures may explain why relatively few men claim the Invalid Care Allowance (ICA) (restricted to those under retirement age) which is paid to those who give up paid work to provide at least 35 hours of care a week. Men and women also differed in the amount of responsibility they carried: two-thirds of women and half of men carried the main responsibility for care and women were more likely than men to care for someone outside the household. Not surprisingly, the amount of care provided for someone outside the carer's household was less: three-quarters of carers spent less than 20 hours. Conversely, 45 per cent of carers living in the same household spent more than 50 hours per week and among carers aged over 65 years the proportion was even higher: 59 per cent. Men and women are just as likely to be looking after a spouse, but women are far more likely than men to be looking after a parent or an adult child.

The Audit Commission in Britain calculated that in 1985 carers saved the Government over £3,000 a year per elderly person cared for, and therefore concluded that 'carers have needs and rights—since their work is important to the economy and health of the Health and Social Services' (Audit Commission, 1986, p. 43). It is thus estimated that Britain's 6 million carers currently provide about £20 billion worth of support annually (Family Policy Bulletin, No. 6, January 1989). However, recognizing their needs and rights would cost money, and though policies in the 1970s did begin to recognize carers' financial contributions—the ICA was introduced in the 1975 Social Security Act, and carers' state pension rights were protected—policies in the 1980s have eroded even these modest steps.

For example, the earnings threshold (above which, eligibility for ICA is lost) has been increased only once in twelve years and is currently £12 a week. It should be three times that amount. More important, eligibility for the ICA has recently been extended to include married women as a result of a European Court ruling in 1986 that to restrict it to single women and men contravened the EEC Directive on Equal Treatment in Social Security. At the time the decision was made, the 1986 Social Security Bill was still going through Parliament and immediately the Government moved to limit the impact of the decision by making changes in other benefits for the disabled. In particular, eligibility for the additional premiums for disabled people receiving the means-tested Income Support will depend on the severity of the disability. Those who are sufficiently ill or infirm to qualify for an attendance allowance (i.e. requiring a 'wakeful and watchful presence' day and/or night) will qualify for the higher premium. However, they will also have to show that no one is getting an ICA in respect of the care they need. In other words, since April 1988 anyone who gives up their job to care for a disabled person and applies successfully for an ICA will see that person's social security benefit reduced by exactly the same amount (£26.20 in April 1989, representing one-sixth of female gross average weekly earnings). This is very different from the other rules which apply to overlapping benefits. In this case the claimants are different people, not necessarily living in the same household. One benefit is based on some recognition of loss of earnings and carries with it protection of basic state pension rights, the other is based on additional needs arising from chronic sickness or disability. The amount of care required to qualify for an ICA is 35 hours per week but the person needing care must be receiving an attendance allowance which presumes the need for between 84 and 168 hours of care per week. In short, the state is forcing the carer to forgo the ICA and a future right to a state pension, or making the person who is dependent on another's care pay for it. In 1986 30,857 people received the ICA. As a result of the EEC ruling in 1987 the numbers trebled to 91,392. Will the numbers fall in 1988 as carers give priority to preserving the income and the feelings of the person being cared for? These are complex issues and it illustrates the conflicting needs of caregivers and their dependants.

Such a move also illustrates the enormous reluctance to give carers within the family a measure of financial independence. The new Income Support scheme pays a premium in addition to the basic personal allowance. This depends on the characteristics of the household; for example, families with children or with a disabled member receive a premium. There is no premium for carers. For women the link between caring and dependency is still very strong and the closer the caring situation resembles a family situation the less likely it is that financial support will be forthcoming. Much of the caring which goes on within the family has remained invisible—the GHS survey of informal care mentioned above is the first national study of its kind. However, it is interesting to note that this study *excluded* time spent on call while sleeping. At the time of writing junior hospital doctors are campaigning to get their long shifts on call reduced because they rightly argue that repeated nights of broken sleep impair their ability to work and damage their health. When this happens within the family it is not even counted, although the GHS survey did find a high proportion of carers in *every* age group in poor health.

Proposals for reorganizing responsibilities for the statutory community care services were published in March 1988, in the Griffiths Report *Community Care: Agenda for Action.* The main recommendations were based on giving local authorities responsibility for co-ordinating the services which an individual needs, but not necessarily providing them. A mix of statutory, voluntary, and private sector services is envisaged. However, as the Government has been busy stripping local authorities of resources and responsibilities, this Report did not initially meet with favour and how its proposals will be implemented remains unclear. Meanwhile families are being left to care for their infirm, handicapped, and chronically sick members with dwindling support from the statutory services and little recompense for the financial costs concerned. Even worse is the fact that those whose earnings have been reduced because of their caring responsibilities will receive lower state pensions than would have been the case under the 1975 Pensions Act. This is because from April 1988 the amount of the earnings related pension will be based on average *lifetime* earnings, not on the best *twenty* years.

FINANCIAL SUPPORT FROM THE FAMILY

Central to the post-war social security scheme was the assumption that, once married, a woman was and indeed *should* be dependent upon her husband. She therefore had the right to state benefits *derived* from her husband's contributions to the state scheme. For example, her pension in old age or when widowed was based on *his* contributions and her claim to the maternity grant could be based on his contributions if hers were insufficient. The 1975 Social Security Act and the 1975 Pensions Act began to treat women irrespective of their marital status as individuals in their own right, although it was recognized that for older women economic dependency had been a reality and widows in particular should continue to receive pensions derived from their husband's contributions. Thus under the State Earnings Related Pension Scheme (SERPS), introduced in the 1975 legislation, widows could inherit *all* of their husband's earnings-related pension and add it to their own earnings-related component, subject to a ceiling. In the social security review, ten years later, this was thought to be 'too generous' in spite of the fact that elderly widows are one of the poorest groups amongst pensioners. From April 1988 widows over retirement age will only be able to inherit *half* their husband's earnings-related component. Divorced women were not treated as generously as widows unless they were over retirement age when the divorce occurred. Neither the 1975 nor the 1986 social security reforms have addressed the question of what claims, if any, women—and men— should have on a former spouse's entitlements to state and occupational benefits. As long as marriage and child-bearing interrupt and depress women's earning capacity (by between 25 per cent and 50 per cent) and therefore their opportunity to build up their own benefit entitlement, this is an important question.

Meanwhile the common law obligation on husbands to maintain their wives has ended. The 'self-sufficiency' of each spouse is the objective of financial settlements on divorce, and maintenance for wives will be even more closely associated with continued responsibility for caring for children. The 'obligation to maintain' never was a 'meal-ticket for life' as some have claimed because only a tiny minority of divorced wives relied on maintenance as their main source of income. Nevertheless, the change in the law has weakened women's claims on their husbands at a time when many find themselves in an increasingly precarious position within the labour market *and* when the state social security system is failing to meet their needs, because entitlement to benefit is based on *full-time* activity in the labour market. It should be noted, however, that conversely women are becoming responsible for their husband's (or cohabitee's) debts. For example, a loan from the new Social Fund is recoverable from either the claimant *or* his or her spouse/cohabitee. Similarly a spouse or cohabitee will be responsible for the unpaid community charge of their partner. In other words, marriage now entails weaker claims by wives to maintenance from husbands but strong claims by the state for their husband's debts.

Overall, the picture is a gloomy one which, although concentrated in inner-city areas, is not confined to them. Moreover, it is a picture which is becoming more rather than less gloomy as growing numbers of people have to depend on lower wages, lower benefits, and less family support.

References

Atkinson, A., and Micklewright, J. (1988), 'Turning the screw: Benefits for the unemployed 1979–1988', Paper given at the Institute of Fiscal Studies, Apr.

Audit Commission (1986), *Making a Reality of Community Care* (London).

CSO (Central Statistical Office) (1989), *Social Trends 1989* (London).

Department of Employment (1988), *Employment for the 1990s*, Cmnd. 540 (London).

DHSS (Department of Health and Social Security) (1981), *Growing Older*, Cmnd. 8173 (London).

—— (1985), *Reform of Social Security*, Cmnd. 9518 (London).

Kahn, A. J., and Kammerman, S. B. (eds.) (1987), *Child Support: From Debt Collection to Social Policy* (London).

Low Pay Unit (1988), *The Poor Decade: Wage Inequalities in the 1980s* (London).

Martin, J., and Roberts, C. (1984), *Women in Employment* (London).

Matthewman, J., and Calvert, H. (1987), *Guide to Social Security Act 1986* (London).

OPCS (Office of Population Census and Surveys (1989), *General Household Survey 1986* (London).

Tinker, A. (1981), *The Elderly in Modern Society* (2nd edn., London, 1984).

Treasury (1989), *The Government's Expenditure Plans 1989–90 to 1991–92*, Cmnd. 621 (London).

7

The Implications of the Reform of Local Government Finance for the Inner Cities

John Gibson

INTRODUCTION: THE POST-ELECTION 'FLAGSHIP'

Despite Mrs Thatcher's immediate attention to the inner cities on the night of her third election victory, it was the poll tax which she labelled as the 'Flagship' policy of her third term of government in June 1987. However, there is a strong link between the two subjects. This is because the stated purpose of the reform of local government finance is to remove what the Government has perceived as major weaknesses in local accountability—with the worst weaknesses in the inner cities. This chapter will show that the reforms will exert their most substantial effects in the inner cities.

First, it would probably be helpful to many readers to provide some data on the scale of local government expenditure and finance.[1] Table 7.1 shows that total local authority public expenditure in Great Britain amounted to nearly £40,000 million in 1987/8. This was 23 per cent of general government expenditure. However, these are net expenditure figures from which income from charges and capital receipts have been subtracted, and they understate the relative importance of local authorities due to the fact that these sources of income have been proportionately much greater for local government than for central government.

Current expenditure is over five times larger than gross capital spending. The relative current expenditure on various services by English authorities is shown in Table 7.2. Nearly 50 per cent of

---

[1] Helpful because there is relatively little consideration, in the large literature on the inner cities, of local government finance. Exceptions are the survey by Kennett, 1980—now unfortunately dated—and Kirwan, 1986.

Table 7.1. *Total public and local authority expenditure, Great Britain, 1987/1988* (£ million)

Local authority public expenditure	
Relevant expenditure	32,005
Other current	4,383
Total current	36,388
Gross capital	7,219
Receipts	−3,656
Net capital	3,563
Total local authority expenditure	39,520
Planning expenditure planning total	145,744
General government expenditure	171,829

Source: Treasury, 1989, ch. 21.

Table 7.2. *Current expenditure on services, English local authorities, 1987/1988* (£ million)

Education	12,711
School meals and milk	469
Libraries, museums, etc.	474
Personal social services	2,927
Police	3,149
Fire	721
Other Home Office services	438
Transport	1,868
Employment and consumer protection	174
Non-HRA housing	184
Housing benefits	199
Environmental services	3,060
Agricultural services	137
TOTAL	26,511

Note: HRA = Housing Revenue Account.

Source: Association of County Councils (1988).

net current expenditure is accounted for by education. In addition there are substantial shares of expenditure on police, transport, personal social services, and environmental services.

Table 7.3. *'Total' expenditure and its financing: English local authorities 1987/1988 budgets* (£ million)

Expenditure	
RSG Net Current Expenditure	26,386
RCCO	−90
Loan charges	2,656
RFC to HRA	395
less interest receipts	−550
Relevant expenditure	28,797
Net non-relevant expenditure	262
less specific & supplementary grants	−3,298
'Total' expenditure	25,841
Income	
Rates[a]	16,039
Domestic rate relief grant	717
Block grant	8,677
Other specific income	36
Drawings from balances	372
'Total' income	25,841

Note: RSG = Rate Support Grant; RCCO = Revenue Contributions to Capital Outlay; RFC = Rate Fund Contributions; HRA = Housing Revenue Account.

[a] Includes rate rebates.

Source: Return of Expenditure and Rates, 1987–8.

The relative importance of local taxation and central government grants in financing the total expenditure of English local authorities is shown in Table 7.3. One point to note is that general grants are much larger than specific grants. Thus even for the inner cities receipts of block grant in 1987/8 were, despite cutbacks in the 1980s, still over ten times larger than receipts of specific urban aid grants.[2]

To complete this brief picture it is worth stressing that there were large differences in spending levels per head between areas. Spending levels were much higher in inner London than elsewhere. Partly this reflected differences in Grant Related Expenditures (GREs)—the central government's assessment of the cost of providing a comparable standard of services in different areas. In 1987/8 the range in GRE was from £514 per adult in Tandridge in Surrey to £1,344 per adult in Tower Hamlets in inner London (CIPFA, 1988). However, spending above GRE also tended to be much higher in some of the high 'needs' areas. As we shall see later this will have major consequences in the new system of finance.

The plan of this chapter is as follows. First I explain why the Government has decided to scrap domestic rates and introduce poll tax and its associated reforms. Second, I explain the difference between the present and the new system at local authority level, putting particular emphasis on the changes in the tax contributions of domestic taxpayers to local authorities' finances. Third, I examine the changes in the distribution of local domestic taxation between households in different income groups and also living in different parts of the inner-city local authorities. Fourth, I predict the effects these changes will have upon the spending of local authorities. Fifth, I analyse the effects of the changes in the non-domestic rating system. Sixth, I analyse the implications of two other reforms which will have significant effects within the new local finance system on residents of the inner cities, namely the abolition of the Inner London Education Authority (ILEA) and the 'ringfencing' of Housing Revenue Accounts (HRAs). Finally I draw some brief, and relatively stark, conclusions.

---

[2] Data given in a Parliamentary Written Answer on 30 June 1987 showed that urban programme grants given to inner area partnerships were £70.3 million in 1987/8 but block grant received by the partnership local authorities was £740.1 million.

The Reforms: Description, Background, and Rationale

There had for some time been a desire by many in the Conservative party to abolish domestic rates. Mrs Thatcher herself was strongly identified with this wish because she had been Shadow Environment Secretary in the Autumn of 1974 when a commitment to abolish domestic rates had been included in the Conservatives' general election manifesto. When the Conservatives eventually came to power in 1979 a combination of grant cutbacks and newly elected Labour-controlled local authorities committed to high levels of service provision resulted in particularly large rate increases. This resulted in fresh pressure for reform or abolition of the rating system and in 1981 the Government published a Green Paper exploring alternative local taxes (DoE, 1981). However, the Government's 1983 Rates White Paper rejected all alternative local taxes and settled instead for legislation to cap rates in selected authorities (DoE, 1983).

This looked as if it would be the end of the search for the elusive replacement for domestic rates. However, after criticism of the grant system by the Audit Commission (1984) an internal review of local government finance had been set up in the autumn of 1984. This, like previous inquiries, was not expected to lead to any major reform in local taxation. It was the unanticipated furore in Scotland in 1985, resulting from the disturbance to rates bills caused by a rating revaluation, which led the Government into the decision finally to scrap domestic rates. In January 1986 the Green Paper *Paying for Local Government* (DoE, 1986) was published, setting out the radical proposals for the reform of the system of local government finance in Great Britain based on the scrapping of domestic rates and their replacement by a poll tax.

The rationale of the proposed changes in the system is to overcome what the Government sees as 'serious shortcomings which significantly weaken local accountability', shortcomings which it claims were always inherent but were revealed now because 'a Government, for the first time since the war, has been seeking to exercise significant restraint over local authority spending' (DoE, 1986, para. 1.32).

The Government diagnosed three problem areas contributing to a weakness in local accountability (DoE, 1986, pp. 5–7). I shall now list the problems and the proposed reforms sequentially.

(1) Local electors: the gap between those who vote and those who pay
The problem. The most important weakness in local democratic accountability is the gap between those 'paying for local services and voting in local elections' (DoE, 1986, para. 1.52). Over half the electorate do not directly pay full rates: in England out of over 35 million electors only 18 million are liable to pay rates, and 3 million of these receive partial rebates and a further 3 million full rebates. It is claimed that spouses who do not directly pay rates and other non-paying adult members of households also have little appreciation of the real burden of increased local authority spending.

The proposed reform. The solution proposed was to replace domestic rates by a flat-rate 'community charge' i.e. poll tax, to be levied upon each adult (person aged over 18). The level of the charge, although the same for each adult within a local authority, will vary between local authorities according to spending levels.

In addition it was also planned to end full local tax rebates and ensure that even those with the lowest incomes and receiving Income Support would pay a minimum of 20 per cent of the full local tax for their area. This proposal came into effect in April 1988.

(2) The contribution from non-domestic rates
The problem. On average 54 per cent of rate-borne expenditure is met by non-domestic rates and in some local authorities the non-domestic ratepayer 'provides as much as three quarters of the income raised locally. Authorities therefore find themselves in a position to increase spending on services for the voting domestic ratepayer largely at the expense of the non-voting, non-domestic ratepayer' (DoE, 1986, para. 1.35).

As well as the deleterious effects on local accountability caused by non-domestic rates there were a number of additional problems. Business representatives had expressed concern about the real increase in the level of non-domestic rates particularly in the early

1980s, the sometimes erratic year to year changes in rate demands, and the large differences in rate poundages between locations: the range of rate poundages had widened since 1978/9 when the ratio of maximum to minimum poundage was 1.77, to 2.26 in 1985/6 (Bennett, 1986). The Government argued that one effect of the recent experience of non-domestic rates was a reduction in efficiency and competitiveness. This was likely to have affected the level of employment, and higher rate poundages in some high-spending urban areas leads to distortion in location and other investment decisions as well as placing unfair burdens on those businesses which are tied to a particular area.

The proposed reform. The conversion of non-domestic rates from a tax levied at variable rates by different local authorities according to their spending levels into a nationally uniform tax with the proceeds distributed to local authorities on an equal amount per adult basis. This removed the differences in rate poundages between areas. Greater stability in the year-on-year changes in non-domestic rates was also to be achieved by tying increases to the level of increase in the RPI.

(3) The grant system

The problem. The objective of the present system is to enable local taxpayers in all areas to finance similar standards of service, measured by expenditure per head in relation to GRE—at the same rate poundage.[3] This requires the present block grant to be used to compensate fully for differences in rateable values per head—resources equalization—and also to compensate fully for differences in GREs per head—needs equalization. Needs equalization is achieved by giving more grant to high needs areas. Resources equalization is achieved by different rates of grant support on increments in expenditure, with the rate depending on rateable values per head of authorities. This makes grant levels depend on expenditure and increases the complexity of the grant

---

[3] Within London the effective rate poundage at GRE was lower: by a minimum of 29.3 per cent in inner London and 19.2 per cent in outer London in 1987/8. This reflects a political judgement that rate bills in London would be unfairly high if they were based on the national standard rate poundage schedule applied to London's higher domestic rateable values.

system. The use of the grant system to achieve rate poundage equalization means that because rateable values differ between areas rate bills are higher in areas where housing is expensive for equivalent spending levels, and also 'to pay for a similar increase in spending, authorities in areas where rateable values are low need to increase their rate bills by a smaller amount than high rateable value authorities' (DoE, 1986, para. 1.41). This is held to be unfair.

The GREs are lengthy because they are built up on a service-by-service basis and also complex because they have been increasingly refined in an attempt to reflect special higher-cost factors. Changes in the GRE formula which have occurred have also led to instability because they have had 'a powerful impact upon the grant of individual authorities that are most affected, producing significant changes in the amounts which they need to raise from rates which are related to changes in their expenditure' (DoE, 1986, para. 1.40).

The proposed reform. (*a*) the simplification of the grant system by conversion of the present block grant with its implicit general fixed and matching components into two lump-sum grants: a needs grant to compensate for differences in assessed spending needs per adult between local authorities; and a standard grant, providing an additional sum from national taxation towards the cost of local services, distributed again as an equal amount per adult; (*b*) a reduction in the present lengthy formula for assessing needs to a simpler assessment based on a few key indicators.

The accountability problem in the inner cities

These, then, were the perceived defects and problems of the present system and the reforms to be introduced. It is worth pointing out that Government Ministers have perceived the weaknesses in local accountability to be particularly severe in the inner cities. For this they have given two reasons. First, the problem of non-paying voters was alleged to be largest in the inner cities. Thus Michael Howard, the Minister given special responsibility for explaining the reforms, asserted: 'In Liverpool only one voter in four pays rates directly and in full. In Manchester the proportion may be slightly lower.'[4] Second, there was often a very large contribution from the non-domestic ratepayer, particularly in the case of some of the Government's least favoured Labour-controlled local authorities in inner London: 'In Camden, for example, for every £1 contributed by the domestic ratepayer the non-domestic ratepayer contributes £4' (DoE, 1986, para. 2.18). It was this greater weakness in local accountability which, according to Ministers, led to the choice of high levels of spending by many of the inner cities. Thus when the Secretary of State noted in the second-reading debate that since 1979/80 local spending had increased by 18 per cent in real terms he also added, 'but by much more than that in many of our cities run by the Labour party'.[5]

REDISTRIBUTION OF DOMESTIC TAX BURDENS

At authority/tax area level

The change in the domestic tax base from rateable values to adults, combined with the change in non-domestic rates from a local discretionary source of finance into a centrally fixed assigned revenue and the switch to fixed grants, brings in a very different structure of finance. This will result in large changes in the domestic sector's total local tax contribution in different areas,[6] at present levels of spending, with the largest increases in some of the cities, especially in Labour-controlled parts of inner London. Indeed the changes are so large that the Government intends to impose 'safety nets' which will initially reduce the change in average bills at local authority level. These safety nets will then be phased out over a period of four years. However, I shall concentrate here mainly on the ultimate changes in bills which are implied by the new system, because they better describe the long-term changes in incentives facing local authorities.

---

[4] From 'Mr Howard's speech to the ADC', Association of District Councils, County Branch Consultative Meeting, 17 Sept. 1987, p. 3.

[5] House of Commons, Parliamentary Debates, 17 Dec. 1987.

[6] The poll tax will, of course, be collected at district level and the change at this level will reflect the net changes on the local authorities and joint boards at each tier in each tax collection district.

Table 7.4. *Impact on average domestic tax bills of switch from domestic rates to poll tax (£ per year)*

	average rate bill per household	per adult			% change in bill for two–adult household with average rate bill
		basic poll tax	spending above GRE	poll tax	
England	440	178	46	224	+1.8
Main areas					
Shire areas	419	178	14	192	−8.3
Metropolitan areas	424	178	53	231	+9.0
Inner London	594	178	399	577	+94.3
Outer London	517	178	48	226	−12.6

Source: Parliamentary Written Answer, 29 June 1987.

Table 7.4 compares average rate bills per household by the main areal subdivisions of local authorities for the 1987/8 pattern of local authorities' expenditure and aggregate grant totals. The poll tax in each area in England would have been £178 per adult for spending at GRE. However, we can see that the average level of poll tax would have been £224 per adult, because the average level of spending was £46 per adult above GRE. The poll tax would have been much larger in inner London—£577—than elsewhere: over double the metropolitan average and three times the shire average (£192), reflecting the average level of spending above GRE in the different areas. Although rate bills are higher at present in London, the difference is much lower than that for poll tax and this shows in the calculated figures for changes in bills for two adult households with average rate bills and poll taxes for their areas. These fall by 8.3 per cent in the shires and by 12.6 per cent in outer London, and rise by 9.0 per cent in the metropolitan areas and by 94.3 per cent in inner London.

However, these figures mask much larger variations at tax collection area level. Table 7.5 gives the figures for the inner cities—that is tax areas where there are partnership or programme

Table 7.5. *Impact on average domestic tax bills of switch from domestic rates to poll tax—inner cities (£ per year)*

	average rate bill per household	per adult		poll tax	% change in bill for two-adult household with average rate bill
		basic poll tax	spending above GRE		
Inner London[a]					
Hackney★	765	178	513	691	80.7
Hammersmith and Fulham	404	178	287	465	130.2
Islington★	552	178	305	483	75.0
Lambeth★	536	178	369	547	104.1
Tower Hamlets	548	178	461	639	133.2
Wandsworth	399	178	256	435	118.0
Outer London					
Brent	676	178	104	283	−16.3
Metropolitan					
Bolton	381	178	24	202	6.0
Manchester★	492	178	94	272	10.6
Oldham	334	178	23	201	20.4
Rochdale	363	178	58	236	30.0
Salford★	450	178	64	243	8.0
Knowsley	517	178	88	267	3.3
Liverpool	500	178	123	301	20.4
Wirral	542	178	66	244	−10.0
Sheffield	371	178	69	248	33.7
Gateshead★	359	178	85	263	46.5
Newcastle★	479	178	114	292	21.9
North Tyneside	427	178	87	265	24.1
South Tyneside	353	178	76	254	42.8
Sunderland	379	178	84	262	38.3
Birmingham★	496	178	8	186	−30.0
Coventry	472	178	41	219	−7.2
Sandwell	389	178	−3	175	−10.0
Wolverhampton	501	178	26	204	−18.6
Bradford	369	178	59	238	29.0

Leeds	341	178	57	235	37.8
Non-metropolitan					
Middlesborough	479	178	98	277	15.7
Blackburn	273	178	15	193	41.4
Hull	332	178	70	248	49.4
Leicester	362	178	42	220	21.5
Nottingham	368	178	29	207	12.5

[a] ILEA's spending above GRE: £252 per adult.
* inner area partnership authorities.

Source: as Table 7.4

local authorities. Inner-city authorities usually spend higher in relation to GRE and would have had average poll tax bills larger than is typical of the class of area—metropolitan, inner London, outer London, shire—in which they are located. There is also a strong tendency for average tax bills to increase—the percentage increase being particularly severe for the inner London areas. However, there is some heterogeneity. Thus the metropolitan authorities in the West Midlands experience reductions in the average bill.

The inner-city areas can be contrasted with the figures for a range of suburb and shire areas given in Table 7.6. Here there is a tendency for bills to fall with especially large reductions in the affluent areas of the South-East spending below GRE, with average bills set to fall by a third in many areas and by a half in areas such as South Buckinghamshire. However, there is again heterogeneity with bills tending to rise in the North, with its low rateable values, especially in tax areas where spending is well above GRE.

In general, it is these two factors—domestic rateable value per adult and spending in relation to GRE—which are the cause of such large differences between the fortunes of the average domestic taxpayer in inner cities and other areas. However, there are also some important special factors or 'quirks' in the present system which make a full explanation necessarily complicated. It is best to explain the mechanics of the redistribution in two parts,

Table 7.6. *Impact on average domestic tax bills of switch from domestic rates to poll tax—selected suburban, shire, and other metropolitan areas (£ per year)*

	average rate bill per household	per adult			% change in bill for two-adult household with average rate bill
		basic poll tax	spending above GRE	poll tax	
Inner London					
Westminster	811	178	218	396	−2.3
Outer London					
Barnet	655	178	44	222	−32.3
Bromley	430	178	−6	173	−20.0
Redbridge	427	178	−8	170	−20.4
Metropolitan					
Sefton	500	178	32	210	−16.0
Trafford	429	178	−22	156	−27.3
Solihull	529	178	−15	163	−38.4
Non-metropolitan					
South Bedfordshire	591	178	58	236	−22.8
South Buckinghamshire	825	178	28	206	−50.1
South Cambridgeshire	516	178	−12	167	−35.3
Copeland	320	178	79	258	61.3
Epping Forest	571	178	6	184	−35.6
Tewkesbury	435	178	−6	173	−20.5
Worcester	401	178	−29	149	−25.7
St Albans	627	178	26	204	−34.9
Tunbridge Wells	353	178	−26	152	−13.9
Ryedale	317	178	3	181	14.2
South Oxfordshire	535	178	23	201	−24.9
Taunton Deane	371	178	2	180	−3.0
North Shropshire	357	178	−2	177	−0.9
Mole Valley	501	178	−9	169	−32.5

Source: as Table 7.4.

first examining the change if authorities were spending at GRE and second the difference in domestic tax cost or saving for actual spending differences from GRE.

So first let us examine the position at GRE. At 1987/8 levels of grant and yield of non-domestic rates we have already seen that the poll tax would have been £178 per adult in all tax areas in England. In comparison the rate poundage which the block grant enabled outside London was 228 pence, and at the average domestic rateable value per adult of approximately £104 we can see this gives a rate bill per adult at GRE of £237. Thus if spending were at GRE there is a reduction in average bills of £59 in areas with the national average domestic rateable value per adult. However, there are much larger reductions in high rateable value areas like Surrey where average domestic rateable value per adult is £139 (average rate bill at GRE, £317). There are also low rateable value areas in the North, such as Durham, where average domestic rateable value per adult is £67 where bills rise even for spending at GRE (average rate bill at GRE, £153). In general, the northern inner cities have below average domestic rateable value per adult (Manchester £86, Liverpool £85, Sheffield £70, Newcastle £83, Bradford £65) which contributes to their relative disadvantage under poll tax. Average domestic rateable values per adult in London are much higher—£170 in inner London and £138 in outer London—but gains from these high domestic rateable values are not as high as implied by the above argument. This is because the Government presently sets the rate poundage at GRE in London below the standard 228 pence level outside London—it is a minimum of 30 per cent lower in the borough tax areas of inner London and at least 15 per cent lower in outer London.

The above describes the change in average domestic tax bills if authorities spend at GRE. The other component of change in average domestic tax bills is the difference in domestic tax cost or saving for actual spending differences from GRE. Under the poll tax system the domestic tax cost or saving of each £1 of spending difference from GRE is simply £1 because of the major structural simplification of converting grant and the proceeds of the non-domestic rates into lump sum form, fixed at the start of the financial year.[7] In contrast, under the present system the domestic tax cost of an extra £1 of spending varies greatly between authorities. Table 7.7 provides data for a selection of authorities which represent the full range of difference between authorities in the cost to domestic ratepayers of the marginal £ of expenditure.

Column (1) shows that under the present system (1986/7) for the authorities in receipt of block grant an additional £1 in expenditure leads to losses in block grant shown in Column (1). This means that the cost to ratepayers as a whole (i.e. domestic plus non-domestic), shown in Column (2), of spending an extra £1 is greater than £1—it is £1 plus the loss of block grant on each £1 of spending. The range of grant loss is from 2.5p for Kirklees with the low rateable values per head typical of West Yorkshire to 346p for Kensington and Chelsea with its high rateable values per head, hence the range of ratepayer cost is from 102.5p for Kirklees to 446p for Kensington and Chelsea. This variable loss in grant in Column (1) reflects the resource equalization properties of the present system, achieved by setting through the block grant formula a common rate poundage cost for an extra £1 per head of spending. The unique feature of the English (and Welsh) system is that the differential variation in grant is negative, rather than positive, reflecting the Government's overriding objective of attempting to discourage expenditure whilst still retaining the resource equalization properties of the system.

The total cost of an extra £1 of spending shown in Column (2) must be borne by ratepayers and is shared between the domestic and non-domestic sectors according to their share of aggregate rateable value. The net result for the domestic sector is shown in Column (3) and for the non-domestic sector in Column (4). Column (3) shows that there is a substantial variation between authorities receiving block grant in the cost to domestic taxpayers of a £1 of spending under the present system from just over 50p

---

[7] Given that the local tax base is to be moved from rateable values—domestic plus non-domestic—to adults, there is by definition no longer any difference in taxpaying capacity per adult between areas and therefore no need for matching grant to equate the cost of providing an extra £1 per adult of services between authorities.

Table 7.7. *Cost to domestic sector of extra £1 of spending under domestic rate system (1986/1987 data) and poll tax system* (in pence)

Domestic rate system

	Change in block grant	Total extra cost to local ratepayers	Extra cost to domestic ratepayers	Extra cost to non-domestic ratepayers
	(1)	(2)	(3)	(4)
Buckinghamshire	−93.2	193.2	108.8	84.4
Cleveland	−73.9	173.9	73.2	100.7
Northumberland	−33.0	133.0	65.1	67.9
Suffolk	−46.5	146.5	80.3	66.2
Manchester	−149.9	249.9	93.0	156.9
Liverpool	−100.3	200.3	90.1	110.2
Newcastle upon Tyne	−118.6	218.6	92.5	126.1
Birmingham	−108.3	208.3	96.9	111.4
Solihull	−71.9	171.9	112.3	59.6
Kirklees	−2.6	102.6	52.1	50.5
ILEA	0.0	100.0	25.8	74.2
Camden	0.0	100.0	23.8	76.2
Hackney	−57.8	157.8	77.8	80.0
Kensington and Chelsea	−346.3	446.3	234.8	211.5
Westminster	0.0	100.0	16.1	83.9
Barnet	−80.8	180.8	119.3	61.5
Newham	−106.8	206.8	96.0	10.8

Poll tax system

	Change in block grant	Total extra cost to local taxpayers	Extra cost to poll tax-payers	Extra cost to non-domestic ratepayers
All authorities	0.0	100.0	100.0	0.0

Source: Author's computations.

in Kirklees with very low rateable values to nearly £2.50 in Kensington and Chelsea with its high rateable values.

Now let us look at the authorities, ILEA, Camden, and Westminster, which do not suffer any losses in block grant on marginal expenditure because they receive no block grant. The reason why these authorities do not receive any block grant is because their rateable values are very high and their expenditure is more than sufficient to have exhausted their entitlement to block grant. In fact, ILEA (rateable value £517 per head) loses all grant at an expenditure below its GRE and Westminster's huge rateable value per head (£1,789) ensures that it receives no block grant whatever its level of expenditure.[8] With no grant penalties at the margin the cost of an extra £1 of spending is simply £1 for these authorities. In addition, because the non-domestic sector is such a large proportion of the total rateable value in these authorities the end result is extremely low domestic ratepayer marginal costs: in ILEA and Camden this is in the 25p per £1 region—less than half the figure for the lowest rateable value authorities outside London. This helps explain the Government's particular concern about Labour-controlled inner London authorities supporting what it regards as their excessive expenditure at very little expense to their domestic ratepayers and largely at the expense of the non-domestic ratepayer.

This change in the domestic marginal contribution is the reason why the new system has by far the biggest impact in inner London, with ILEA's overspend costing £1 per £1 under poll tax compared to 25p per £1 under the present system. Not only this, but the spending above GRE is much larger in inner London than elsewhere, with ILEA alone spending £252 per adult above GRE in 1987/8. For the provincial cities, especially those with lower domestic rateable values like Sheffield and Gateshead, there is a less dramatic, but often sizeable loss through this higher cost of spending above GRE.

This then provides the bulk of the explanation for the fact that average poll tax bills rise markedly in inner London and in many of the northern cities. Finally, to put the impact of the poll tax

[8] In 1987/8 ILEA lost its entitlement at a level of expenditure below its GRE. See CIPFA, 1987.

into perspective, the doubling of average tax bills in some areas should be set against the fact that the largest increase in average bills, caused by shifts in block grant in the 1980s, was barely above 10 per cent in real terms.

Redistribution between households

However, we must in turn quickly put this large change in average bills at area level into perspective by giving some figures which show that the change between individual households is much greater than the change in local authority average bills. A Parliamentary Written Answer stated that 3 million households in England would face an increase of more than 50 per cent in their tax bills when poll tax replaces rates. This implies that 6 million households will face bill changes above 50 per cent: i.e. 35 per cent of English households.[9] Compared to this the 1987/8 based figures showed only 19 areas (with 1.2 million households) out of 369 tax collection areas where the average bill change per adult would have been greater than 50 per cent. The reason for this is that there is a much larger variation between individual households than there is between local authorities' averages in the relative amounts of the two factors which affect the distribution of tax bills under the present and new system: rateable values and the number of adults. We will now look at the nature of the redistribution by household type, and then examine the relative regressivity characteristics of the poll tax compared to domestic rates.

Table 7.8, reproduced from the 1986 Green Paper (DoE, 1986), shows the clear tendency for household local tax bills to fall under poll tax for single adult households and to rise for three adult households, with a more even pattern for two adult households. However, there is considerable variation within each household type and this is caused by the large differences in rateable value between households. Households with low rateable values (for their size of household) tend to lose, and those with high rateable values (for their size of household) tend to gain, under poll tax.

[9] Data given in a Parliamentary Written Answer, 25 Nov. 1987.

Table 7.8. *Households (thousands) gaining and losing with full replacement of domestic rates by the poll tax, Great Britain, based on 1984/1985 data*
(£ per week)

	Single pensioner	Other single adult	Two adults	Three + adults	All households
Losers					
10+	—	—	0	50	50
5–10	—	—	75	425	500
2–5	0	75	1,325	1,125	2,525
1–2	25	100	1,625	425	2,175
0–1	375	275	3,750	325	4,725
TOTAL	400	475	6,800	2,350	10,000
Gainers					
0–1	1,700	775	2,800	200	5,475
1–2	250	350	1,275	100	1,975
2–5	350	600	1,400	100	2,450
5–10	75	100	350	25	575
10+	25	25	50	0	100
TOTAL	2,400	1,850	5,875	425	10,575

Notes: 0 = less than 12,500. Numbers may not add due to rounding.
Source: DoE, 1986, Fig. J7.

The relative regressivity of poll tax and domestic rates is shown in Table 7.9 which gives the relationship between tax bills and 'equivalent' net household income—that is household income adjusted for differences in the number of dependents. The bottom row shows how net bills rise for the lowest income groups, apart from the very lowest, but then fall for those groups above £200 per week by increasing amounts as income increases. For the very highest income group (over £500 per week) there are gains of nearly £7 per week.

Table 7.9. *Relationship of rates and poll tax to net household income (England 1986/1987 prices)*

	Under 50	50– 75	75– 100	100– 50	150– 200	200– 50	250– 300	300– 50	350– 400	400– 500	500+	All
	Ranges of equivalent net household income (£ per week)											
Gross												
Rates	6·07	6·17	6·72	7·32	7·95	8·31	8·72	9·27	9·95	10·54	13·64	7·40
Poll tax	6·00	6·36	7·27	8·03	8·12	8·01	7·59	7·36	7·09	7·42	7·00	7·41
Net												
Rates	1·64	3·04	5·94	7·18	7·90	8·29	8·71	9·27	9·95	10·50	13·62	6·37
Poll tax	1·63	3·13	6·31	7·64	7·91	7·89	7·52	7·31	7·03	7·34	6·89	6·25
Difference	−0·01	0·09	0·37	0·46	0·01	−0·40	−1·19	−1·96	−2·92	−3·16	−6·73	−0·12

Source: Parliamentary Written Answer, 25 Jan. 1988.

The 'within-city' pattern of redistribution

Not surprisingly these regressivity characteristics are mirrored in the pattern of redistribution of local tax burdens within the cities, with households in deprived inner-city wards faring much worse than those in the suburbs. Let us take Birmingham as an example. Table 7.10 gives the data at ward level for Birmingham based on a comparison between a domestic rate poundage of 242·3p and a safety netted poll tax of £249.50 for its 1987/8 spending, a level at which there is very little change in average household bills at local authority level. This gives a fairly clear picture of the quite dramatic contrast between inner-city wards with core area definitions, especially those including priority areas, and the outer wards, with very large gains in all three wards of Sutton Coldfield and in Edgbaston. There is some ambiguity, however, because wards such as Edgbaston combine the most luxurious private housing areas with small pockets of multi-occupied run-down housing. Thus the table also includes data on the Conservative proportion of the Conservative plus Labour vote in the 1988 local elections and this shows a strong trend towards wards where the Conservatives are strong (the linear correlation coefficient between poll tax gains and the Conservative share of the vote is 0.78). Other local authorities with inner-city areas

Table 7.10. *Impact on average household domestic tax bills of switch from domestic rates to poll tax—Birmingham by ward level*

	average gain/loss per household (£ per year)	percentage of households gaining	Ward characteristics	
			Con. share of Con. plus Lab. vote[a]	Inner area definition
Sutton Four Oaks	348.5	86.5	88.1	—
Edgbaston	239.5	79.2	60.8	P (part)
Sutton Vesey	191.3	78.0	82.2	—
Sutton New Hall	125.6	74.8	77.4	—
Quinton	78.7	67.6	60.3	—
Kings Norton	61.9	62.2	36.2	—
Hall Green	56.5	64.9	75.0	P
Weoley	44.9	62.2	45.1	—
Harborne	42.3	57.0	59.8	—
Moseley	25.8	54.8	41.9	P (part)
Brandwood	15.7	59.2	49.1	—
Erdington	14.4	57.9	47.5	P
Northfield	10.7	58.1	55.8	—
Kingsbury	9.4	61.7	28.3	P
Bartley Green	7.5	59.3	51.3	—
Shard End	1.3	50.8	29.8	P
Billesley	−1.9	50.8	42.1	P (part)
Bournville	−2.1	51.1	48.5	—
Ladywood	−3.4	56.9	25.9	C & Pr
Hodge Hill	−6.4	47.9	44.9	P
Longbridge	−6.9	52.0	38.0	—
Sheldon	−17.7	47.3	50.3	P
Sandwell	−21.2	55.3	45.2	P & Pr
Yardley	−28.3	53.2	48.4	P
Perry Barr	−41.4	36.4	54.1	P
Oscott	−44.6	40.9	50.4	P
Aston	−46.5	49.6	12.6	C & Pr
Selly Oak	−55.6	40.4	47.5	—
Stockland Green	−58.7	51.4	36.7	P & C (part)
Fox Hollies	−70.3	45.5	32.4	P & C (part)
Kingstanding	−76.2	41.4	29.8	P
Acocks Green	−88.0	38.2	42.5	P & C (part)
Nechells	−94.4	43.9	18.3	C & Pr
Handsworth	−97.5	44.3	18.1	C & Pr
Washwood Heath	−104.7	35.0	21.7	C
Sparkhill	−115.3	49.5	28.4	C & P (part)

Soho	−126.0	35.9	13.3	C & Pr
Sparkbrook	−153.5	31.0	15.8	C & Pr
Small Heath	−197.4	22.4	32.6	C
Birmingham average			44.6	

Notes: P = Partnership area—area for economic regeneration.
C = Core area—high levels of economic, physical, and social deprivation.
Pr = Priority ring where the greatest concentration of deprivation exists.

ᵃ 1988 local elections.

Source:Birmingham City Council, 1988*a*.

have also carried out the same type of study and have found similar results.[10]

There is also a tendency for ethnic minority households to fare much worse than the average. This is because on average they have households with relatively high numbers of adults compared to the rateable value of property occupied. A study conducted by Newcastle upon Tyne found that a much higher proportion (78 per cent) of households with Asian heads were losers compared to those with UK heads (56 per cent). Also, as Table 7.11 shows, there was an even greater relative disparity towards heavy losses.

Table 7.11. *Poll tax impact on ethnic minorities—Newcastle upon Tyne* (£ per year)

	Households with UK-born heads (%)	Households with Asian-born heads (%)
Gainers	44	28
Losers	56	72
Loss under £100	16	12
£100–£250	18	19
more than £250	20	41

Source: Newcastle upon Tyne City Council, 1988.

[10] See Birmingham City Council, 1988*b*.

EFFECTS ON LOCAL AUTHORITIES

The redistribution of the tax burden which we have described is important in its own right because it will have a substantial impact on the budgets of many poorer households. In addition, the impact tends to be worse for poorer households in the inner cities than equivalent households living outside the cities, because the ratio of poll tax to the present rate poundage is higher in authorities spending above GRE.

However, it is highly likely that these bill changes will then generate reactions from local authorities. One source of reaction is that some authorities will receive extra external finance and some will receive less. This transfer means that authorities in the suburban South-East and other suburbs will be able to spend more for present domestic sector contributions and the opposite will apply to many of the cities. This will make some impact on improving services in the suburbs and reducing them in the cities. However, superimposed on this is a powerful incentive to reduce spending due to the fact that (1) the total tax cost of local spending will be higher for a majority of the electorate, and (2) the marginal tax cost of spending will be higher for an even larger majority of households. The reasons for (1) are that poll tax tends to hit those households with below average incomes and a sizeable majority of households have below average incomes, and also the poll tax hits those households with lots of electors (adults). The marginal tax contribution for most households rises simply because, as we showed in Table 7.10 above, the gross marginal domestic tax cost increases in most authorities. The relevant theory of public finance (Buchanan, 1967) would lead one to expect that this combination of increases in marginal and average tax rates will lead a sizeable majority of the population to favour some reduction in present levels of local authorities' spending.

This is not a novel scenario, it is the one described in the Government's Green Paper, where it is anticipated that either existing councillors will reduce services and tax bills or, if they do not, the newly sensitive electorate will ensure that they are replaced by councillors who will.[11]

[11] For a fuller discussion see Gibson, 1987.

The above factors suggest that residents of inner areas are going to have their local tax bills increased and see their services deteriorate. The Government could offset this to some extent by directing more grant to the cities; indeed, there has been some movement in this direction already in adjustments to GREs which favoured the cities in 1988/9. However, it seems unlikely that this Government will wish to enhance significantly the ability of inner-city authorities to protect service levels. Indeed, recent expenditure levels set for the inner-city rate-capped authorities implied large cuts in services and were the main reason for lower poll tax levels for these authorities based on the 1988/9 budgets.

We must now consider other relevant changes such as the introduction of the uniform business rate. There are also the changes in housing finance and the abolition of ILEA which have important effects on the poll tax system.

Changes in non-domestic rating

The local tax payments of the non-domestic sector will be affected both by the structural change to uniform non-domestic rate poundages and the first revaluation since 1973. Both these changes are to be phased in over five years from the start of the new system with a ceiling placed on the year-on-year increases facing individual properties.

The switch to a uniform business rate poundage brings changes in local tax bills for the non-domestic sector which depend upon the difference between the present local rate poundage and the national average rate poundage which raises the equivalent yield from the non-domestic sector. In 1987/8 the national non-domestic rate poundage would have been 224.1 pence. In the majority of areas the 1987/8 poundage was within 10–15 per cent of this average figure. Thus out of 366 local tax areas the rate poundage was below 190 pence in only 18 areas and above 250 pence in only 83 areas. Business rate poundages will tend to reduce most in the northern metropolitan areas with reductions of over 30 per cent in Manchester, Liverpool, Newcastle upon Tyne, and Bradford and in many other districts with reductions of over 20 per cent. However, there is no significant beneficial effect in inner London because present poundages (but not rate bills) are mostly at or below the national average.

The effects of the revaluation are uncertain until the new values are published. However, the 1986 Green Paper gave a general indication that the relative values of shops would increase, with rate bills for prime shops increasing by an average of 50 per cent. It also expected increased bills for some period office buildings, new large industrial premises, and warehouses. Bills were expected to fall for older industrial and warehouse properties. Superimposed on this average pattern was expected to be a relative fall in non-domestic rateable values in the North.

It is fair to say that these changes provide some encouragement to private sector employment prospects in the inner cities outside London. However, even taking into account the significant effect of differential rate poundages on the rates of return on capital invested in different local authorities (Bennett, 1986), it is still unlikely that the change will have much impact on unemployment in the inner cities.

Other interacting changes: ringfenced HRAs and the scrapping of ILEA

The Government plans to ringfence HRAs from the rate fund from 1 April 1990 and this will have major effects on poll tax levels in a number of authorities, especially in the inner cities. The size of the effect depends upon the extent to which the rate fund contribution to (or from) the HRA is greater than the GRE allowance for these contributions. At a national level the GRE for contributions was £420 million in 1987/8 which was heavily concentrated in inner London with much lesser amounts in the provincial cities, while the vast majority of areas had zero GREs.[12] Analysis by CIPFA (1988) showed that the major effects were also concentrated in inner London with reductions in poll tax levels of £133 in Camden, £119 in Lambeth, £107 in Southwark, £96 in Hammersmith and Fulham. There were increases in poll tax

---

[12] Political consideration, not logic, governed the decision to allow authorities where the DoE identified potential HRA surpluses to have zero, rather than the computed negative GREs.

levels of £63 in Wandsworth, £50 in Barking & Dagenham, and £47 in Tower Hamlets. Poll tax levels tended to fall in the provincial cities but generally by less than £20 per adult.

The Government's plans for ringfencing have been heavily criticized elsewhere but the main point here is that the concentration of poll tax reductions from this source markedly reduces the level of poll tax in some of the inner London boroughs. However, it must be remembered that where there are gains for the poll tax payers there is an equivalent loss of financial support from the rate fund borne by a relatively smaller number of tenants.

Finally we must mention the decision to scrap ILEA. This will also have a major impact on the poll tax levels of the inner London boroughs. The gap between spending and GRE was £252 per adult in 1987/8, and an analysis by CIPFA (1988) has shown that without spending cuts the overspend (and therefore poll tax per adult level) will rise in many of the more deprived inner London boroughs: by £11 in Lambeth, £12 in Southwark, £26 in Lewisham, £34 in Tower Hamlets, £51 in Greenwich, and £53 in Hackney.

CONCLUSION

These must be sobering figures with which to finish our survey of the effects of the reform of local government finance on the inner cities. The startling increase in local tax bills shortly to face most households in the less affluent wards of inner-city areas does not seem to constitute a policy either (1) to increase the welfare of those households or (2) to revive the economies of the inner cities or (3) to reflect the Prime Minister's election night concerns, to secure an increase in the Conservative vote in the inner cities. The effects of the poll tax are likely to be a reduction in the levels of provision of major public services like education and personal social services.

The reforms in local government finance can best be understood as an important policy component within what Young (1989) has described as the larger political strategy followed by Mrs Thatcher's Government. This sees the main objective of policy as an attack on 'the culture of dependency' and to 'free people from the trap of municipal dependency'. The poll tax will be a powerful weapon in this attack.

References

Association of County Councils (1988), *Rate Support Grant (England) 1988/9* (London).

Audit Commission (1984), *The Impact on Local Authorities' Economy, Efficiency and Effectiveness of the Block Grant Distribution System* (London).

Bennett, R. J. (1986), 'The impact of non-domestic rates on profitability and investment', *Fiscal Studies*, 7, 34–50.

Birmingham City Council (1988*a*), *Impact of the Community Charge on Households in Birmingham: Report of the City Treasurer to the Finance and Management Committee* (Birmingham).

—— (1988*b*), 'Summary of studies of the impact of the poll tax on individual authorities', Treasurer's Department (Birmingham).

Buchanan, J. M. (1967), *Public Finance in Democratic Process* (Chapel Hill).

CIPFA (Chartered Institute of Public Finance and Accountancy) (1987), *Block Grant Statistics 1987/88* (London).

—— (1988), *Paying for Local Government: Community Charge and 'Ring-fenced' Housing Revenue Accounts* (London).

DoE (Department of the Environment) (1981), *Alternatives to Domestic Rates*, Cmnd. 8449 (London).

—— (1983), *Rates*, Cmnd. 9008 (London).

—— (1986), *Paying for Local Government*, Cmnd. 9741 (London).

Gibson, J. G. (1987), 'The reform of British local government finance: The limits of local accountability', *Policy and Politics*, 15, 167–74.

Kennett, S. (1980), *Local Government Fiscal Problems: A Context for Inner Areas* (London).

Kirwan, R. (1986), 'Local fiscal policy and the inner city', in V. Hausner (ed.), *Critical Issues in Urban Economic Development*, vol. 1 (Oxford).

Newcastle upon Tyne City Council (1988), 'The distributional impact of poll tax', Report to Policy & Resources Committee (Newcastle upon Tyne).

SCT (Society of County Treasurers) (1988), *Block Grant Indicators* (Reading).

Treasury (1989), *The Government's Expenditure Plans 1989–90 to 1991–92*, Cmnd. 621 (London).

Young K. (1989), 'Inner city policy', in D. T. Cross and C. Whitehead, *The Planning Yearbook* (Newbury).

8

Challenges for Education:
The Needs of the Urban Disadvantaged

David Mallen

INTRODUCTION

The most important background fact relevant to education about
what is happening in the inner city at the moment is that the
skilled working classes are moving out, so we have in the inner
cities in most parts of the country a much greater concentration of
the poor and the handicapped—I mean handicapped and not
disabled, using the term in the sense of what society does to particular people, magnifying the disadvantages they have already.
In inner London there are five out of ten of the economically most
deprived boroughs in the country, seven out of ten of the most
socially disadvantaged, seven out of ten with the worst housing
problems.

There is also an intensity of life in the inner cities. If we
consider the number of people who live in inner London, we find
there are over 81 people per hectare, compared with Liverpool
with 46.6, Manchester with just over 40, and Birmingham with
just under 40. But this misrepresents the picture in these other
major cities. If, instead of taking Birmingham or Manchester as a
whole, you look at their inner city (the Inner London Education
Authority (ILEA) serves, in the main, the inner-city part
of London), you would find that the intensity goes up quite
dramatically, excluding the leafy suburbs of Edgbaston or
Didsbury or wherever. This very concentration of people also
leads to major problems as far as young children are concerned,
with restricted play space and a lack of open space for them to
enjoy.

We have more than 180 home languages in inner London. It is

the most polyglot city in the world now—far greater than New York. Again, that has a major impact on schools. Some schools have an overwhelming majority of, for example, Sylheti speakers (a branch of Bengali); in other schools it's not so much that any one particular language dominates the school, but the variety of the pupils' home languages. So Pimlico school, near Victoria, has nearly fifty languages spoken by the children in the school. To them English is the second language. This is both an advantage and a disadvantage: bilingual children, provided their English is good enough, obviously have a tremendous additional asset, but for those whose English is not fluent (that is, one in six of the children in our schools) it is clearly a major handicap.

About half the pupils are eligible for free school meals. That is an increasing number; four years ago only about a third were eligible. That is reflected in the inner areas of the other major cities.

One child in four in our schools comes from a one-parent family. The families that we are talking about in the inner cities have high mortality rates and higher illness rates (and obviously that reflects on children's absence from school as well as the support they are able to get from their parents) (CSO, 1988).

There is, therefore, an intensity of problems which the chidren have to cope with before they actually turn up at school. Eric Midwinter (the distinguished educationalist, who did much work in Toxteth, Liverpool 8) always said that the thing that confused him was when people started to pretend that London was part of England. There is a danger in extrapolating inner London figures and you certainly will not find the intensity of inner London problems in the other inner cities, but the sort of problems affecting inner London schools are the ones that affect the inner cities referred to.

THE EDUCATION DEBATE

We need to go back ten years in the debate that reached a climax with the 1988 Education Reform Act. In 1976 James Callaghan, when he was Prime Minister, made a speech at Ruskin College, Oxford outlining his concerns that the education service was not addressing the needs of the country as an industrial and commercial society. Shortly afterwards the Department of Education and Science published a paper which highlighted the problems of the education service which the then government perceived. They had four main anxieties:

1. There were unacceptable differences from school to school in the content and quality of children's learning and this in turn implied inequality of opportunity.
2. The curriculum had become overcrowded in response to constantly expanding demands and arguably the attempt to meet social needs had been at the expense of more strictly educational goals. In other words, as comprehensive schools had come in, they were deeming themselves to have a social role as well as a strictly educational one. It was a Labour government that first challenged the validity of that.
3. Not enough young people are equipped with the skills, knowledge and understanding of our economy which are essential to our country's well-being.
4. In a much more mobile society different teaching approaches or methods between schools can lead to a break in learning on the part of the child simply because she/he had moved from one area to another. There we have the beginnings in government terms of the move towards a national curriculum.

That was published in 1977. The Labour Government talked for the rest of its period of office, had lots of meetings up and down the country, but in fact nothing came of it during Labour's term. There was no Education Act after the 1976 Education Act which was the one requiring local authorities to submit comprehensive proposals. This was immediately repealed when the Conservative Government got into power in 1979—one of its very first acts. That was all that was seen from Labour about the 'Great Debate'.

Since the Conservatives have been in power, there has been the 1980 Act which legislated on school government: the procedures to be followed when there is a proposal to open, close, or change the nature of the school, admissions policies, school meals policies (opening up discretion), school milk, and a whole variety of little issues. In 1981 there was a major Act regarding special education which led to greater integration of many children into mainstream schools and the introduction of a more formal and detailed process leading to the assessment of the special educational needs and the educational policies to meet them for pupils with disabilities. In 1986 there was another major Act, which concerned itself with governors, curriculum, discipline in school, finance, parents' meetings, and again a whole variety of other issues. In 1987 there was one of the biggest of them all, the School Teachers' Pay and Conditions of Service Act, which completely changed the way that teachers' pay was calculated and, for the first time, linked pay and conditions of service. That in its turn is leading to major changes in the way secondary schools, in particular, are organized.

Now there is the 1988 Education Reform Act, the most radical of them all, aiming, in the words of the then Secretary of State for Education and Science, Kenneth Baker, to 'inject a new vitality' into the education system. It seeks to do this by, on the one hand, giving major powers to the Secretary of State and so reinforcing the concept of a 'national' service; and, on the other, transferring powers from the local education authorities (LEAs) to the governors of schools and colleges and to individual parents. The Act contains sections on a national curriculum; testing and assessment; admissions up to the available capacity of a school; devolution of the management of finance and staffing to schools and further education colleges; grant maintained schools, which allows schools to opt out of the LEA system by becoming maintained by the Government instead of by the LEA; the establishment of the University Funding Council and the Polytechnics and College Funding Council (which will 'encourage and reward approaches by higher education institutions which bring them close to the world of business' and will enable the Government to impose *its* priorities on the system of higher education in England and Wales); and the abolition of the Inner London Education Authority, with the transfer of responsibility for the education service to the twelve inner London boroughs and the City of London.

In summary, during the period of office of the Conservative administrations since 1979 we have seen a number of huge education Acts, compared with a period of lethargy on the part of the Labour administration which preceded it.

The Education Reform Act was not the only piece of legislation enacted in 1988 which will affect the education service; local government finance is also to be changed radically in 1990. The property tax on homes, the rates, is to be abolished and replaced by the community charge, perhaps better known as the poll tax. Business rates will no longer be determined by the local authority but by the national Government and will be distributed by the Government to the local authorities. There will continue to be government grants distributed according to the Government's assessment of the 'needs' of a particular authority. This is not the place to go into a detailed discussion of local government finance but it is important to point out one feature of the new system: the local authority will, in broad terms, be able to vary only one-quarter of its income, that from the community charge. The remainder will be determined by the Government. This means that, to increase its expenditure by 1 per cent the local authority will have to increase the community charge by about 4 per cent. Conversely, a reduction of 1 per cent will lead to the poll tax being reduced by 4 per cent. The incentives for the authorities to reduce their expenditure will thus be considerable, which is what the Government intends. In the past, Labour local authorities have been prepared—indeed, have wanted—to have high levels of expenditure because businesses bore the brunt and because poorer residents could be exempted from payment. Neither premiss will be true after 1990 and it is difficult to see how high-spending local authorities will be able to withstand political pressures to reduce their expenditure. These authorities are, almost invariably, responsible for the inner-city areas, towards which they direct additional resources. If we take in the additional fact that education (once described as 'the cuckoo in the nest' of local government) accounts for nearly half of the tax-borne expenditure of local authorities, it becomes clear why I regard this as a crucial element in the debate about the future of education in the inner cities. Money will not resolve all the problems of inner-city education, but we can safely predict that, without sufficient resources, many of the urgent needs of the children and their families will not be met.

Let me now return to the Education Acts themselves. This Government is, as it regularly reminds us, committed to the view that market forces should be a much greater factor in the determination of priorities in the public sector. In the sense that this means switching power from the providers to the 'consumers', the concept has won much public support. When Kenneth Baker argued, in his opening speech on the Education Reform Bill, that the service had become 'producer-dominated', he was echoing a criticism that was wide-spread across the political spectrum (though, when pressed, the critics would usually concentrate their fire on *organized* teacher opinion, chiefly the trade unions, rather than on the individual teacher).

Where the debate has been much less clear is on the issue of *how* to promote the interest of the consumer. The free marketeers themselves are clear enough: provide parents with a voucher with which they can 'buy' a place at any school they wish. They will only wish to buy the best. Good schools will get fuller and bad schools will fold up. Therefore, all children will go to good schools. QED.

Others are not convinced. For a start, markets work primarily for the benefit of the strongest: those with most money, with the best information, with the capacity to shop around, are the ones who get best value for their money. Will schools give priority to those children whose parents can 'top up' the value of the voucher? Will the parent who has failed in the system be in the same position to judge success in a school as the graduate who can see the full potential of the system? Does the child whose parent can use the family car to transport her to a distant 'good' school not have greater opportunities than the child who is needed to help look after younger brothers and sisters and must therefore go to the nearest school in order to be able to fulfil the caring, family role?

There is another weakness in the market concept so far as schooling is concerned: it ignores the value of a school as a community. Very often it is the quality of the community that parents choose when selecting a school with their child. And yet unbridled market forces might destroy the very qualities being valued. Some of the most popular secondary schools are small and their smallness is seen as a virtue. Others serve particular religious communities and the shared values of faith are highly prized. Still others seek to serve particular geographical communities and establish links with other groups in the locality in order to strengthen the feeling of 'belonging'. In each of these examples, simply to insist that the school admits anyone who seeks a place might be to destroy the very institution being valued.

This argument can be taken a stage further to demonstrate the limitations of the market philosophy in determining educational provision. If I am buying a good, the worst I can do is to deny another person the opportunity to buy it. If it is the last one, the third and fourth person would not have been able to buy one anyway. But that is not the case with schools. In inner London we have tried to plan our secondary schools so that wherever you live your child will have reasonable access to big schools and small schools, single-sex and mixed, county and church. We have also tried to give a good geographical spread, in the belief that schools provide a valuable community resource—for example, for adult education, youth clubs, meeting places—beyond their prime purpose. But suppose thirty parents of boys in a small single-sex school decide to switch them to the nearest mixed schools (by no means unlikely: girls-only schools are far more popular than boys-only). The boys' school might then be too small to be viable and have to close, denying the opportunity of a single-sex school to the parents of the other boys. In addition, the mixed school might become unbalanced between boys and girls, which is not what those who wanted a mixed school would have had in mind. Cap all that with the fact that the school building as a resource might be lost, and it can be seen that the losers not allowed to choose can be far greater in number than the winners who were.

The Government has stopped short of a market system but has taken moves in that direction. Is it likely that the Education

Reform Act and its predecessors will benefit a majority of the 'consumers' or only the well-organized minority? I should like to highlight four main areas: opting out, parental involvement, the curriculum, and resourcing.

Grant Maintained Schools and City Technology Colleges

The 1988 Act allows for two new kinds of schools: Grant Maintained Schools and City Technology Colleges. The idea behind the former is that schools which feel oppressed by the LEA which maintains them can apply to the Secretary of State to be allowed to opt out of the LEA system and be maintained by a grant from the central government. It harks back to the old direct grant schools abolished by Labour as part of the move away from selective education. Views differed as to how many would opt out: Mrs Thatcher had visions of wholesale transfers (which reflects her own contempt for local government), Mr Baker was more modest in his claims. To date—but it is early days—his has been the more accurate forecast. Interestingly enough, there are as many schools wanting to opt out of Conservative LEAs as Labour ones and Democrats have had their share too. The reason for wanting to opt out has just as often been to avoid reorganization as any other motive. Meanwhile, the Secretary of State has been putting pressure on LEAs to reorganize their secondary schools to take out of use the surplus places resulting from the fall in birth rates in the seventies.

Whatever can be said about Mr Baker's ability to forecast the number of schools wanting to opt out of LEAs, it cannot seriously be argued that his predictions so far as CTCs were concerned were accurate. His vision was to establish in the inner cities new schools with a strong technological bias which would serve as beacons of good practice forcing up standards in neighbouring schools. 'All or most' of the start-up costs would come from industry. The reality is very different. Industry, for the most part, would not co-operate and the schools would cost the taxpayer about £140 million with only about a quarter of the start-up costs coming from the private sector. Several are not in the inner cities at all, and some of those that are will simply replace successful existing schools. In any case, the concept is based on a false premise: there is no evidence that high performance in one school raises standards in another. Indeed given the huge government financial input (often several times greater than the total capital allocation for *all* other schools in the LEA) the other schools have been provided with a ready explanation for different levels of performance. Not surprisingly, the Treasury has pulled the plug on the scheme and there will be no more government-sponsored CTCs after the first phase.

In my judgement, what will happen as a consequence of opting out and CTCs will be the re-introduction of selection: not necessarily as we have traditionally known it—at least in the state sector— but, I think, by social qualification. Whilst grant-maintained schools might not initially accept only the cleverest children, they will accept those children who are the most compliant, whose parents are supportive, whose parents are seen to have something to offer to schools as well as the children. We might then see other schools less committed to the belief in the benefits of opting out but who could feel the need to acquire similar powers in order to protect themselves. We will see a much greater split in schools, probably especially in London but in other places as well, between middle-class schools and working-class schools, *and* (if America is anything to go by) we might well see schools which have a large proportion of black 'underclass' and white 'underclass' pupils and other schools which have more privileged members of both communities. Given there is a much higher proportion of privileged white people than privileged black people, I think we will see some schools predominantly serving black children and others white children, a retrogressive step. As argued above, markets act in favour of the advantaged— the ones with choice; the disadvantaged are those who have to accept, willingly or unwillingly, what is left after the advantaged have made their choice. If my worst fears come about we could see a number of reactions: greater alienation on the part of 'the underclass'; still poorer academic results in the inner-city schools than before; still poorer staying-on rates beyond the minimum school-leaving age of 16 (already huge differences can be seen in the staying-on rate between inner-city schools and suburban schools), restricting possibilities for those who do not go on to higher education; poorer employment rates (there is historical evidence for this: youngsters from one school have a decided advantage over ones from another school simply by saying on the application form that they have been to such and such a school); and, finally, but by no means least in importance, poorer quality of staff in the inner-city school than in the more privileged areas, as the odds against success in the former begin to stack up.

Parental involvement

I believe passionately in the involvement of parents in their children's education. I have worked in Coventry where we devoted a lot of time and effort to developing community schools with, I think, a great deal of success in the involvement of parents. I have tried similar things in inner London without, I have to say, similar success, although there have been some improvements—a reading scheme and a maths scheme, intended to involve parents in the development of early skills with their children, are steps forward. We have, in London, developed the 'London Record of Achievement'. This is going to be a selection, in an important-looking folder, of children's work, of their own assessment of what is happening to them, and teachers' assessment of how they are developing. This will be shared with the children and with their parents on a regular basis, building up a sort of portfolio of each child's life in the school so it can be used when they are applying for jobs or applying to go into further education. The Record of Achievement is an important development for two reasons. First, it gives credit for a whole range of achievement over an extended period as opposed to the single certificate showing GCSE results as if that summarized an entire school career. Secondly, it depends for its success on the close involvement of parent and child: it provides a mechanism for developing a partnership.

I believe also that parents are important in the government of the school. We need parent governors, and I am not against government moves on that front. But the Government's assertion that the way to give parents greater involvement in their children's education is to increase the number of parent governors, or to have a once-a-year parents' meeting to be addressed by the governing body does not correspond with how parents see what they want. Parents are interested, obviously, to see that the school is run well, and if they can influence its direction there are some of them who want to do that. The parents I know say they want to understand what is happening to their own child or children and be involved in the development of that; if they are interested in the general running of the school it is in its academic and pastoral organization and not, as the Government seems to think, in a wholesale 'management' of the business side of the school. School governors are going to have to make very important financial decisions which many people, and indeed many business people, say they do not want to get involved in. The time commitment involved in doing that—and doing it well—is phenomenal, even if you have the skills. And at this point we must return to the inner cities where very many of the parents either do not have the skills or do not have the confidence that they have the skills—which is just as important. They will not wish to be involved and what may well happen is that middle-class and political activists will emerge and take over this supposed right of parents to control the way that their children are educated and the running of the school. The urban working class will once again be represented by those who purport to have their interests at heart, short of actually listening to them and responding to the anxieties they express. What parents need for support is increased contact time with their child's teacher, and support in under-standing what the school is trying to achieve, which has worked in some very deprived areas, in particular in Coventry. Patience is needed to get them to come in the first place, because often people who themselves failed in school do not feel welcome there, and it needs a careful approach. We should be trying to help them to help their younger children and give them the confidence to have a much more active role in, for example, maths and reading schemes. That is one of the major advantages middle-class parents give to their children, that they are able to help them in the development of those early skills and get them off to a flying start.

Curriculum

I am in favour of a national curriculum. I would have preferred a better debate amongst professionals and parents about the content of the national curriculum but I can understand the impatience of the Secretary of State that the debate was meandering along and it was time for some decisions. However, he should have set clear limits on the discussion period with a stated intention to introduce a bill in the following session in Parliament. That way there might have been a much greater feeling of consensus about the way forward and a greater commitment towards the idea by the teachers. That commitment could be won but has not yet been.

I am worried, I have to say, about the way that this Act enhances the powers of politicians and bureaucrats in curriculum matters. The final decision on the national curriculum is taken by the Secretary of State, who is to be advised by a National Curriculum Council (NCC), but he appoints that Council. It is not difficult to see that people who want particular elements to go into the curriculum of schools can achieve it without any great effort. Indeed, we have seen the Secretary of State tell the NCC, before they had considered the matter, what his criticisms of the report of his maths working group were. 'Please advise me. This is the advice I want.' The fact that the national curriculum is controlled by politicians, not really answerable to anybody, is very worrying.

There is a fundamental concern. Are we moving, step by step, to a 'dual system': education for the most able and training for the *hoi polloi*? I do not think this Act actually takes us there, but there are signs in the way vocational education (which, in context, is a good thing) is having a greater place in the Government's thinking. It might be welcomed or at least accepted by inner-city residents that what schooling is about is preparation for a job rather than preparation for life. This is the opposite end of the pendulum swing from the position in many schools that there should be no contact at all with the world of work, it should not influence what happens in school at all, a ridiculous state of affairs. 'Education has different aspects: the development of character and capabilities; the acquisition of specific skills; the enhancement of intellect; the enhancement of mind, body and soul; and the training of the social human being.' That quotation from a conference 'Education 2000' is, I think, a good description of what education ought to be about. I think the pendulum has swung to a fairly sensible point. It is now generally accepted that there is a need to balance the education offered to children amongst those different aspects. My worry is that the pendulum is still swinging and we might see, at least for some children, a move to a purely mechanistic curriculum: one that is supposed to prepare them for a job and for work. I am minded of Sir Alec Clegg (the great education officer in the old West Riding of Yorkshire) saying: 'there are two purposes in education, one is to cook a pot, the other is to light a fire, and you have to choose which you believe to be the prime purpose.' If we cannot enthuse our young people with a quest for knowledge and self-development in whatever form it comes for each child, I believe we have failed them. If in eleven years we cannot light a single fire of enthusiasm, then we have failed to prepare the child for a fulfilling adulthood.

The Government in its testing and assessment proposals has missed the point of what we could do, because of the dominance of the market philosophy. If you test children you can do it for a variety of purposes: for a diagnostic purpose, to identify what help the child needs in order to acquire skills, in order to develop; for screening, to try to work out what general areas of knowledge are missing with a particular group of children; or, and this is what the Government is doing, you can do it in order to prove that all youngsters have reached a particular level of knowledge and you can add up all those achievements and turn it willy-nilly into what the school is supposed to have achieved. I do not think that what the Government is proposing is reasonable. To use the analogy of health and doctors: a doctor who works in an inner-city area will have a higher failure rate than one who works in suburban areas if you take illness among the patients as a way of proving success or failure—that is a fact (CSO, 1988). A heart surgeon who has a number of patients dying is not necessarily a worse surgeon than an ENT surgeon who has no patients who die. You cannot simply take one set of statistics without taking into account all the other factors around the case to prove success or failure. What the Government is proposing, by adding up exam passes or grade assessments, will work to the disadvantage of urban schools because they will never ever achieve the same level of 'success' as the middle-class schools. In ILEA we tried, with regression analysis, to assess the actual achievement of schools by taking into account input factors like middle-class/ working-class, language problems, home deprivation, and so on. What it shows is that there are schools which appear to be very successful but are in fact failing the children, because they are not achieving the average results of the authority as a whole. The 'value added' by the school was less than it should be but the fact could be disguised by other favourable inputs.

Resourcing

I have already referred to the fact that the middle classes are able to make considerable input into their children's education, by helping with early skills, by having a knowledge of the system, by being able to duck and weave and work the system to their advantage, by recognizing the value of education which most of them have, and by the general support that they give to their children and to the education service as a whole. We must enhance the ability of the disadvantaged to make similar contributions for their children.

The middle classes can also spare some of their resources to increase the resources available to schools. You see that very regularly if you go into schools—computers, mini-buses, visits that the children make organized by the school, visiting groups or individuals such as theatre groups and musicians who come to schools to enhance what the school has to offer. But if the family income is already at marginal levels of subsistence, clearly none can be spared for extras no matter how valuable those might be perceived to be by the family. We face a time when the capacity of the LEAs to provide for the difference will be diminished, both because of the inexorable squeeze on resources that LEAs are facing, and have faced for many years now, and also because of local financial management. Decisions will be made not by the LEAs but by the people in each school. There are strong signs that what the Secretary of State wants is for all schools to be funded, for the most part, on a per capita basis. The advantages and disadvantages that the children suffer will only to a limited extent be taken into account. We therefore face the very real prospect of schools with the greatest need having the fewest resources. As so often, because few adults visit schools, it will be a social change of major proportions about which the public will not feel aroused because they will not experience it.

But, in my experience, the overwhelming majority of parents are well aware of the opportunities which a good education offers to their children and are keen for their children to take full advantage. Middle-class parents have known for long enough that they have an important role to play. There must be a systematic attempt to give all parents the support they need in developing either their skills or the confidence to use skills they already have. I mentioned earlier that since 1987 teachers' pay and conditions of service have been linked together: teachers can now be required to take part in parents' meetings. I would go a stage further and build a guaranteed right for parents to meet with teachers, individually and in groups, and offer the teachers an increase in pay in recognition of its importance. That way a reforming government could do something to increase the effective power of all and demonstrate a real commitment to the extension of parents' rights. The response of the mandarins in the Department of Education and Science, to increase the parents' numbers and role in the governing body, can be only part of the answer. Parents must be given individually the support they need to help their children benefit from schooling and collectively the confidence to recognize that their views are different from but as important as those of the professional educators.

The squeeze on resources available to urban local authorities is bound to reduce educational opportunities for the poor urban communities. There will be fewer of the nursery classes which have proved to be a valuable means to expand the experiences and language of many disadvantaged children. The limited, and yet very successful trials of using mother tongues as well as English with small children seem unlikely to continue at present levels, let alone be replicated in other areas. Community education, involving parents, will remain a limited opportunity. Access courses, which bring adults who 'failed' in school back into education and, indeed, into higher education, are further examples of success stories, meeting real societal as well as personal needs; such courses are struggling to survive when they should be expanding year on year. Although much is made of 'inflated bureaucracies' and 'Loony Left' causes, the truth of the matter is that the overwhelming majority of the additional spending by urban authorities is on schemes such as I have just mentioned. To achieve the levels of reductions now being required by the Government, the LEAs will have to abandon some of the support they give to the disadvantaged and will have to reduce their resourcing levels nearer to national averages, despite the overwhelming concentration of disadvantage in the major cities and towns.

I shall pass quickly over the abolition of the Inner London Education Authority because, whatever I write, the cynical will simply say, 'Well, he would argue that, wouldn't he?', whilst those who know the work of the Authority (and I have *never* claimed that it did not have faults) will share my sadness at its demise. But, as there is no realistic prospect of its being revived in the foreseeable future, if ever, we must concentrate our efforts on helping the boroughs make the best fist of it that they can. That my colleagues and I, with full support of the Members, are doing.

Finally, I must say a few words about education for 16–19-year-olds. No political party in this country has a coherent policy for this age-group and yet it seems absurd to talk of a comprehensive system of education which, for a good half of the population (and a much, much higher proportion of the working class), ends at 16. In the United States what we call 'school leaver', they call 'drop-out' and that says it all. This Government has put together a Youth Training Scheme which, despite many weaknesses, particularly for young people with disabilities, could form the basis of a training and education programme. For example, bodies have been set up to consider the hotchpotch of vocational qualifications and A levels (report rejected); a ministerial committee considered the organization of this phase but its nerve failed and its impact was negligible; new examinations and courses are dreamt up. But no one tries to relate the bits to each other, nobody knows what we should be trying to guarantee young people and how to achieve it. I accept it is complicated: it involves the relationship between schools and further education colleges on the one hand, and business and higher education on the other; it involves education *and* training (now the responsibility of different ministries!); it needs to consider the integration of young people with special educational needs and the improvement of their life chances; financial support for the poor must be part of the package. But we simply cannot afford, as a nation, to accept the continuation of the present mess. We cannot afford to allow young people to leave school believing 'that's the end of that'. How many times will they have to change jobs, develop new skills during their lifetime? They will be living in a period of enormous change and if they as individuals and we as a nation are to take advantage of it, there must be better education—not just up to 16 but through their lives.

CONCLUSION

To sum up: those political parties who believe in a comprehensive system of education need to do three things. First, to pass a one-clause Act which makes the admissions policies of grant-maintained schools the responsibility of the LEA in which they are situated. That's all: the rest of the powers are already in place. Secondly, they need to commit more resources to the poorer areas. Priorities need to be considered and the powers to make specific grants—another gift of the present Government—used to direct effort on those priorities. And, finally, they need to work out a comprehensive policy for the education and training of 16–19-year-olds—and a resolution in favour of tertiary colleges or denouncing A levels simply will not do. Their present policies simply mock those who are being failed.

　　The sad thing is that none of this is happening. Nor has it been happening in the university departments of education whose contribution to the education debate over the past decade has been pitiful. However, several of them have now recruited high-quality people who actually know how the system works. The smart politicians will be seeking their help.

Because this Government acted upon the real and proper concerns—those described in the introduction to this chapter— outlined in the 1977 White Paper, which were being expressed by those earlier governments, we have a strange debate taking place at the moment. It is a debate in which there is broad, though, it has to be said, not total agreement about problems, but only one set of proposals, the Market set, is being considered as a remedy. Other politicians seemed paralysed into inactivity. I have tried to sketch out ways in which the urban disadvantaged will, far from having an improvement in their education, face the prospect of a real deterioration in the quality of schooling which they receive. The task for those who believe that education is a service which should respond to the needs of all, which is a right for all, where equality of opportunity is vital, is to address the problem and propose realistic alternatives to those presently on offer.

To pretend that all is for the best in this best of all possible worlds, to accept that the education professionals should be allowed to return to their inward-looking perspectives, is as unacceptable as a market-oriented approach will prove to be. I see very few signs that new thinking is high on the non-market policitians' political agenda.

Reference

CSO (Central Statistical Office) (1988), *Social Trends 1988* (London).

9

Housing Conditions, Problems, and Policies

Nick Raynsford

THE PROBLEMS

Any consideration of housing issues in the inner cities has to start with a definition of the term 'inner cities'. In housing terms this raises several difficulties. A geographical definition alone is inadequate. Belgravia and Kensington are certainly parts of the inner area of London, but by no stretch of the imagination can they be said to exhibit the characteristics normally associated with the term 'inner cities'. Conversely, overspill estates on the periphery of conurbations, such as Knowsley in relation to Merseyside, can be described in almost every respect, except for their location, as displaying inner-city problems. In other areas, for example Greater Manchester or Glasgow, almost the whole conurbation, both inner area and outer estates, could be discussed under the general heading of inner cities. The city centre and the periphery would both be embraced by any serious analysis of the area's housing problems. So in approaching this subject, I will be using the phrase 'inner cities' loosely to cover housing in an urban context rather than specifically housing in what could be defined literally as the inner city.

The second priority is to define the key housing problems and conditions in the urban areas. There is no single problem, nor one overriding issue. Housing conditions in our cities are varied, and problems come in some quite surprising forms. For example, the use of the words 'inner cities' conjures up an image of dereliction, and perhaps of decaying council estates. Yet arguably the worst symptoms of housing in the urban context at the moment are to be found behind substantial stuccoed Victorian mansions, in areas like Bayswater, where sums of £200 or more a week are being paid for a single room. That would not initially suggest an acute housing problem, until it is made clear that I am referring to the concentration of homeless families in 'bed and breakfast' hotels. So the words 'inner city' can be misleading, if they prompt stereotyped images, because in reality urban housing problems are much more complex and varied.

Shortage

The key problems, in my view, are fourfold. The first is shortage. In the 1970s it became fashionable for academics and politicians to say that the shortage of housing was a problem of the past. This was always an over-simplistic argument, because it depended on a crude 'balance-sheet' approach which ignored local shortages, and the extent to which properties may not be available to the people who need them. Put in simple terms, there is no advantage in a large supply of houses for sale at a high price if the shortage is experienced by poor people who cannot afford them. Equally, a large supply of housing in the North of England is of no great use if there is insufficient local employment and people are moving away—encouraged to get on their bicycles—in search of a job. Indeed, this process could well be exacerbating the problem if there are not enough homes in the areas to which they are moving. So it was always a suspect argument, and it has become much more so in the course of the last few years, because of the serious loss of rented housing in Britain.

At the end of December 1987 there were 1.3 million fewer rented homes in Britain than eight years previously (Treasury, 1988). This is one of the most remarkable yet least quoted social trends in the last decade. (I have deliberately taken the period from 1979 because it is a direct consequence of government policy.) There are two main reasons. On the one hand the Government has encouraged the sale of council houses without adequate replacement; and on the other, despite its claimed attempts to stimulate private lettings, the Government has presided over a continuing steep decline in the private rented market. Previously, indeed for most of this century, the decline of the private rented sector was offset by increasing provision of public rented housing, initially mainly from local authorities and New Towns, and more recently from local authorities and housing associations. However, the position has changed dramatically since 1979. There has been a reduction of around 800,000 council homes, and around 650,000 privately rented homes, offset by about 150,000 extra housing association homes, giving a net overall loss of 1.3 million. Yet there has been no comparable reduction in the demand for rented housing.

Against that background it is hardly surprising that there is a homelessness crisis. The problem bears most heavily on people with low incomes who cannot afford to buy and need rented accommodation, yet who are confronted by a diminishing supply of rented homes. So the rise in homelessness in recent years, with the number officially accepted by local authorities in England rising from 57,000 in 1979 to 118,000 in 1988, can be related directly to the shortage of adequate housing available to rent at prices that the people who need it can afford (Audit Commission, 1989; Thomas and Niner, 1989).

The problem is not unique to the inner cities—it is in fact a nationwide phenomenon. However, its scale and degree is much more acute in the urban conurbations, and above all in inner London. There an explosive combination of exceptionally high house prices, a chronic shortage of rented housing, and the magnet effect of the capital, particularly for young single people, has fuelled the already serious homelessness problem with predictable and very visible consequences.

Economic mismatch

The second major problem can be seen as an extension of the first one. It is the mismatch between the cost of housing and people's resources. One aspect has already been outlined: people who cannot find homes they can afford, because their incomes are too low. The problem however goes wider than that. It may be helpful to approach it by looking back at the attempts that have been made by governments of different persuasions over the last forty years to tackle the gap between people's resources and the cost of housing.

The main policy approach during the early post-war years was rent control, which was seen as a means of keeping rented housing, the bulk of which was then provided by private landlords, available for people of modest incomes. So rents were not allowed to increase dramatically; indeed in the first fifteen years of the post-war period there was little increase at all. Then after the Conservatives' 1957 Rent Act, rents began to rise. In 1964 an incoming Labour government instituted a new system of rent control, based on the 'Fair Rent' concept, which has continued in force, at least for part of the rented housing stock, until the 1988 Housing Act ended Fair Rents on all new lettings, and opened the door once again to unrestricted market rents. While the effect of rent control may have been to protect certain tenants, and keep rents within their reach, it clearly was not a framework in which there was any on-going prospect of rented housing being provided by private landlords for people in need. It could, therefore, only work in a context in which other agencies, mainly local authorities, were generating the supply of new lettings that were needed. They too required subsidy so that the rents on their lettings were not beyond the means of their tenants and prospective tenants. As the public sector progressively replaced the private sector as the main source of rented housing, so the importance of, and scale of, these subsidies increased.

The other approach, designed to tackle the mismatch, has been based on providing subsidies directly to individuals in need, initially through National Assistance (later Supplementary Benefit), then through a plethora of local rebate schemes, until in 1972 a national Rent Rebate and Rent Allowance scheme was introduced, which covered private tenants for the first time. That led on to Housing Benefit from 1982 onwards. This approach is the one favoured by the Government which criticizes general subsidies to tenants (though not to owners) as expensive and indiscriminate. It believes instead in 'targeting' subsidy to tenants on those most in need through a means test. This approach has proved singularly unsuccessful. Take-up has been very patchy, particularly in the private rented sector. When the costs of benefit payments began to escalate in the early 1980s, partly because of increased rent levels, the responsible government department, the Department of Health and Social Security, grew alarmed and consequently instituted a series of cuts in the benefit programme. Between 1983 and 1988 Housing Benefit was cut on eight separate occasions (Ward and Zebedee, 1989). So we now have a truncated Housing Benefit system which is substantially less generous, and less effective than the scheme that was introduced fifteen years ago, and which is certainly not ensuring that people can afford higher priced accommodation that otherwise would be beyond their means.

This process however is by no means over. One of the great dilemmas for the Government is created by their ideological commitment to market rents in the private sector and much higher rents for tenants of councils and housing associations. This will inevitably increase Housing Benefit costs, but the Department of Social Security (DSS) has shown no willingness to pay the bill. So there is a straight conflict between the financial concerns of the DSS and the Treasury on the one side, and the market rent ideology of the Department of the Environment on the other. The people who are losing out as a consequence are the very people who depend on some kind of assistance to keep housing costs within their means. Once again this is not a problem unique to the cities. It applies more widely, but there is a special inner-city dimension, largely because of the concentration of poorer households in certain parts of the inner city, and also particularly in Greater London, with its exceptionally high accommodation costs.

Social polarization

The third major problem is one which most people would recognize as a classic inner-city problem: the concentration of disadvantaged households in certain areas of the city, and often in the worst housing conditions. It used to be argued that council housing had broken the historic link between bad housing and poverty. The thesis was that the provision of council housing had ensured for the first time that poor people did not have to live in bad housing. I was always a bit sceptical about that claim and I am even more so now! Council housing in its early days did not often meet the needs of the poorest; it tended to be allocated to the slightly better off, for example industrous artisans, to use the language of early twentieth-century housing managers. Even in the post-war era, applicants were usually inspected to see that their standards were suitable before they were offered council housing. Many of the poorest families were left in privately rented accommodation and lodgings. So there was always a degree to which council housing did not meet the needs of the very poorest. But more recently that has changed, partly as a result of legislation. I think particularly of the Housing (Homeless Persons) Act 1977, which imposed duties on councils to house certain homeless people, many of whom are among the poorest and most disadvantaged members of our society. However, this change has coincided with other far-reaching changes in the nature of council housing.

As has already been mentioned, the size of the council stock in Britain has been diminishing over the last decade, essentially as a consequence of the Right to Buy. Many better-off council tenants have bought themselves out of the tenure. This process has also often resulted in the best and most attractive properties being sold, including the cottage estates and individual houses in the outer suburban areas. In turn this has meant a smaller and generally less desirable stock being available for people in need. The problem has been exacerbated by the deterioration in conditions on many council estates, some of which were badly designed and shoddily built, others of which have not been properly maintained. Cuts in budgets, reducing local authorities' abilities to improve and maintain properties, have of course accentuated the problem. The outcome is a tendency towards the concentration of poorer and more disadvantaged households in less desirable property. The process if it continues will inevitably lead to council housing performing a residual and stigmatized role as the 'dumping ground' for people who have no other options.

Additionally, in some cities, and particularly in London, a lot of poor households still live in private rented accommodation, where conditions are generally the worst of all tenures. Social polarization is also seen in the concentration of some ethnic minority groups in poor condition owner-occupied housing in inner-city areas. All of these trends are tending to reinforce patterns of correlation between poverty, social disadvantage, and bad housing in many inner-city areas.

Condition of the stock

That leads naturally to the fourth problem, the condition of the housing stock. The post-war emphasis on clearance of slums, followed by a swing of the pendulum from the late 1960s onwards in favour of rehabilitation, contributed substantially to the removal of the worst slum conditions inherited from the Victorian era. It also virtually eradicated what was seen in the immediate post-war era to be the core problem, the absence of basic amenities like baths, WCs, and basic sanitation in housing. The number of houses without standard amenities is now miniscule, but at the same time the pattern of poor conditions in the housing stock has been changing. There has been a growing problem of disrepair, seen not just in the private rented stock where the worst housing has traditionally been found, but increasingly in owner-occupied housing, which now accounts for 50 per cent of London's sub-standard homes (AMA, 1987). This reflects the growing number of poor home-owners, both elderly and not-so-elderly, who are not able either to pay for or to organize the repairs or improvements that are needed to their homes.

At the same time there is a serious backlog of repairs and clear evidence of deterioration on many council estates. This has arisen either because of inadequate expenditure on maintenance, or as a consequence of design and structural problems, many reflecting the over-optimistic faith in the value of the prefabricated construction systems so popular in the 1960s and 1970s. Tackling this legacy calls for a great deal of expenditure, either for demolition and replacement, or for rehabilitation. In some instances it will require the replacement of types of provision which are unsuitable for family housing and which pose special problems to households on low incomes. These include high-density and high-rise estates, and many other dwellings with inherent defects such as inadequate insulation, or abnormally high heating costs. Improving and modernizing the sub-standard parts of the public sector stock to create safe, modern, and energy-efficient housing is a major task for the coming decade.

TACKLING THE PROBLEMS

What ought we to do to tackle these problems? In endeavouring to answer that question I propose to review current government policies, which are in many respects counter-productive, as well as spelling out my own views on the necessary and appropriate housing policies for the 1990s.

Shortage

New house building. The first priority must be an expanded house-building programme to reduce the shortage, and meet the rising tide of homelessness. In particular, we must provide more homes for renting at a cost that people on modest incomes can afford. How are these homes to be provided? The Government has made it clear that it does not want to see any more council housing built for general housing needs. It has succeeded in reducing the council house building programme from around 100,000 a year in the late 1970s to less than 30,000 a year currently, and its latest financial projections indicate the programme falling to as few as 6,000 a year by the early 1990s (Treasury, 1988, 1989). Although the Government is expanding the Housing Corporation budget to finance housing associations, the increased housing association programme will not be sufficient to fill the gap. Indeed, the Government's projections suggest an annual output of only 24,000 new housing association homes by the early 1990s, a lower level than was being achieved in the mid-1970s (Treasury, 1988, 1989).

The private rented sector. In parallel, the Government claims to be seeking to revive the private rented market but few people believe this is going to happen. The private rented market has been in decline since the beginning of the century for essentially economic reasons. The rate of return necessary for a landlord to justify keeping his investment in housing would require a rent level beyond the means of those low-income households who have been the principal tenants of private rented housing in the past. If indeed they could afford it, they would be far better advised to buy, not only because they would not have to pay a profit element to the landlord, but because they would qualify for mortgage interest tax relief. No comparable subsidy is available for rental payments.

The previous Conservative attempt to revive the private rented market by reducing tenants' rights in 1957 failed spectacularly. The market continued to decline as landlords sold up and re-invested elsewhere. But the erosion of tenants' rights opened the door to a particularly odious form of exploitation, associated with the Notting Hill landlord Peter Rachman. The 1988 Housing Act repeats the same mistakes as in 1957. Reducing tenants' rights with so-called 'Assured' and 'Assured Shorthold' tenancies is unlikely to stimulate the market. Nor will the increased penalties for harassment prove an adequate safeguard against the activities of latter-day Rachmans.

The tax incentives provided through the extension of the Business Expansion Scheme (BES) to 'Assured' tenancies by the 1988 Finance Act are also unlikely to provide any significant long-term growth in rented accommodation. The prospect of a tax-free capital gain at the end of a five-year investment period is prompting BES managers to look for what they euphemistically describe as 'exit routes'—in other words, means of getting the tenants out to realize the capital gain (Nationwide Anglia Building Society, 1988). In the meantime rent levels on BES schemes are likely to be far in excess of the means of low-income households looking for rented housing.

There are of course bound to be some exceptions in subsections of the private rented market. The most obvious are lettings to business people and young single people sharing. For example, in certain university towns you can find a viable specialist private rented market because a number of single people sharing have sufficient disposable income to meet the costs, and landlords have a realistic expectation of continued high occupancy levels.

Up-market lettings to business people and tourists are also likely to remain economically viable.

However, apart from these relatively small sections of the market, the only way in which a private rented sector can be maintained is through generous subsidies to bridge the gap between the level of rent a landlord needs to justify keeping his or her money in rented housing and the amount that the prospective tenant can afford to pay. Even if there was clear and unambiguous indication (which there is not at present) that the Treasury and the Department of Social Security would be happy to meet that gap through Housing Benefit, the question would obviously arise: 'Is this the most sensible way to use public money? Are there not better ways of achieving the objective of housing people on modest incomes than providing very large subsidies which help landlords to make profit?' The answer is, of course, that there are far more efficient ways. The advantages of the rent pooling system that has applied to council housing make it possible to achieve an affordable rent for a council tenant for a much lower subsidy than would be necessary to pay an individual private landlord.

Other housing agencies. The answer does not lie in the private sector. But this does not mean simply going back to a monolithic public sector, dominated by council housing, as the only answer. There is a need to increase the output of council housing from the hopelessly inadequate levels envisaged by the Government, but this must be part of a more pluralist approach with rented housing being provided by a number of agencies. Housing associations will clearly continue to play an important role. There is also scope for increasing the role of co-operatives and self-build groups. Indeed, one of the guiding principles behind an effective housing policy for the 1990s must be the close involvement of the 'customer' in the housing process. How many of the mistakes of the system-building era might have been avoided had the architects, housing managers, and other professionals who thought they knew what was best for people, had to listen to and heed the views of the people for whom those homes were built. Involving the public in the design and planning of new housing schemes should apply not just to co-operative and self-building housing schemes but to all housing built by public authorities and social landlords.

There is also a case for the judicious use of specialist agencies along similar lines to the New Town Development Corporations which made an important impact in the immediate post-war era. There has been a strange political about-turn on such agencies, with the political Right seizing on Corporations as a vehicle for privatization, while the Left has become cautious and sometimes frankly hostile because Corporations appear undemocratic. Yet with clearly set objectives and obligations to involve the public in their planning process, new specialist agencies with single-minded social objectives could make a significant contribution, not just to provide homes in specific areas, but perhaps also to tackle intractable problems which spill across local authority boundaries, such as the proliferation of 'bed and breakfast' hotels for the homeless.

While the programme will certainly need to be expanded, it would be a serious mistake to emphasize quantity at the expense of quality. This would be to repeat the errors of the 1960s, when the 'numbers game' tended to dominate housing debates. Sacrificing quality for the sake of a few extra units is almost always counter-productive, leading to additional costs in later years to remedy the inadequacies built-in at the outset.

Economic mismatch

Subsidy. The second key issue is the mismatch between resources and cost. This requires an effective system of subsidizing housing for people who cannot afford the full economic cost. There is no simple, easy mechanism for achieving this. Nor is it just a matter of choosing between general subsidies, which keep the cost of housing down for everyone, or means-tested subsidies to individual people in need. The Government defends its emphasis on means-tested benefits as cost-efficient because this way subsidies go only to people who need them. However, simple dependence on means-tested benefits without any general subsidy would mean massive increases in the level of rents and a serious poverty trap problem for people on low incomes. So for example a couple with two children under 11, claiming Famiy Credit and rent and rate rebates, would lose all except 31p of a £10 a week pay rise taking their gross income from £130 to £140 a week. This involves a marginal tax/benefit rate of 97p in the £, or almost two-and-a-half times the rate of tax applicable to the highest paid earners in Britain (Raynsford and Morris, 1988). Even without Family Credit, the marginal tax/benefit rate for low-income households is 90p in the £, which must act as a serious disincentive to seeking any increase in earnings.

Furthermore, there is a take-up problem, with rent rebates (to council tenants) traditionally estimated to be reaching no more than three-quarters of eligible tenants, and rent allowances (to private tenants) thought to achieve even less penetration (Treasury, 1988). These are the problems associated with dependence solely on means-tested benefits. They are problems which the present Government has not addressed.

Nor has the Government, despite its belief in means-testing and its opposition to general subsidies for rented housing, addressed the issue of general subsidies to home-owners. Mortgage interest tax relief is currently costing £5.5 billion a year in revenue foregone of which more than £1 billion goes to higher rate taxpayers. One might expect this group to be identified as a high priority for subsidy withdrawal, particularly by a government which stresses the evils of dependence on subsidy and 'feather-bedding'. But, of course, they are not.

The need for radical reform. We therefore have to recast the subsidy system. This does not just mean taking subsidies away from home-owners and increasing subsidies to tenants. Ideally we should be aiming for a benefit system which works across the board, applying both to home-owners and to tenants, and concentrating assistance on middle- to low-income groups. Among the latter there are two particular groups of home-owners in need. First, there are those who are meeting the initial high costs of buying for the first time, especially in expensive areas. For them some initial subsidy is probably necessary, but there is no reason why this should continue indefinitely. Their position will, in general, have been transformed after ten years for the cost of their repayments as a proportion of their income will have fallen dramatically. Secondly, there are poorer home-owners who do not have adequate means at the moment to maintain and repair their homes. In both these instances there is a case for more subsidy for home-owners but not the indiscriminate subsidies provided by mortgage interest tax relief and exemption from capital gains tax. A progressive withdrawal of these indiscriminate subsidies, and their replacement by more appropriate types of assistance, directed more effectively at those in need, are essential.

There are obvious political obstacles which have to be overcome if reform is to be achieved. The spectre of a loss of mortgage interest tax relief has been thought to be a powerful political weapon to be used against any party proposing major reform. Yet the consequences of inertia in terms of cost and misapplication of subsidy are unacceptable. A politically realistic route to reform must be found.

This almost certainly rules out a fundamental root and branch reform. However desirable the concept of a universal housing subsidy scheme may be in theory, the degree of upheaval and the extent of the losses likely to be caused (or feared) almost certainly make this a politically impossible option in the short term.

However, there is no reason why a more gradual and piecemeal approach should not be made towards establishing a fairer and more effective subsidy system. Tax relief to owners should be restricted to the standard rate (currently 25 per cent) so as to end the additional unjustified bonus which higher income groups currently receive. New mortgages for first time buyers could qualify for subsidy on a different formula, giving higher relief (perhaps 35 per cent) in the early years, but declining over a period of time to nothing. This would help concentrate subsidy when it is most needed in the early stages, but avoid an ongoing open-ended commitment. The extra costs of the higher initial subsidy would be covered to start with by the withdrawal of higher rate tax relief and the phasing down of subsidy in later years would generate significant savings. Over a period of time all mortgage relief would transfer to the new system, but in a way which avoided any immediate short-term loss to standard rate tax payers.

Subsidies for rented housing. In parallel, subsidies to the rented sector need to be revised to ensure a 'level playing field' for all social housing providers. So local authorities, housing associations, tenant co-operatives, and Development Corporations would be able to create new homes at rents which would be broadly comparable and within the reach of people in low-paid employment. A degree of rent pooling is essential to avoid unacceptably high subsidy costs of unaffordable rents on new buildings. Broadly comparable rent levels would allow a pluralist framework to thrive with the various agencies competing in terms of quality of service but without the temptation to cut maintenance costs to reduce rents.

Housing Benefit should then revert to its appropriate 'safety net' role for those on very low incomes rather than as the main subsidy to the rented sector. The poverty trap problem would be reduced by rent levels which would be affordable to most people in employment without dependence on means-tested benefit and by the gentler withdrawal of entitlement (or 'taper') as a claimant's income rises.

House prices. At the same time we have to address the issue of house prices. It is unsatisfactory from the point of view of economic efficiency as well as social objectives, if it proves impossible for many people to move from the North to the South because of the differential in house prices, and if it is impossible for people on modest incomes to buy in whole areas of the South of England because house prices are beyond their means. Leaving the market to run free is simply intensifying the problem.

Tackling this requires general economic measures and also specific housing measures. Reducing the shortage of rented housing will help to reduce the pressure for owner-occupation which is forcing up prices. Separate planning designation for social housing will safeguard housing for low-income groups in high cost urban areas as well as rural areas, where there is heavy market pressure on the small available stock. It will also avoid prohibitive costs of land acquisition in high price areas. Finally and more radically, we must raise once again the question of whether people's capital assets in their houses should not be subject to taxation. This would, of course, be a way of exercising a direct influence on house prices, assuming a direct correlation between value and tax liability under a land or property value taxation system.

Attacking social polarization

The third task is to break down the rigid social divisions in our cities, which lead to the concentration of the poorest people in the worst housing. This is not a problem for which there is a simple solution. We have to remember that some groups, and I think particularly of some groups from the Asian subcontinent, have very compelling reasons for wanting to live in close proximity. The evidence from areas in East London such as Spitalfields shows that many people of Asian origin feel much safer living together in a community than if they were dispersed. So it is not just a question of taking the easy option of a dispersal policy. Some ethnic minority groups do not want that. But they should not have to live in concentrations of poor housing.

This reinforces the need to tackle the problems of bad housing conditions. It will require a more effective grant system to help people improve conditions in owner-occupied homes. In the rented sector it means extending choice so that people can choose to move to a new home or a different area and do not end up concentrated in the worst quality housing because they are the poorest and most disadvantaged. This is very much dependent on the supply of homes.

A short supply coupled with statutory requirements to house those with the greatest needs means that those people will go into the only available housing. In a contracting council sector with a large backlog of unmodernized homes, this will often mean poor-condition housing. By contrast, in an expanding council sector in which new properties are being built and properties are being improved, there is a better prospect of people being offered a wider choice, and there will be less risk of a concentration of the most disadvantaged people in the worst housing.

The right to buy. That leads to the question of the 'Right to Buy'. Some people would argue that as this has a polarizing tendency, with wealthier tenants buying and the less well off left behind, it ought to be repealed. I do not agree. The 'Right to Buy' policy should be maintained but with certain amendments to remedy its failings. It needs to be coupled with a duty on local authorities to replace every unit sold while there is still a need for rented housing in that area. Local authorities must have the freedom to reinvest the receipts from sales in the provision or acquisition of new homes, and a specific subsidy to make up the difference between the discounted sale price and the market price so that councils can replace those units. Such an approach would sustain freedom of choice, because people who wanted to buy would be able to do so, but at the same time it would not penalize the homeless and the badly housed, because the loss of units through sale would immediately be made good.

There are two further strong arguments for this approach. First, it would compel reluctant authorities like Westminster and Wandsworth, currently selling properties to reduce their stock of council housing, to replace them. Secondly, it would tend to break down some of the current social polarization between people living in council estates on the one side and others in private housing on the other. In many of the inner-city areas the easiest way to replace would be to buy, rather than to build new homes. A process under which some of the council stock is sold and at the same time other property is acquired will begin to reverse this polarization between council tenants living in one section of the town and owner-occupiers in another.

Stock transfers. What about stock transfers encouraged by the provisions of the 1988 Housing Act? These take three different forms: first, compulsory acquisition by Housing Action Trusts (HATs); secondly, transfer of individual properties on estates as a result of tenants asking for another landlord; and thirdly, large-scale voluntary sales by councils to other landlords.

The first of these options is unlikely to have a wide impact. There has been fierce tenant opposition to HATs in all of the first six areas proposed for this treatment (Shelter and the London Housing Unit, 1988). The Government has in consequence been forced to scale down the HAT programme and allocate more investment into the few chosen areas. To allay tenants' fears of large-scale property sales and 'gentrification', the Government is likely to have to make further concessions on the extent to which speculative private investment will be permitted. The more HATs become a call on public investment, the less will be Government commitment to them. Indeed, there are far better models for collaborative projects bringing together government, local authorities, housing associations, and tenants to achieve significant area-based improvement schemes. The HAT programme is no signpost to the future.

The so-called 'Tenants' Choice' scheme under which tenants can opt for another landlord is also fatally flawed. The motive is so transparently one of privatization (there is no right to opt back if the tenant does not like the new private landlord), and the voting system is so grotesquely rigged (the freehold of a block can be transferred even if, for example, five times as many tenants vote against the new landlord as in favour) that the scheme has engendered widespread hostility among tenants' groups throughout Britain. It will not prove the popular stablemate to the 'Right to Buy' that the Government hoped. It also involves an absurdly complex and long drawn out procedure that will frustrate even some tenants' groups who do fancy a change of landlord. It is not, therefore, the appropriate means for extending genuine tenant choice and will need to be replaced.

The third type of transfer, the voluntary disposal under which councils can pass over all or part of their housing stock to another landlord, is also problematic. It has been most favoured by Conservative-controlled local authorities with relatively small-scale housing stocks. In other words, it is not an inner-city phenomenon. At the time of writing only two of these transfers had been approved by tenants' ballot (in Sevenoaks and Chiltern Districts) while a much larger number had been rejected (for example in Rochford, Salisbury, Arun, Gloucester, Three Rivers, and Torbay) (Platt, 1989). Although advocates of such local transfers have stressed the advantages of freedom from local authority capital investment controls, and enforced rent increases, the prime motivation has also appeared to be an ideological preference for private rather than public sector provision. It also involves an irrevocable step taken on often very short-term appraisals of the respective merits of disposing or holding on to the stock. If local authorities continue to bear responsibilities for meeting housing needs within their areas, then it is a curious move to divest the authority of all its housing and depend on agreements with the alternative landlords to provide homes for those in need.

Selective transfers of part of the stock to other owners, and indeed to tenant-controlled co-operatives, as in Glasgow, can be a positive and appropriate response, particularly where a local authority is facing difficulty in managing a large stock. However, wholesale transfer of all the stock to another landlord looks suspiciously like abnegation of responsibility. Those authorities which have succeeded in such transfers will only have themselves to blame if they are faced with expensive replacement costs to enable them to meet statutory obligations in the 1990s.

Housing management. A great deal more needs to be done to improve the standard of service and quality of management of public sector housing. For too long there has been a tendency towards insensitive, authoritarian management and in recent years cuts in resources, coupled with increasing demands, have created a position in which too many authorities have tried to meet a whole range of housing needs in their area, when they have not been able to do so. This creates the worst of all worlds. It leads to disillusionment as the public see no prospect of getting help from a public authority and it leaves the councillors disillusioned and frustrated because they want to be able to house and help people, yet they see the council failing. In turn this can easily lead into a depressing cycle of pessimism and recrimination, in which councillors blame the staff, and at the same time the staff blame the councillors.

To break that cycle we need to ease the situation in which excessive demands are focused on local authorities. I have already advocated a more pluralist approach towards provision of housing in the future. I would like to see more responsibilities extended to housing associations and indeed to other bodies, including corporations, so that local authorities can be allowed more freedom and scope to improve their performance. This should make it possible for them to concentrate on providing good quality housing, and managing it well, rather than being crushed by excessive demands that they cannot meet.

Satisfying the customer. We ought to be aiming for a framework where customer satisfaction is the key criterion. What a sign of progress it would be if the local authority was able to put a notice on the door of the housing department saying 'The customer is always right' without this generating cynical and hilarious laughter—which it would do at the moment. That requires much more sensitivity towards the public. Local authorities will need to see their role increasingly in terms of satisfying the needs and aspirations of the customers rather than administering rules which they themselves determine. In part this means new initiatives such as decentralization to make the services more accessible to the public. It also means encouraging more tenant participation, devolving some power to tenants, and helping tenants who want to do so to assume a greater degree of control over the running of their homes and their estates through local management agreements, estate budgets, and co-operatives.

Mirroring a more pluralist framework in the rented sector, there needs to be a wider range of tenancy options in the council stock, embracing at one extreme tenant management co-operatives wholly responsible for the day-to-day management of their homes, through to traditional tenancies where the council assumes full management responsibility and performs this efficiently. In between, tenants should be free to choose tenancy conditions, including or excluding repairing obligations and a range of special services, which suit their needs at that stage in their life. Of course, these may well change over time, and the option of buying in extra services as needed, such as help with cleaning, cooking, or care, should be readily available. Nor should local authorities be deterred from offering such services to home-owners. Such a pattern of provision would both help to meet needs more effectively and contribute to breaking down the social polarization already discussed.

As an incentive to efficient management and as a safeguard for tenants against poor performance by their landlord, there must be accessible and effective means of redress. Standards of performance will need to be clearly defined and tenants must have a swift remedy, perhaps through a housing court, if the landlord fails to meet these standards. Persistent failure could lead to an enforced transfer of the management or ownership of the properties to another body, controlled by the tenants themselves, or to another landlord. This framework would provide a real enhancement to tenant power and choice in contrast to the involved, complex, and bureaucratic 'Tenants' Choice' scheme introduced by the 1988 Housing Act. Unlike the provisions of that Act, it should apply to all non-resident landlords, including housing associations and private landlords, whose tenants may have good grounds for wanting a change of landlord.

Improving the condition of the stock

Finally, we need to take remedial action on the condition of the stock. This requires additional investment; investment in the public sector to tackle the backlog of bad condition properties, and investment through other agencies like housing associations, and indeed corporations, to supplement that work. Financing that investment is going to be expensive, but it is not just a question of seeking additional finance from central government. We have to look rather more creatively at the assets of public authorities. Any private business, sitting on assets the size of our public authorities' housing stocks, would be borrowing money against the security of those assets in order to maintain, renovate, and modernize them, because they would see that as prudent. Instead, Britain is shackled by Treasury conventions which restrict such borrowing through public expenditure controls. At least in respect of housing associations, it has now been accepted that loans raised from private financial sources and matched with government grants should not be treated as public expenditure. A similar approach should be adopted in respect of local authority borrowing, within limits set to ensure that borrowing does not exceed prudent limits in relationship to the value of the authority's assets.

We also need an improved and simplified grant system to tackle the problems confronting in particular poor and elderly home-owners. This should be supplemented by agency schemes to assist people who have not got the necessary technical skills, or the ability, to go through the many stages of getting their home improved, such as obtaining planning consents, seeking tenders from builders, and supervising the building work.

We should recognize that there is no long-term future for the bulk of the private rented stock. The private landlord cannot be revived as a realistic means of providing affordable homes for low-income groups. The private rented sector also still contains a concentration of bad condition housing. The sooner that is acquired by responsible landlords, improved and made available to people in need, the better. The transfer of the bulk of the remaining privately rented stock, apart from the small sections of the market which are economically viable, should be achieved as quickly as possible.

CONCLUSION

Contrary to the views of the Government, there is a major role for public sector agencies and for the Government both in prompting and in taking action to tackle the problems. Investment is essential both to build new homes and tackle the backlog of disrepair, as is a reform of the subsidy system to create a fairer and more effective bridge between cost and resources. So too is a more pluralist framework which ensures more choice for the consumer and a better standard of service. These are the key objectives I believe we should be aiming for in the inner city and these are the principles which should underpin an effective urban housing policy for the 1990s.

References

AMA (1987), 'Greater London home condition survey', Association of Metropolitan Authorities (London).

Audit Commission (1989), *Housing the Homeless: The Local Authority Role* (London).

Nationwide Anglia Building Society (1988), 'Memorandum inviting participation in Nationwide Anglia First Rented Housing BES Fund' (London).

Platt, S. (1989), 'On the home front', *New Statesman and Society*, 31 Mar.

Raynsford, N., and Morris, G. (1988), Unpublished exemplifications prepared for the National Federation of Housing Associations.

Shelter and the London Housing Unit (1988), 'Housing Action Trusts (HATs): The struggle begins' (London).

Thomas, A., and Niner, P. (1989), *Living in Temporary Accommodation: A Survey of Homeless People* (London).

Treasury (1988), *Housing and Construction Statistics 1977–1987* (London).

—— (1989), *The Government's Expenditure Plans 1989–90 to 1991–92*, Cmnd. 621 (London).

Ward, M., and Zebedee, J. (1989), 'Guide to Housing Benefit and Community Charge Benefit', SHAC and the Institute of Housing (London).

10

Urban Renaissance? The Arts and the Urban Regeneration Process

Franco Bianchini

> The arts create a climate of optimism—the 'can do' attitude
> essential to developing the 'enterprise culture' this Govern
> ment hopes to bring to deprived areas. Inner city economic
> stagnation is a downward spiral . . . The arts provide a
> means of breaking this spiral and helping people believe in
> themselves and their community again.
>
> (Arts Council of Great Britain, 1988)

This chapter outlines the process by which the potential of the
arts in urban regeneration was recognized, and describes how the
cultural policies adopted by some British cities during the last
decade relate to local strategies for economic, social, and physical
development. After a discussion of the political and economic
implications of current forms of 'arts-led' urban regeneration, the
chapter sets out the case for democratic, locally accountable
'cultural planning' in Britain's towns and cities.

THE NATIONAL CONSENSUS ABOUT THE ARTS AND URBAN SOCIAL INTEGRATION

In many respects, a nineteenth-century definition of 'the arts' and
of the role of the arts in urban policy dominated policy development in Britain until the 1980s. The term 'art' had long been used
in English to mean any sort of human skill but, by the end of the
last century, the phrase 'the arts' had been restricted to music,
theatre, painting, sculpture, and literature. The fields of activity
chosen by the Arts Council after its creation in 1946 largely
coincided with the Victorian redefinition of the arts. Indeed, the

Arts Council did not admit until 1967 to its canon of 'art' worthy of public subsidy such popular, twentieth-century cultural forms as jazz and photography, and it established its own Film, Video, and Broadcasting Department as late as 1987.

The belief in the arts as a vehicle for social integration in urban areas, which emerged in the turbulent 1840s (Minihan, 1977, pp. 85–95), also became part of the Arts Council's ideological inheritance. The Arts Council has traditionally attributed a civilizing, ennobling value to 'the arts', and has seen them as important to achieve the integration of different social groups and identities into a supposedly politically neutral 'national culture'.

A concrete demonstration of this stance was provided in the 1970s, when the Arts Council had to respond to the challenge of the developing 'community arts' and 'ethnic arts' movements. Both movements were very active in deprived inner-city areas and both questioned the Arts Council's distinction between 'high' and 'low' culture. They often used contemporary art forms and believed that the public's involvement in the creative process could help bring about social and political change.

By 1975 the Arts Council had responded to these pressures and had begun to fund community arts groups. It did so on the advice of its own Community Arts Working Party, chaired by Harold Baldry, whose report was published in June 1974. The Baldry Report, which was written with the specific purpose of persuading the Arts Council bureaucracy to fund community arts, deliberately overlooked some of the more subversive aspects of the community arts movement. The report enabled the Arts Council to stress the 'educational' function of community arts, and neutralize the radical potential of the movement, by redefining community arts as simply an intermediate stage in the march towards the appreciation of 'high' art (Kelly, 1984, pp. 15–25).

The concept of 'ethnic arts' was coined by Naseem Khan in *The Arts Britain Ignores* (1976), a book commissioned by the Arts Council, the Gulbenkian Foundation, and the Community Relations Commission. It was the first comprehensive survey of the cultural life of ethnic minorities in Britain; the Arts Council welcomed its recommendations, and contributed £5,000 towards the establishment of a Minority Arts Advisory Service (MAAS).

Black commentators, however, strongly criticized the 'melting pot' approach adopted in *The Arts Britain Ignores*. Kwesi Owusu (1986), for example, argued that 'to equate Black and White immigrant communities is a mistake . . . Naseem Khan justified this approach by attributing to all cultures and traditions a common problem: that of integration into the mainstream of British culture' (pp. 56–7).

The Arts Council's 'pre-electronic' definition of the arts and its belief in the 'integrationist' function of participation in cultural activities were part of a wider consensus, which encompassed the Labour party. For example, in 1977 the Arts Study Group of Labour's National Executive Committee (NEC) published *The Arts and the People*, a background paper which subsequently formed the basis for a NEC policy statement approved at that year's party conference. In keeping with the consensus, *The Arts and the People* clearly implied that ethnic and community arts could help achieve social cohesion, particularly in the inner cities. It recommended, for instance, that more 'ethnic minority arts projects' be funded under the Labour Government's Urban Aid Programme and stressed that 'local authorities should be made to realise how helpful community-based artistic creativity can be in building up a unified and harmonious neighbourhood' (Labour Party, 1977, p. 57).

This consensus view on the role of the arts in urban policy did not include any serious consideration of the potential contribution of the arts to local economic development. This attitude was largely the product of a widespread tendency among cultural policy-makers to 'define culture as a realm separate from, and often actively opposed to, the realm of material production and economic activity' (Garnham, 1983, p. 1), the origins of which can once again be traced back to the nineteenth century (Williams, 1958).

FROM SOCIAL INTEGRATION TO ECONOMIC DEVELOPMENT: THE CONTRIBUTIONS OF THATCHERISM AND THE 1981–1986 GLC

The separation between the cultural and the economic sphere in British arts policy increasingly came under attack in the 1980s.

The attack on the arts policy consensus was launched by two very different, even conflicting political forces: the post-1979 Conservative governments led by Margaret Thatcher, and the Labour Left which gained control of the Greater London Council (GLC) in 1981.

In the arts, the Thatcher governments reduced the role of public subsidy, at the same time as enhancing reliance on the private sector. From 1979 to 1985, the Treasury grant-in-aid to the Arts Council grew in real terms by a mere 0.6 per cent per year. It was the smallest annual rate of increase under any government since the institution of the Arts Council itself, whose difficulties were made more serious by the fact that inflation in the performing arts is higher than in other sectors of the economy (Baumol and Bowen, 1966). One of the Arts Council's crucial responses to the crisis was *A Great British Success Story* (1985), which marked an important shift of attitudes by making the case for increased public funding for the arts more on *economic* than on moral or social grounds. The document, written in the style of a business prospectus, explicitly identified the potential role of the arts in the economic regeneration of the inner cities, in attracting tourists and foreign currency, and in creating employment. Its impact, however, was probably limited by the decision to concentrate on the narrower argument that the arts provided 'a very good return on the public's money' (Arts Council, 1985, p. 6), through VAT on tickets, income tax, and national insurance payments. *The Times*, for one, found this argument 'uncomfortably reminiscent of the all-too-familiar proof that there is no such thing as an uneconomic coal mine' (6 March 1985).

The Arts Council and the national arts policy establishment were clearly induced to reconsider their views on the relationship between the arts and the economic sphere primarily by the political pressures of Thatcherism. However, the single most important influence on the cultural policies of urban local authorities in the 1980s was the GLC under Ken Livingstone's leadership (1981–6).

The GLC formulated and implemented its cultural policies primarily through its Arts and Recreation Committee (ARC) and Industry and Employment Committee (IEC). The two committees shared important features. For example, they employed a much wider definition of 'the arts' than that adopted by the Arts Council, and prioritized contemporary cultural forms, including photography, video, electronic music, and community radio. There were, however, some crucial differences between the two committees' ideological and policy approaches.

The ARC's initiatives on community and ethnic arts targeted certain 'communities of interest'—blacks, the women's and gay rights movements, the Irish community, youth groups, the elderly, and the disabled—and developed a radical critique of 'social integration' as an objective for arts policy in inner-city areas. The committee was innovative in many respects, especially in creating policy-making and grant-allocating structures which devolved power and resources to those 'communities of interest' themselves. But, like the Arts Council, the ARC allocated grants to clients on the basis of annual deficit funding (Bianchini, 1987). The IEC, however, explicitly rejected this traditional notion of the economics of the arts. Its strategy deserves—for the purposes of this chapter—a more detailed examination than that pursued by the ARC.

The IEC had been set up by the Livingstone administration in 1981 to attempt to increase the range and choice of jobs open to Londoners, by stimulating as well as directly providing investment in both manufacturing and services. The GLC also established the Economic Policy Group (EPG), a small unit of economists whose duty was to help the IEC draw up a new 'London Industrial Strategy', which would be implemented by a new interventionist agency, the Greater London Enterprise Board (GLEB). Nicholas Garnham, Professor of Communications at the Polytechnic of Central London, worked with the EPG to develop a 'cultural industries strategy' within the wider industrial strategy. Garnham defined the 'cultural industries' as 'those social practices which have as their primary purpose the transmission of meaning' (GLC, 1983, pp. 1–2). These included the performing arts, sports, the music industry, advertising, broadcasting, the film, video, and photographic industry, and printing and publishing.

The cultural industries strategy was more important for its

conceptual innovations than for its practical achievements. The GLC's and GLEB's total expenditure on it in 1984 and 1985 was only £600,000. By way of comparison, the revenue expenditure of the ARC on its cultural policies exceeded £20 million in the single financial year 1983–4.

Nevertheless, under Garnham's guidance, the EPG lucidly demonstrated the economic importance of the cultural industries. Its research showed that in 1983 London's cultural industries sector employed about 250,000 people—112,000 in printing and publishing, a further 50,000 in film, video, and broadcasting, and about 20,000 in advertising. The EPG also articulated a major critique of the policy of deficit funding pursued by both the Arts Council and the ARC. This was most cogently expressed in *Cultural Industries Strategy* (June 1984), a report which argued that public cultural policies tended to have 'a relatively marginal impact' on consumption of cultural commodities and services, since they had traditionally been directed at activities which could rarely be commercially viable. The report concluded that the only way for the public sector to have an impact 'both on economic and employment patterns and on "culture" in its broadest sense' would be to intervene 'through and not against the market'.

The alternative approach advocated by the EPG was embodied by a Cultural Industries Unit, established within GLEB in the summer of 1984. The Unit's work was based on investments through loans and equity rather than subsidy. It supported only arts bodies which seemed likely to become commercially viable enterprises, and provided them with 'common services' typical of the commercial sector—marketing, management consultancy, advice on the introduction of new technology.

The importance of the IEC model was that it showed how cultural policy could form an integral part of the local economic development framework. Nevertheless, it failed to integrate cultural policy into a wider *urban regeneration* project. Its strategy was confined to the economic sphere. It did not address the questions of the physical and social regeneration of the inner city. To find examples of the use of the arts to lead a broader process of urban regeneration, we have to turn to the experience of other

Labour-controlled cities, such as Sheffield, Birmingham, Liverpool, Newcastle upon Tyne, and Glasgow during the 1980s, where arts initiatives became an increasingly visible part of local responses to the decline of manufacturing industry and steep rises in unemployment.

THE ARTS AND URBAN REGENERATION: THREE POLICY MODELS

The GLC experience initially raised awareness of the potential of the arts in economic development in all five cities. As in London, bodies responsible for economic development took the lead on a range of cultural policy issues.

More specifically, the GLC model had a considerable influence on the policies adopted by the five city councils for the development of local cultural industries. In most cases, however, policies inspired by the GLC's cultural industries strategy—with its emphasis on production and distribution—coexisted with a more 'consumerist' approach to 'arts-led' regeneration. The single most important source of inspiration for this approach was the experience of many American cities in the 1970s and 1980s.

The growth of arts funding in the United States, from both corporate and federal sources (particularly after the establishment of the National Endowment for the Arts in 1965), contributed to a remarkable expansion in the number and range of cultural activities and organizations during the 1970s, which in turn created a pressure for the construction and renovation of arts facilities. In many American central cities, arts groups became partners in 'growth coalitions' that included local government, corporations, financial institutions, preservationists, and developers. They were largely extensions of the kind of coalitions which had been formed in some major cities around the aim of downtown development, for reasons aptly described by Norman and Susan Fainstein (1982, pp. 161–2):

At least in a number of prominent places such as New York, Boston, San Francisco and Denver . . . downtown has become a source of profit once more as its uses have changed—the factory, the port and the working class district have been replaced by the office, the tourist centre and the upper class neighbourhood.

The arts appealed to downtown growth coalitions for a number of reasons. They could strengthen cities in the intense inter urban competition for the lucrative and growing tourist trade. They could enhance public perceptions of downtown real estate developments and their long-term appreciation potential. They provided local government not only with an increased tax base, but also with opportunities to create new employment and revitalize under-used areas. Opera, ballet, classical music, and other 'high' art forms, in particular, reinforced the central city's appeal to crucial economic élites. Lastly, both high art and more popular forms of cultural animation (street theatre, for instance) attracted consumers to downtown shops, hotels, and restaurants and helped the city centre fight off competition from the new out-of-town shopping developments.

Two of the products of the participation of the arts to downtown growth coalitions were the inclusion of cultural facilities in mixed-use developments (MXDs) and the creation of 'cultural districts'. Both the MXD and the cultural district combine the arts with a variety of mutually supportive revenue-producing uses, such as office, residential, hotel, retail, and recreation. The various components are functionally and physically integrated, and are developed according to a coherent plan. MXDs and cultural districts were a reaction against the 'splendid isolation' of arts facilities from the rest of city activities, which was a common feature of many American arts centres built in the 1950s and 1960s. Arts organizations, in conclusion, benefited from their integration into MXDs and districts designated also for commercial and residential uses, because they came into contact with potential new audiences, with people who normally would not have attended arts events. But two even more important incentives for arts groups were the possibilities of finding new premises and of achieving long-term financial viability. In some cases both of these opportunities were provided by intermediary non-profit making organizations in which the arts community was represented jointly with the local authority, the developers, and other partners. Their duty was to manage, maintain, and promote the MXD or the cultural district (Snedcof, 1985).

A third strand of policy-making, which had some influence on developments in the five British cities under consideration, was the use of cultural policy to transform the city centre into a focus for civic identity. This approach derived from the experience of Left-controlled local authorities in Italy and other Southern European countries since the late 1970s. Its primary object was not to regenerate the local economy, but rather to encourage residents to 'rediscover' the city centre. This was achieved by making the city centre safer, more accessible, and more attractive, through a strategy which encompassed policies not only on cultural animation but also on public transport, policing, planning, and environmental improvements.[1]

We shall now return to the arts-led urban regeneration process in our five British case-studies and examine how the three external policy influences described above interacted with local strategies.

LOCAL EXPERIENCES

Glasgow

Of the five British cities examined here, Glasgow was the first to implement successfully a 'consumerist' arts-led urban regeneration strategy. The pragmatic, Labour-controlled Glasgow District

---

[1] The experience of the Communist-controlled City Councils of Rome (1976–85) and Bologna influenced the development of policies by the 1981–6 GLC. The first was probably a direct source of inspiration for the GLC's cultural animation policies (the festivals on the South Bank, for instance), while the second may have inspired the GLC's introduction of cheap fares for London's underground and bus services. According to Raphael Samuel (*New Left Review*, Nov.–Dec. 1985, p. 19) a reading of Jaggi, Muller and Schmid, *Red Bologna*, published by Writers and Readers co-operative in 1977, was part of the preparatory work of the new [Labour] group. The example of the Communist administration in Rome, with its splendid summer programme of open air films and festivals, was also very much in the mind of the GLCers in one of their happiest innovations, the linking of municipal socialism to public gaiety. The influence of the Bologna and Rome examples was felt also outside London. *Red Bologna* increased awareness of the radical potential of local government among Labour

Council (GDC) realized that the city should reconstruct its own image (which was frequently associated with violence, drunkenness, and urban decay) in order to attempt to compensate for lost manufacturing jobs by attracting new companies and business investment, and by expanding the financial sector, tourism, and related consumer service industries. The arts played a key symbolic role in furthering the process of transformation of the image and the economic base of the city. In 1987 Arts Minister Richard Luce designated Glasgow as the UK choice for the title of 'European City of Culture' for 1990 (following such prestigious places as Athens, Florence, Amsterdam, West Berlin, and Paris): an award which GDC subsequently trumpeted as the clearest proof of the city's renaissance.

However, Glasgow's achievement was the result of policy initiatives which went well beyond the arts field and which involved not only GDC but also other agencies.

Of the three models for policy-making outlined in the previous section, the cultural industries approach was the most marginal to the urban regeneration process in Glasgow. The American model was much more influential. In Glasgow, as in many American cities, local public and private sector forces were united in using the arts as a vehicle for economic regeneration. The Glasgow coalition was supported by national public sector bodies such as the Scottish Arts Council and the Scottish Development Agency (SDA). The main local partners were GDC, Strathclyde Regional Council, and Glasgow Action, a 'private-public' partnership, the formation of which had been specifically influenced by American models such as Pittsburgh's Allegheny Conference on Community Development.

Glasgow Action was one of the products of two major studies, conducted by consultants McKinsey & Co. and published in 1984 and 1985, on the development potential of Glasgow city centre. Following the McKinsey reports, Glasgow Action adopted a strategy with three targets: 'continuing to update the City Centre environment', 'improving the image of the city', and 'building

activists and local councillors throughout the country. And there are distinct echoes of the cultural policy of Rome City Council (described in my article in *New Socialist*, Apr. 1987) in Liverpool City Council (1987a).

Glasgow's tourist industry' (Boyle, 1988). The partners in the local coalition took a number of individual and joint initiatives towards the achievement of the three targets.

Physical improvements in the inner city had begun in 1976, when the SDA launched Glasgow Eastern Area Renewal (GEAR). Jointly with GDC, the SDA also carried out various land renewal and environmental improvement schemes, including the cleaning of many fine sandstone buildings, which again contributed to altering the public's perception of the city. Another important initiative was taken by Glasgow Action. With support from GDC and the SDA, it rejuvenated the section of the city centre known as 'Merchant City' (an area of formerly derelict warehouses), by promoting fashionable housing and retail schemes.

The single most effective contribution to the 'city marketing' effort was probably the 'Glasgow's Miles Better' advertising campaign, co-ordinated by GDC and launched by former Lord Provost, Michael Kelly. It was, once again, based on an American model—the successful 'I Love NY' campaign—and featured the smiling Mr Happy, a cartoon character from Roger Hargreaves' *Mr Men* books. Advertisements were placed in London in 1984 (on buses, taxis, in underground and railway stations) and in various publications aimed at the international business community.

However, the contribution of the arts to the development of the tourist industry was much more significant than in the field of physical renewal and more directly measurable than their role in enhancing the city's image. The key actors in the tourism strategy were GDC, Strathclyde Regional Council, and the Greater Glasgow Tourist Board (GGTB).

'Arts tourism' was given a major boost in 1983, with the opening of the Burrell Collection and the launch of Mayfest, Glasgow's major annual arts festival. GDC owns and operates the Burrell museum, which attracted over 1,100,000 visitors in 1984 (Myerscough, 1988*a*, p. 175). Mayfest came into existence largely as an initiative of the Scottish trade union movement, but the main funding for it has traditionally been provided by GDC. The Burrell Collection and Mayfest further strengthened Glasgow' cultural infrastructure, which was already quite powerful in the performing arts field. For example, in addition to prestigious national arts institutions (Scottish Opera, Scottish Ballet, the Scottish National Orchestra, and the BBC Scottish Symphony Orchestra), the city hosts various drama companies, including the internationally renowned Citizens' Theatre. After the opening of the Scottish Exhibition and Conference Centre in 1985, Glasgow Action, the GGTB, and GDC co-operated with the Scottish Arts Council, Strathclyde Regional Council, and the city's myriad arts groups to create a programme of cultural animation for the summer months, when theatres and other arts venues and places of entertainment were closed. This included a series of new international festivals of choral and folk music, jazz, dance, and street theatre, and was aimed at making Glasgow more competitive on the international convention tourism market. After Glasgow's nomination as 'European City of Culture' in 1987, GDC established its own Festivals Unit, to co-ordinate a three-year programme of celebrations, performances, exhibitions, publications, and conferences culminating in the 'European cultural capital' celebrations of 1990. GDC plan to spend an additional £6 million on arts projects for 1990, around £200,000 of which would be devoted to commissioning new work—including two new operas.

In conclusion, the style and the goals of the Glasgow coalition resembled those typical of 'growth coalitions' which had involved the arts in the regeneration of some American cities. But, by the late 1980s, the leading actor in the arts-led regeneration process was clearly Glasgow District Council. GDC is now endowed with its own distinctive cultural policy, and is able to set the arts investment agenda for other local—public and private—funding bodies. In this sense, Glasgow is moving towards the model of cultural policy-making which prevails in major cities in France, Italy, West Germany, and other West European countries, where local authorities often commission new cultural work and co-ordinate an annual programme of arts events to which other public and private funding bodies can respond.

Sheffield

By the end of the 1980s, Sheffield had adopted Glasgow's strategy of exploiting the arts to shed its negative image as a declining industrial city. But there were clear differences between the two cities, in terms both of policy approaches and of the actors who took the lead. Unlike Glasgow, in Sheffield there was no coalition of public and private sector forces, supported by national funding agencies. By contrast, cultural policy was developed chiefly by the City Council's Department of Employment and Economic Development (DEED), which had been set up in 1981 in response to the rise in local unemployment from 5 per cent in 1979 to 11 per cent. As in the GLC case, the political initiative behind the new employment strategy came from a group of councillors on the Left of the party, under the leadership of David Blunkett.

Between 1983 and 1987, the Council adopted a GLC-style cultural industries strategy, demonstrating how this could play a leading role in the revitalization of part of the city centre. It created a 'Cultural Industries Quarter' in a previously run-down industrial area in the southern section of the city centre, with two main complexes: the Leadmill and the Audio-Visual Enterprise Centre (AVEC). The Leadmill opened in 1982 as a venue mainly for rock bands, but has expanded into an adjoining former cutlery factory now transformed into an arts and media training and exhibition centre. The AVEC is linked with Red Tape, Britain's first municipal recording studios and rehearsal rooms, and houses the Untitled Photographic Gallery and Workshop and recording studios owned by two of Sheffield's best-known rock bands. The complex will be extended to provide new premises for the Anvil, a successful 'civic cinema' opened by the Council in 1983, and for Sheffield Independent Film, an umbrella organization for local independent film and video-makers. The council also plan to attract a whole range of small arts enterprises to the Quarter and to forge links with the adjacent Science Park, to initiate research into the development of new technology in image and music recording.

The outstanding feature of Sheffield's cultural industries strategy is the creation of local structures for production, distribution, employment, and training, with an emphasis on contemporary cultural forms—electronic music, film and video, broadcasting, fashion, and graphic design. But the Council is also developing a second cultural district in the heart of the city, in Tudor Square, focused around more traditional, 'pre-electronic' art forms. Tudor Square is to be transformed into an 'arts square' featuring the Crucible Theatre, the restored Lyceum Theatre, the Ruskin Crafts Gallery, the city's Central Library, and a proposed new hotel and art gallery. Unlike cultural districts in the United States, the square is to contain only a minimal number of shops and no offices and residential units. Rather, it is designated to create a 'continental European' civic square: 'a place for people in which events, both planned and spontaneous, can be enjoyed' (RHWL Partnership, 1988, p. 41). The Cultural Industries Quarter and Tudor Square will be the focal points of a major youth-oriented cultural festival during the World Student Games, which will be hosted by Sheffield in 1991. The Games themselves are seen by the Council as an excellent opportunity to project internationally the new image of Sheffield as both a reborn, enterprising city, and a mecca for sports and youth culture.

In Birmingham, Newcastle, and Liverpool there were—just as in Sheffield—attempts to develop the local cultural industries infrastructure. But they were accompanied by more 'consumerist' strategies, focused—more as in Glasgow—upon 'prestige' arts developments.

Birmingham

After Labour took control in 1984, Birmingham City Council adopted both the cultural industries and the 'consumerist' approach to arts-based regeneration. The Council felt that the arts could contribute to enhancing the image, the amenities, and the distinctive character of the city centre. After a series of post-war planning disasters, the condition of the city centre was widely perceived as the main problem Birmingham had to tackle in order to improve its own overall image, and market itself as an international business centre.

The focus of the cultural industries strategy is in the Digbeth district, where the council have created a 'Media Zone'. The launch of a Media Development Agency (in December 1988) will be followed by the establishment of a Media Enterprise Centre, to promote the formation of media–related businesses, and encourage them to locate in Digbeth. A longer–term target is to set up a Design and Media Centre, a major venue for the exhibition and promotion of design and media activities and products.

The area of the city around the new International Convention Centre (ICC), to be opened in 1991, is the major physical focus for the 'consumerist' approach, which is particularly aimed at expanding business tourism. The ICC will include facilities for up to 1,500 delegates and a new concert hall for the City of Birmingham Symphony Orchestra (CBSO). The hall is the Council's reward for the CBSO's successful work as a cultural ambassador for the city. The redevelopment of the ICC area will be completed with the construction of Brindley Place, an MXD which will comprise three office buildings, an American–style 'festival shopping' centre, a hotel, open canalside areas, the National Aquarium, and the National Indoor Sports Arena.

In short, the Council hopes that the city's new cultural 'aura' will help improve its credibility in international business circles. To this purpose, the Council is supporting annual festivals of jazz, film, and television, in addition to the CBSO. The Council's vision of Birmingham's future is also at the basis of its plans to create Parisian–style quarters in the city centre: the Media Quarter in Digbeth, Chinatown, the Jewellery Quarter, the theatre and entertainment district, the Gun Quarter, the civic and business districts.[2]

[2] On Birmingham City Council's strategies for the cultural industries and the city centre see Comedia, *Birmingham Audio-Visual Industry* (April 1987), *Birmingham City Centre Review* (Apr. 1987) and the proceedings of the *City Centre Challenge Symposium*, held in March 1988. On the Brindley Place MXD see *Birmingham Business Today* (autumn 1988). For a critique of the Council's plans for the city centre see Birmingham for People, *What Kind of Birmingham?* (Jan. 1989).

Newcastle upon Tyne

Newcastle City Council, like Birmingham, was controlled by a moderate Labour group. Under the leadership of Jeremy Beecham, who was elected in 1976, the cultural policy of Newcastle City Council was chiefly aimed at enhancing the quality and variety of local opportunities for cultural *consumption*. Such a target was consonant with the local Labour leaders' traditional belief in the necessity of reasserting the function of Newcastle as a regional capital, with a catchment area of about 3 million people. Both Beecham and his predecessor T. Dan Smith, the leader of the Council from 1966 to 1974, were part of this tradition. The Labour leadership's aspirations help explain why the Council adopted a cultural policy which one commentator has defined as ' "auditoria"-led' (McKellar, 1988). The Council helped renovate and relaunch the Georgian Theatre Royal, the Victorian Tyne Theatre and Opera House, and the Tyneside Cinema. It also contributed to the conversion of a group of ten derelict listed buildings into the Newcastle Arts Centre, an MXD which houses media workshops, exhibition spaces, and a studio theatre.

The Council's regional capital vision was shared by The Newcastle Initiative (TNI), an organization formed in June 1988 as a result of *Initiatives Beyond Charity*, a report on the role of business in urban regeneration by the National Task Force of the Confederation of British Industry. TNI works with public sector bodies, including the City Council, but is firmly controlled by the private sector. Its Board consists exclusively of senior members from local business and the academic community, and its Chairman has to be chosen from the business element of the Board. One of TNI's 'flagship' projects to promote Newcastle's role as 'a vibrant and stylish regional capital' (TNI, 1988*a*) is the creation of a 'Theatre Village' in the West End of the city, an area which the restored Tyne Theatre and the newly opened Newcastle Arts Centre are beginning to revitalize. The 'task force' set up by TNI to implement the Theatre Village scheme is chaired by John Hall, the entrepreneur who built the giant Metro shopping centre at Gateshead, whose conception was clearly influenced by the carefully planned 'festival atmosphere' pervading many shopping developments in the United States. The study on the potential of the Theatre Village, commissioned by Hall from the Northern Region of the Royal Institute of British Architects (RIBA), proposed the creation of an American-style cultural district with cultural industries components (TNI, 1988*b*).

Liverpool

Liverpool City Council's first ever arts and cultural industries strategy was published as late as November 1987. This initiative was very much a product of the May 1987 local elections, when a new Labour group rose to power. It replaced the forty-seven Labour councillors (about a quarter of whom were associated with Militant, the Trotskyist intra-party faction) who had been surcharged and banned from office in March that year, when the House of Lords turned down their appeal against being punished for setting a rate too late in 1985. Under the Militant-controlled Labour administration (1983–7), both cultural policy and economic development had been neglected. The 'urban regeneration strategy' co-ordinated by the Chair of the Finance Committee, Tony Byrne, prioritized the renewal of the city's housing stock. The Militant-controlled Council had also been fundamentally hostile to the Merseyside Development Corporation (MDC), which had been established by Conservative Environment Secretary Michael Heseltine in 1981. Such hostility extended to the restoration of the warehouses of the city's Albert Dock, the largest group of Grade 1 listed buildings in Britain, which the MDC successfully transformed into an MXD with a strong arts component. By 1988 the complex housed the Tate Gallery in the North, a Maritime Museum, Granada TV's regional news centre and several offices, shops, restaurants, exhibition spaces, and residential apartments. In marked contrast with the attitudes prevailing during the Militant era, one of the first urban strategy documents issued after the new Labour group gained control recognized that the regeneration of the docks provided 'an asset to the city' (Liverpool City Council, 1987*b*, p. 32), and stressed the need to strengthen the visual and physical links between the Albert Dock and the city centre.

One of the main objects of the Council's new cultural industries strategy, not unlike in Sheffield and Birmingham, is to create local facilities for cultural training, production, management, distribution, and marketing. For instance, the Council has helped establish Music City, an agency for the development of the local pop and rock scene. Two other interesting initiatives are the appointment of Britain's first municipal Film Liaison Officer, to encourage film-makers to use Liverpool as a location, and the launch of the Hope Street Project, a theatrical training scheme attached to the Everyman Theatre.

The most innovative aspect of the Liverpool approach is probably the way in which arts and cultural industries strategy is integrated into both the overall economic development framework and the city centre strategy formulated by the Council (see concluding section of this chapter). This augurs well for the future development by the Council of a coherent and detailed arts-based strategy for the regeneration of the city.

The Politics of 'Arts-led' Urban Regeneration

As we have seen, the role of the arts in urban regeneration is increasingly considered by local élites as crucial in improving a city's chances to enhance its image, in attracting tourists, and in boosting a new service-based economy. A new political consensus has emerged, particularly around the usefulness of 'prestige' arts projects. Labour local authorities of different political orientations broadly agree on the aims of prestige arts-led development. But such consensus goes much wider than Labour-controlled local councils. Both the Arts Council (as shown by this chapter's opening quotation) and Conservative Arts Minister Richard Luce have wholeheartedly embraced the concept of arts-led urban regeneration. Indeed, Luce recently defined the arts as 'the heartbeat of urban regeneration', since arts projects can create 'individual and community optimism and pride, feelings of hope and possibilities where perhaps before there was none' (*Glasgow Herald*, 19 October 1988).

The Thatcher Government itself, in the 1987 document *Action for Cities*, recognized that 'arts projects which attract local support make places much more pleasant to live and work and encourage commercial development' (DoE, 1987, p. 25). The document indicated Bradford as one of the cities where the regeneration potential of the arts had been realized. The City of Bradford Metropolitan Council is indeed an interesting example of cross-party consensus about the use of the arts in urban regeneration. Under Conservative control, the Council negotiated the de-centralization of part of the facilities of London's Science Museum, and co-ordinated the subsequent opening of the National Museum of Photography, Film and Television, in a redundant theatre building in Bradford city centre (1983). The Conservative administration also established an Economic Development Unit (EDU) in 1979, which adopted the title 'The Mythbreakers' and launched a campaign to reconstruct the image of the city. After Labour took control in 1986, it continued to support the work of both the EDU and the National Museum, which in 1987 attracted about 750,000 visitors. Building on the successful refurbishment of the Alhambra Theatre by the Conservative-controlled Council, Labour launched in November 1986 an ambitious plan for the transformation of the West End of the city into a cultural district. This would contain the National Museum, the Alhambra, and the northern touring base of the National Theatre, together with a media centre, a multi-screen cinema, a 1,250-seat bingo hall, a bowling alley, and a 'speciality' shopping centre. The West End would be linked with Little Germany, the city's historic merchant quarter, which Labour planned to upgrade with new offices, restaurants, shops, and housing, as well as art galleries, crafts workshops, design and performance centres. After a by-election in September 1988, the Conservatives regained control of the Council. They immediately pushed through a £5.8 million cuts package, dramatically reduced the social services and education budgets, and planned to privatize various leisure centres and to sell fifteen old people's homes. Remarkably, however, the new radical Thatcherite Council, which broke with the policies of its Labour predecessor in almost all fields, continued to support the West End and Little Germany projects, and the related tourism strategy.

This bipartisan consensus is certainly based on the fact that, as

confirmed by our case studies, the arts can contribute positively
to both the physical renewal and the economic regeneration of
the inner cities.

Physical renewal

The contribution of the arts to urban renewal has taken two main
forms. The first is the inclusion of arts facilities into programmes
of renovation and conversion of buildings and districts. In some
cases, the rise in the value of property and land generated by
arts activities has attracted developers and financial investors to
previously run-down urban areas. The second main kind of
contribution is the use of the visual arts and the crafts to enhance
buildings and districts aesthetically, particularly in the city centre.
In some cities, local authorities have co-ordinated programmes
of 'urban beautification' and 'place making', involving the introduction of 'percentage for art' and 'public art' schemes. Examples
of this kind can be found in Birmingham—where the City
Council, in 1983, decided to spend 1 per cent of the construction
costs of the International Convention Centre on artworks within
the building—and, more significantly, in Dundee and Swansea,
two other Labour-controlled cities.[3]

Economic regeneration

The first aspect which must be considered here is the impact of
arts policies on training and employment. The number of arts
jobs which have been created as a direct result of the arts policies
of the five cities under consideration is relatively small. It is also
probably too early to assess the impact of local cultural industries
strategies on job creation. What can be said is that participation in

---

[3] On 'place making' see R. Lee Fleming and R. Von Tscharner, *Place Makers:
Creating Public Art That Tells You Where You Are* (Cambridge, Mass., 1981).
'Percent for art' ordinances (currently adopted by 22 states and over 80 cities in
the USA) normally require that 1 per cent of a local authority's capital improve-
ment budget be earmarked for artworks in public places. On public art
programmes in Swansea and Dundee see Swansea City Council, *Swansea
Maritime Quarter* (1988), and Dundee Public Arts Programme, *Public Art in
Dundee 1985–1988* (1988).

arts activities can encourage people who have not been adequately catered for by formal education to undertake further education and training. More specifically, cultural industries projects targeted at the unemployed—Sheffield's Red Tape, for instance—did offer a contribution to the development not only of vocational skills, but also of 'personal effectiveness' and 'enterprise skills'. These can help unemployed people to find work, if not in the cultural industries sector, then in other sectors of the economy (Centre for Employment Initiatives, 1988).

John Myerscough's studies have provided some insight on arts employment and on the number of jobs created by the spending of arts organizations and their customers in Merseyside and Glasgow, in 1985 and 1985–6 respectively (Myerscough, 1988*b*; 1988*a*). These studies have some limitations in that they refer to a period *before* major initiatives were taken. Myerscough's findings, however, usefully illustrate the economic importance of the arts, and their potential for future regeneration initiatives. For example, 3,242 people were employed in the arts and cultural industries in Merseyside and 10,550 in Glasgow. Spending by arts organizations and their customers sustained a further 3,405 and 4,185 jobs respectively. Total 'direct' and 'indirect' arts employment amounted to 1.23 per cent of the economically active population in Merseyside and 2.25 per cent in Glasgow. Each job in the arts generated 2.8 jobs in the rest of the economy in Merseyside and 2.7 in Glasgow (Myerscough, 1988*c*, p. 140). The arts not only sustained jobs in retailing and other personal service industries, but also contributed to the tourism industry. Glasgow's cultural renaissance was certainly a factor in the increase in the annual number of tourist trips to the city from about 1.85 million in 1985 to nearly 2.1 million in 1987.[4] More specifically, Myerscough has calculated that cultural amenities were the 'sole reason' in the decision to visit Merseyside and Glasgow by 28 per cent and 23 per cent of all tourists respectively. Cultural amenities were a 'very important' to 'fairly important' reason for a further 38 per cent in Merseyside and 63 per cent in Glasgow. (Myerscough, 1988*b*, p. 35; 1988*c*, p. 72).

[4] Figures supplied by the Greater Glasgow Tourist Board and the Scottish Tourist Board.

Finally, Myerscough's surveys of Merseyside and Glasgow middle managers and technologists shed some light on the contribution of the arts to improving a city's public image, and to appealing to business and labour élites. 'Museums, theatres, concerts and other cultural facilities' were an important factor affecting the selection of the place in which to live and work for 80 per cent of those interviewed in Merseyside and for 77 per cent in Glasgow, and were regarded as an important reason for enjoying working in the area by 68 per cent and 79 per cent respectively (Myerscough, 1988*c*, p. 140). Myerscough's conclusions are that although 'cultural amenities were never an overriding consideration in the thinking of mover firms . . . they could be an important supplementary factor'. Cultural amenities were regarded as 'a strong factor assisting the recruitment and particularly the retention of senior and scarce managerial personnel' (Myerscough, 1988*c*, p. 145). The varied range of studies on different aspects of the economic impact of the arts in American cities points to conclusions which are broadly similar to those reached by Myerscough's research on Britain.[5]

Questioning the consensus

The long-term viability of the prestige arts-led model as a formula for economic regeneration is, however, certainly not unquestionable. Myerscough has argued that public spending on the arts is a very cost-effective means of generating employment. He has calculated that the net cost to the Exchequer per person removed from the unemployment count through arts spending was £1,066 in Merseyside and £1,361 in Glasgow. These figures compare very favourably with national figures indicating the cost of creating one job on the Community Programme (£2,200) and in education and local government (£10,400) (Myerscough, 1988*c*, pp. 108–9). Myerscough's figures include the 'customer effect':

[5] See, for instance, *The Arts in the Economic Life of the City* (New York, 1979); C. Violette and R. Taqqu (eds.), *Issues in Supporting the Arts* (Washington, 1982), esp. pp. 12–34; *The Arts as an Industry: Their Economic Importance to the New York–New Jersey Metropolitan Region* (New York, 1983).

those jobs arising in the local economy from spending by people attending arts events. The problem with estimates of this kind is that employment due to the customer effect of the arts (which is particularly strong in sectors such as retailing and hotel and catering) is frequently low-paid, part-time, and characterized by de-skilling and poor levels of job satisfaction, legal rights, and working conditions. There is also some evidence that 'new' part-time jobs in, for instance, retailing are created at the expense of full-time equivalent posts (Montgomery, 1987, pp. 24–35; Northern Region Low Pay Unit, 1988).

As more and more cities compete to sell themselves as tourist and business centres, it is going to be increasingly risky to rely on 'consumerist' models of arts-led regeneration. As Hendon and Shaw (1987, p. 209) point out: 'the politics of urban develop-ment . . . has taken on some of the characteristics of a zero-sum game . . . if there are to be winners . . . there must also be losers.' The success of regeneration strategies that use the arts in order to boost retailing and other consumer services, to expand tourism, and to attract new firms and external investment, increasingly depends on factors over which cities have little or no control. These include variables ranging from foreign exchange rates, airfare prices, and perceptions of political instability to changes in the international financial markets and in the level of residents' disposable income.

The American experience suggests other potentially contro-versial political implications of the prestige model of arts-based urban regeneration. For example, some of these are pointed out by Sharon Zukin in *Loft Living*, one of the first books to analyse the role of cultural producers in processes of urban restructuring (Zukin, 1988). *Loft Living* examines New York's Greenwich Village, where during the 1970s the artists led the way for the conversion of former manufacturing space into residential units. The artists' presence contributed to increasing property values and rents, and to the subsequent displacement of lower-income residents—including, by the end of the decade, many of the artists themselves. The arts helped to further the reconquest of downtown by the new urban middle class, not only in New York but also in other American cities undergoing deindustrialization and a transition to a service-based economy. A study by the US National Endowment for the Arts confirms that the cities with the highest rates of downtown gentrification also have the highest percentage of artists in the workforce (Zukin, 1988, p. 199).

Zukin construes arts-based regeneration in the United States as part of a strategy for the legitimization of urban redevelopment coalitions led by the private sector. In this sense, the inclusion of arts facilities in redevelopment projects—often combined with corporate sponsorship for the arts—can be seen as an attempt to mollify local resistance to controversial schemes, and to create for business leaders an aura of social responsibility.

In the British context, arts-led regeneration initiatives coexist with the erosion of welfare benefits and the growth of spatially segregated urban 'underclasses'. According to David Harvey (1989), prestige arts-led regeneration projects function as 'a carnival mask that diverts and entertains, leaving the social problems that lie behind the mask unseen and uncared for'. Over a quarter of Strathclyde residents live at or below the poverty line, and poverty in Strathclyde rose by 46 per cent from 1981 to 1986 (Cosgrove and Campbell, 1988). Will they benefit from new arts developments in Glasgow city centre? More generally, will low-income residents be further marginalized by the distinct trend towards the privatization of public space in British towns and cities? Many local councils, tempted with promises of increased rateable values and income from land sales, have allowed the development of privately owned and controlled indoor shopping malls in the town or city centre. Management of the new shopping centres have the right to remove physically or deny access to anyone they consider as 'undesirable'.[6] The privatization of public space, in short, could contribute to the further exclusion from civic life of unemployed young people and other residents with low spending power, and to the reduction of their access to new arts facilities, particularly in MXDs and cultural districts.

In short, MXDs and cultural districts where the arts rub shoulders with other kinds of activities certainly have the potential to expand across class boundaries the audience for cultural events.

[6] On the problem of access to private indoor shopping malls see Birmingham for People, op. cit., pp. 9–10 and S. Lake, letter to the *Guardian*, 13 June 1988.

Yet, at the same time, cities often market these MXDs and cultural districts by emphasizing the association of the arts with 'exclusive' lifestyle. There is certainly a contradiction here, and it cannot be solved without a democratization of both access to arts facilities and of the notion of 'art' itself.

It is also valuable to consider briefly the ideological implications of arts-led urban regeneration. David Harvey argues that the involvement of the arts in urban development projects is part of a trend which he characterizes as the substitution of ethics with aesthetics in British urban policy. For instance, he sees the shift from modernism to post-modernism in the aesthetics of urban development as a means of controlling growing social tensions by artificially re-creating local images of 'community' (Harvey, 1987). It would be wrong to explain quintessentially post-modern phenomena like the explosion of the 'heritage industry' in 1980s Britain (Hewison, 1987) as simply a massive exercise in the production of false consciousness. The heritage industry is un-doubtedly—and perhaps primarily—a way in which post-industrial towns and cities have exploited their industrial past as a tourist attraction. But heritage developments are also in some cases a conscious attempt to reinforce local historical identities, which are threatened by the progressive weakening of the link between economic activity and the history and character of the locality in which it takes place. In the search for 'authenticity', of which heritage redevelopments are part, it often happens that 'the only way to attain the real thing is by fabricating the absolute fake' (Lumley, 1988, p. 13). Heritage urban developments frequently present a superficial, idealized image of the past, and can degenerate into 'museumization', which Edward Relph (1976) appropriately considers as a particular version of 'place-lessness'. In conclusion, the whole heritage phenomenon raises more general questions: can the community influence the aesthetic form of urban development? Who shapes and controls the aesthetics of urban regeneration?

Other problems raised by prestige arts-led strategies concern their implications for cultural production, for community-based arts activities, and last, but not least, for the historic function of the arts as a critical force.

In the current climate of intense competition for prestige arts events, cities tend to prioritize support for 'mainstream' arts organizations and the construction of arts venues, rather than for the promotion of new experiments in cultural production or for the development of new talent. In the long term, this may create difficulties already being felt in the United States, where—as William Hendon and Douglas Shaw (1987) observe—'almost everywhere arts facilities have expanded faster than repertoire' (p. 215).

A related problem is that public funding bodies have tended to concentrate resources on developments in the city centre and on high arts (opera and classical music, for instance), in the hope of attracting further financial support from private sources. This often leads to a contraction of the resources available for more popular cultural forms and for decentralized, community-based arts organizations and activities.

Lastly, one of the functions of the arts has traditionally been to question the status quo, and to create awareness of possible alternatives to it. Now there is a risk that the incorporation of the arts into urban 'growth coalitions' will reduce the freedom which is necessary to perform this essential critical role. The hegemonic status of the belief that 'what's good for business is good for the city' could seriously weaken the ability of the arts to point at alternative notions of 'the good' for both the individual and the community.

In conclusion, prestige arts projects can certainly be used as instruments for urban regeneration, but this could involve relatively high social costs and economic risks, and may have problematic implications for the arts themselves. How can we then explain the broad consensus—outlined earlier—on the prestige model of arts-led regeneration? Is it merely a case of 'conspiracy' among hard-pressed élites in depressed, fiscally strapped cities? More importantly, prestige arts-led regeneration initiatives often sharpen conflicts such as those between private and public space, city centre and periphery, tourists and residents, economic development and quality of life goals, cultural consumption and cultural production. The next section will examine precisely the possibility of an alternative arts-led regeneration strategy, built on existing achievements. The proposed strategy will attempt to marry cultural and economic development objectives, and will give priority to the rediscovery of public space and the fostering of participatory citizenship.

THE DIFFICULT ART OF CULTURAL PLANNING

One of the consequences of the debate on arts-led urban regeneration has been to raise the status of cultural policy on the political agenda. In the United States 'cultural planning' is one of the key concepts associated with the increased importance of the arts for policy-makers, at both local and national level (Porter, 1980). The use of the concept in Britain is, for the moment, confined to the process by which the Regional Arts Association assess their potential role in meeting local cultural needs, and in developing local opportunities. 'Cultural planning' could, however, become a useful byword to urban policy, which would attempt to tackle some of the problems outlined in the previous section.

Consumption vs. production

Our analysis of arts-led urban regeneration initiatives suggests that the goals of boosting cultural consumption and of developing the cultural production infrastructure do not necessarily conflict. In the case of some Labour-controlled city councils the building up of local production facilities supported, or at least coexisted with, consumerist strategies, focused upon prestige arts projects. The RIBA's 'Theatre Village' project in Newcastle shows how the dichotomy between production-led and consumption-led strategies can be overcome. The RIBA propose that the Theatre Village should contain a Business Development Centre for arts-related enterprises, a centre for fashion design, training, marketing, and retailing, along with housing, specialist shops, eating and drinking places, arts venues, and other opportunities for cultural consumption.

Newcastle also provides a good example of the potential role of art and design in the revitalization of manufacturing industry.

The City Council has supported the creation of a Fashion Centre based upon the local Polytechnic, to provide a range of services to clothing firms in the North-East. The Italian experience demonstrates that the contribution of designers, visual artists, and craftspeople is crucial for the success of small firms in such sectors as furniture, pottery, shoes, tiles, and glass-making, in addition to clothing. British architect Theo Crosby (1987) has also argued that, due to changes in architectural style, 'ornament, decoration, skills in finish and detail are once again thoroughly respectable and in demand'. Stronger links are therefore needed between the construction industry and the visual arts and crafts and, one might add, between the latter and another growing industry, the manufacturing of items of 'street furniture'.

In conclusion, there is some evidence that the arts are able not only to assist the conversion of cities into service-based economies—often characterized by problems of low pay, de-skilling, and poor quality of work—but also to help create local networks of small units working in highly skilled, high value-added manufacturing sectors.

City Centre vs. periphery

There are two ways in which democratic cultural planning might address conflicts in the spatial distribution of cultural provision. The first would be to strengthen or, in some cases, create from scratch neighbourhood-based arts facilities. These should be genuinely accessible to all sections of the local community (Lewis, *et al.*, 1986), and properly integrated with other amenities—shops, cafés, restaurants, pubs, libraries, leisure centres—to form 'local centres' of activity.

There is evidence that the arts can help break the spiral of decline which often sets in in disadvantaged and spatially segregated communities, in outer estates and depressed inner-city areas. In some cases, arts projects have provided an organizational focus through which a community has been able to identify its own needs and articulate a programme of action. A good example is the Festival Society formed in 1980 by the residents of Easterhouse, a large housing estate on the periphery of Glasgow with a rate of male unemployment exceeding 40 per cent. The success of a series of arts projects initiated by the Society—for instance, the construction of Europe's largest handbuilt mosaic mural, and the establishment of an annual programme of community celebrations and drama activities—gave local residents the confidence to set up some self-managed business enterprises. It also contributed to the creation of the Greater Easterhouse Partnership, which co-ordinates public, private, and voluntary sector initiatives for the regeneration of the area (Centre for Employment Initiatives, 1988, pp. 29–30).

During 1986 community-based arts and leisure projects received over £20 million from the Manpower Services Commission and £22 million from the Department of the Environment. However, despite the clear social and economic benefits flowing from such public investment, there is evidence that 'as far as possible, central government funds available for such programmes are being frozen, reduced or abolished' (Collard, 1988, p. 12).

The creation of 'local centres' should be complemented by a strategy aimed at making the city centre, where most cultural activities are concentrated, accessible, safe, and attractive for all citizens. This approach was adopted by Liverpool City Council in their arts and cultural industries strategy. The Council argued that the best way for local arts and cultural industries to compete with home-based forms of leisure (such as TV, videos, computers, and DIY) would be to become an integral part of an exciting and stimulating 'urban experience'. This could only be achieved if the city centre 'can be transformed so that residents feel it belongs to them; sense that it is safe to visit, particularly at night . . . ; can visit it cheaply and easily; find it pleasant to visit because of the quality of its appearance and its "street atmosphere"' (Liverpool City Council, 1987*b*, p. 5).

The Liverpool policy-makers outlined an 'integrated approach' to city centre revitalization. According to this perspective, a cultural animation strategy for the city centre cannot benefit all residents unless it is co-ordinated with appropriate policies in fields as diverse as public transport, policing, childcare, housing, retailing, economic development, planning, and environmental improvements.

It is imperative to avoid the scenario aptly described by Geoff Mulgan (1989, p. 25), in which 'conviviality is offered to those for whom it has an economic value . . . while those in less skilled work live an increasingly privatised existence, away from city centres, and dependent on home-based entertainment'. In order to ensure that low-income residents are not excluded from the city's cultural life, the city centre should include elements of affordable housing, along with popular and accessible entertainment, shops, restaurants, and other meeting places. Young people with low spending power, in particular, have in some recent cases been denied access to privately owned indoor shopping malls in the town or city centre. The Cultural Industries Quarter and the World Student Games initiatives in Sheffield show that it is much more fruitful, in terms not only of *community* but also of *economic* development, to regard youth and youth culture as positive assets, rather than potential sources of trouble.

In addition to providing particular groups within the population with special facilities and opportunities for self-expression, the city centre should contain indoor and outdoor public spaces, where people of different ages, social classes, and ethnic origins could come together for such civic celebrations as the festivals successfully organized by Rome City Council and the GLC in the early 1980s. Sheffield's Tudor Square project is an example of how a local authority can create flexible public spaces to provide a focus for civic identity.

In conclusion, the variety of the fabric of the city centre must be protected and enhanced, if necessary by checking the trend towards the development of out-of-town 'shopping cities', which may threaten the health of the central city retail sector. Other problems arise when the city centre is dominated by office blocks and large indoor shopping malls, which tend to transform the areas surrounding them into empty and dangerous places after the afternoon rush hour and on Sundays (Fisher and Worpole, 1988).

If the city centre is to be easily accessible to residents, a network of supporting public services must be provided. The paramount need here is for a cheap, fast, reliable and frequent public transport service. The experience of a number of cities in continental

Europe suggests that the provision of cheap and efficient public transport, particularly when combined with the pedestrianization of sections of the city centre, can reduce traffic, noise, and pollution, and even boost retailing (TEST, 1988). In terms of cultural policy, the main advantage of a good public transport service, running late into the night, is that it could help widen people's 'mental geography' and make the option of going out more attractive, particularly for the least mobile social groups. Other support services would, however, be needed. They should include efficient street cleaning and lighting, community policing, the provision of childcare facilities, 'urban beautification' schemes, and a city centre marketing and information strategy. This last strategy could comprise not only the provision of good signposting and town maps, but also the introduction of 'town cards' which residents could use to book and gain access to arts and leisure facilities, to obtain discounts at certain shops, and to vote at local referenda (Mulgan, 1989).

The role of local government

Effective cultural planning, in Wolf von Eckhardt's definition, 'involves all the arts . . . the art of urban design, the art of winning community support, the art of transportation planning, and the art of mastering the dynamics of economic development' (1986, p. 142). It also involves, as we have seen, the art of forming partnerships between the public, private, and voluntary sectors, and of ensuring a fair distribution of whatever economic, social, and cultural benefits can be obtained from arts-led urban regeneration initiatives. In democratic cultural planning there is certainly scope for co-operation between a range of different agencies, including central government, public–private partnerships, arts organizations, and non–profit making trusts like those governing the development of some American MXDs and cultural districts. It seems clear, however, that the central need is for a democratically elected and locally accountable multi-purpose agency. Studies of both the British and the American experience confirm that local authorities have the potential to perform a key strategic role in urban cultural planning (Collard, 1988; Kreisbergs, 1979; Duckworth *et al.*, 1986).

There is much local authorities could do now, with no need to wait for a change in government, to develop democratic cultural planning strategies. First of all, they could restructure their policy-making so as to overcome 'departmentalization' and move towards the adoption of an integrated approach to arts-based urban regeneration. One possible model is the Economic Development Bureau (EDB) created by Glasgow District Council in 1980, which comprises both elected members and officers, and co-ordinates activities across a range of departments, including Public Relations, Finance, Planning, Estates, and Parks and Recreation.

Secondly, the local government cultural planning process must be responsive to the demands and ideas of individual citizens and community groups. There are at least three ways in which this could be attempted. Local authorities could draw up 'arts plans' modelled on those formulated by the Regional Arts Associations, which would consist of audits of existing cultural resources, of surveys identifying the needs of different sections of the local community, and of studies on the local economic and social impact of the arts. Another possible model, based on the GLC experience from 1981 to 1986, is the devolution of decision-making powers and resources to community groups. In the GLC's case, these groups were the cultural expression of urban social and political movements—such as feminism, black and gay activism, Irish and youth groups—which formed part of the Livingstone administration's new political base. But, perhaps as a consequence of the GLC's lack of an overall strategy for urban regeneration, the emphasis tended to be more on the celebration of the distinctiveness and separateness of the identities of these movements—rather than on the contribution that the ideas of the movements themselves could give to improving the quality of life of the wider community. For instance, in addition to supporting women-only arts projects, the GLC could have translated into policies some of the ideas generated by the feminist critique of urban design (Matrix, 1984). This could have shown how feminist ideas, far from being 'marginal', can help solve important everyday problems.

The GLC experience was interesting also in that the formulation of the Council's policies on sports and on community and ethnic arts was based on extensive consultation. The role of public consultation in democratizing the cultural planning process can be illustrated by two examples.

Some US cities have formed municipal design review boards, which comprise local residents along with design professionals, planners, and local politicians (Page and Cuff, 1984, pp. 16–17). One of their functions is to exert some degree of democratic control over the aesthetics of urban development. These forms of community control are necessary because, as we have seen, even urban redevelopment projects carried out in the name of 'diversity' and avowedly in the observance of local heritage and traditions, can contribute to the standardization of the physical fabric of the city.

The second example is provided by the City of Bradford Metropolitan Council who, during 1988, carried out a major public consultation exercise on their plans to transform the West End of the city into a cultural district. Public opinion on the West End scheme was summarized by the Council in some key requirements. The public wished to be involved on a permanent basis in the development and future management of the scheme. They also wanted the West End to offer a great variety of shops, eating and meeting places, arts and entertainment venues, so as to cater for all citizens; to reflect and take pride in Bradford's rich multicultural fabric and traditions and, lastly, to be physically and emotionally accessible for everyone.

The Council convincingly argued that these were requirements for the success of the West End project, not only in social but also in economic terms. For instance, the Council emphasized that continued public involvement in the West End development would create sentiments of 'ownership' and 'responsibility', which would contribute to preventing abuse and neglect, and to containing maintenance costs.

The Bradford experience shows that the goals of developing the local economy and of improving the quality of life, far from being conflicting, can be mutually supportive elements of an arts-led urban regeneration strategy. In other words, it is wrong to distinguish sharply between policies aimed at tourists and external economic élites, and policies aimed at local residents. Recent research on the quality of life in British cities confirms that what special groups within the population expect from a city does not vary greatly from the expectations of the population as a whole (Rogerson *et al.*, 1988, p. 14).

In conclusion, is there an alternative to the pessimistic notion, all too well documented by recent assessments of arts-led regeneration projects, of the 'city of the spectacle' (Harvey, 1987, pp. 275–6), where the arts only contribute to increasing cultural standardization and commodification, social inequality and spatial segregation? The democratic cultural planning strategy outlined here is an attempt to illustrate the potential role of the arts in strengthening civic identity, a sense of community, and the citizens' active involvement in local affairs. These are among the most important conditions not only for the long-term success of urban regeneration strategies, but also for the reaffirmation of the city as a place for the free exchange of ideas, from which can emerge new ways of organizing and perhaps even alternatives to the present political order.

References

Arts Council (1985), *A Great Britain Success Story* (London).
—— (1988), *An Urban Renaissance* (London).
Baumol, W., and Bowen, W. (1966), *Performing Arts: The Economic Dilemma* (New York).
Bianchini, F. (1987), 'GLC R.I.P. Cultural Policies in London, 1981–1986', *New Formations*, 1, 103–17.
Boyle, R. (1988), *Public-Private Partnerships in Operation: A Case Study of Glasgow Action*, paper presented to the Centre for Urban Studies, University of Liverpool, July.
Centre for Employment Initiatives (1988), *The Arts and the Unemployed*, Jan.
Collard, P. (1988), 'Arts in inner cities', unpublished report commissioned by the Office of Arts and Libraries, Jan.
Cosgrove, S., and Campbell, D. (1988), 'Behind the wee smiles', *New Statesman & Society*, 16 Dec.
Crosby, T. (1987), *Let's Build a Monument* (London).
DoE (Department of the Environment) (1988), *Action for Cities* (London).

Duckworth, R. P., Simmons, J. M., and McNulty, R. H . (1986), *The Entrepreneurial American City* (Washington).

Fainstein, N., and Fainstein, S. (1982), 'Restructuring the American city: A comparative perspective', in N. Fainstein and S. Fainstein (eds.), *Urban Policy Under Capitalism* (Beverly Hills).

Fisher, M., and Worpole, K. (eds.), (1988), *City Centres, City Cultures* (Manchester).

Garnham, N. (1983), 'Concepts of culture, public policy and the cultural industries', paper presented to the conference *Cultural Industries and Cultural Policy in London*, organized by the GLC (London).

GLC (1983), *The Cultural Industries and Cultural Policy in London*, 17 June, AR 1116 and IEC 940.

Harvey, D. (1987), 'Flexible accumulation through urbanisation: Reflections on "Post-Modernism" and the American city', *Antipode*, 3, 26–86.

—— (1989), 'Down towns', *Marxism Today*, Jan., 21.

Hendon, W., and Shaw, D. (1987), 'The arts and urban development', in G. Gappert (ed.), *The Future of Winter Cities* (Newbury Park).

Hewison, R. (1987), *The Heritage Industry* (London).

Kelly, O. (1984), *Community, Art and the State* (London).

Kreisbergs, C. (ed.) (1979), *Local Government and the Arts* (New York).

Labour Party (1977), *The Arts and the People* (London).

Lewis, J., Morley, D., and Southwood, R. (1986), *Art—Who Needs it?* (London).

Liverpool City Council (1987*a*), *An Arts and Cultural Industries Strategy for Liverpool: A Framework*, Nov.

Liverpool City Council (1987*b*), *Liverpool City Centre Strategy Review*, Nov.

Lumley, R. (ed.) (1988), *The Museum Time-Machine* (London).

Matrix (1984), *Making Space: Women and the Man Made Environment* (London).

McKellar, S. (1988) 'The enterprise of culture', *Local Work* June.

Minihan, J. (1977), *The Nationalisation of Culture* (London).

Montgomery, J. (1987), *Trade Winds: The Changing Face of Retailing and Retail Employment in the South East* (Stevenage).

Mulgan, G. (1989), 'A tale of new cities', *Marxism Today*, Mar. 18–25.

Myerscough, J. (1988*a*), *Economic Importance of the Arts in Glasgow* (London).

—— (1988*b*), *Economic Importance of the Arts on Merseyside* (London).

—— (1988*c*), *The Economic Importance of the Arts in Britain* (London).

Northern Region Low Pay Unit (1988), *Britain's Bargain Basement: Shopwork Today* (South Shields).

Owusu, K. (1986), *The Struggle for Black Arts in Britain* (London).

Page, C., and Cuff, P. (1984), *The Public Sector Designs* (Washington).

Porter, R. (ed.) (1980), *The Arts and City Planning* (New York).

Relph, E. (1976), *Place and Placelessness* (London).

RHWL Partnership (1988), *The Lyceum Theatre and Tudor Square, Sheffield* (Sheffield), Mar.

Rogerson, R., Findlay, A., and Morris, A. (1988), *Quality of Life in British Cities: A Summary Report* (Glasgow).

Snedcof, H., (ed.) (1985), *Cultural Facilities in Mixed-use Development* (Washington).

TEST (1988), *Quality Streets: How Traditional Urban Centres Benefit from Traffic-Calming* (London).

TNI (1988*a*), *The Newcastle Initiative* (Newcastle upon Tyne).

TNI (1988*b*), *Theatre Village and Chinatown* (Newcastle upon Tyne).

Von Eckhardt, W. (1986), 'Synopsis', in R. Porter (ed.), *The Arts and City Planning* (New York).

Williams, R. (1958), *Culture and Society 1790–1950* (London).

Zukin, S. (1988), *Loft Living* (London).

11

Local Economic Strategies

Doreen Massey

WHAT KIND OF GROWTH?

Let me begin by being provocative. The economic problem in
the inner cities in the 1990s, if things go on as they are, will be as
much the result of growth as of decline. The 'inner city problem'
of the 1990s will not be the one we have been used to for the last
twenty years.

In part, this probably goes some way to explaining the
attention currently being paid to the inner cities by the Conservatives, quick to spot a likely investment opportunity for the
private sector. It is indisputable that, to Mrs Thatcher and her
Government, inner cities are parts of the country where, perhaps
most importantly, their ideology has not yet reached. It is clear
that a major purpose of the Government's focus on inner cities is
political and ideological. But that on its own is not an adequate
explanation of the attention which they are receiving. There are
many other parts of the country where values contrary to the
Conservative ethos are also still strong, and where the Conservative
vote is very low.

One reason behind the selection of inner cities for special
attention must certainly be the fear of 'social unrest' and of
further uprisings. But there is another reason, too—the additional
attraction of the inner cities as a policy focus is that, unlike almost
all these other areas, they are ripe for new investment. It is clear
that the property sector has a new interest in the inner city. The
areas on which it focuses are small and are carefully selected, but
the investment interest none the less marks a significant shift, and
one which is not confined to London. Further, current changes in
population patterns within cities, in the nature of the leisure

industry and more general consumption, and in the finance
sector, mean that there will be demand for new property investments. Capital, even if only certain parts of it, is rediscovering
the inner city.

What is at issue currently is not only, or not so much, a lack of
growth, but the form which 'growth' is taking. This is true at
national level and looks set to be increasingly the case in many
major cities. This may seem contentious when there are so many
social groups, and so many geographical areas, which remain
untouched by the Government's current 'economic recovery'.
But the point is that the nature of the current economic strategy,
the form of growth itself, is *based* on the exclusion of some, on
polarization, on increasing inequality both socially and spatially.

At national level, the fact of increasing inequality has been
widely documented. In terms of income distribution, between
April 1979 and April 1986, those who were in the top 10 per cent
of earners saw their real wages rise by 25.7 per cent (women) and
22.3 per cent (men) while those in the bottom 10 per cent got
increases of only 8.8 per cent (women) and 3.7 per cent (men).
Evidence on the occupational structure of the labour force points
equally towards a sharpening polarization, between a core and a
periphery, between high-status and highly paid jobs and a downgraded, increasingly casualized, low-paid sector. Moreover, it
should be noted that both these indications of increasing inequality
refer to those *in work*, those who supposedly are part of the
economic recovery. It is further evidence that what is at issue is
the nature of growth. And the picture is sharpened by evidence
from local economies. Local economic studies increasingly point
to more and more acutely dichotomized local labour markets
(see, for instance, Boddy *et al.*, 1986, on Bristol). The most
notorious example is that of London's Docklands where even an
official review committee has reported unease about the sharpness
of the social divide precipitated by this jewel in the crown of Mrs
Thatcher's inner-city policy. Finally, if the gap between the top
and bottom deciles of income-earners is taken as a measure of
inequality amongst those who are employed, then in the United
Kingdom in the 1980s inequality was greater where the average
income was higher and, looking forward to the 1990s, inequality

is increasing fastest in areas where average incomes are increasing most (Massey, 1988). It should not be news that particular forms of economic organization, particular forms of economic strategy, lie behind particular distributional patterns. The path chosen by the Government to dig the UK economy out of stagnation produces as a necessary result, indeed is based on, increasing economic inequality.

Moreover, it is in the inner cities, perhaps more than in any other areas, that the divisive effects of this economic strategy are evident. Here, in a kind of microcosm, and varying in intensity between different cities, it is possible to point to the social effects of an economic strategy focused on financial services and property-development, the impact of the decline rather than the modernization of manufacturing, of a competitive strategy based on cost-cutting and deregulation rather than on quality and training, the rapidly increasing polarization within labour markets between the privileged and highly paid on the one hand and the increasingly casualized and de-skilled on the other, and the growth in social inequality on almost every measure.

Thus, to return to the showpiece of the Docklands, one of the most frequent, and entirely justified, criticisms of Conservative strategy as implemented through the Docklands Corporation and the Enterprise Zone is that the jobs which they will bring will not be much use to local people. Either they will be for 'outsiders' (in other words, they will be upper-income jobs designated as highly skilled and reserved for other social groups) or they will be low-paid and designated as unskilled, resulting in both loss of income in comparison with previous jobs, and de-skilling of the local population. However, while this is correct, the deeper point is that these labour-market characteristics are not a result of the nature of the London Docklands Development Corporation (LDDC) alone. They are intrinsic to the whole nature of economic development in the Britain of today—an increasingly polarized skill-structure and an increasingly polarized labour market. These are the only kinds of jobs which are being created in the economy as a whole.

A comparable phenomenon is happening in the United States, so often looked to for new ideas on inner-city policy. In their detailed analysis of recent changes in income distribution and in the structure of the labour market in that country, Harrison and Bluestone (1988, p. 75) conclude that 'the restructuring has proceeded far enough that the broad outlines of a sharply more polarised society can already be discerned. What is more, after five years of continuous economic expansion since the recession of 1981–82, the trend towards inequality continues—despite the fact that in the past, buoyant economic times were always associated with less inequality, not more.' Moreover, within this inegalitarian boom 'surely one of the most dramatic developments of the last decade has been the wave of downtown redevelopment projects, typically characterized as signifying the revitalisation of the nation's cities. Signs of prosperity seem to be popping up in one urban area after another' (p. 66). Yet, as they demonstrate in general terms for urban America, and as Davis (1987) has graphically shown for Los Angeles and Sassen-Koob (1984) for New York, the 'revitalised' cities reflect perhaps more strongly than any other parts of the country the increasing polarization of society as a whole. In symbolic confirmation of this, and of the social antagonisms to which it can give rise, is the fact that in recent predictions of employment change in 'Boston—the city known above all in the country for high technology, its major universities with their sophisticated computer programmers, and its world-famous hospital system—the number-one growth occupation is *building custodian*, which currently pays about $236 a week' (Harrison and Bluestone, 1988, p. 73, italics in original).

In the long debate over inner cities which has been going on since the 1960s, one of the things which has quite definitely been established is that in a wider structural sense many of the roots of 'urban economic crisis' do not lie within the cities themselves. They lie in changes which have a broader provenance, in the reorganization of national, even international, economic forces. What is now clear is that that conclusion applies not only to quantitative changes in the number of jobs, but also to the very nature of 'economic growth', and indeed of the economy, itself.

One immediate implication of this argument is that many of the policies which will have the biggest impact on 'the inner-city problem' (we shall examine later the appropriateness or otherwise of this term) will not be called 'inner-city policy'. They will have a wider remit. Most generally what is needed is a less divisive model of economic growth at the national level, and labour-market policies which work strongly against the current tendencies towards polarization into core and periphery. At an absolute minimum such a redirection of the economy would have to include different strategic choices about priority sectors—less of a favouring of the City and property-development, more attention paid to a wider range of sectors in both manufacturing and services. And within manufacturing especially it would require a strategy of upgrading and modernization rather than the current option of competing with other economies on the basis of low wages and a lack of social regulations. Such a strategy should lead not only to a more secure competitive base but to a demand for a more highly trained and qualified labour-force. So different national policies would be needed on training, too, to meet this demand, to spread the possession of skills more equally through society, and to begin to undermine the monopoly power currently held by those in the more privileged parts of the UK labour market. Such a change in economic direction would also mean providing a wider range of services through a revitalized and rethought public sector rather than the private sector, thus making possible both a more egalitarian delivery of services to the consumer (both socially and geographically—the inner city would clearly benefit here) and higher-quality jobs and employment-conditions. It would mean a whole range of labour-market policies—to establish minimum wages, to improve the legal conditions for part-time and casual work, to provide a more favourable context of trade-union organization in new sectors. And it would require a whole battery of measures to diminish discrimination in the labour market—policies against racism, legislation on equal opportunities, and proper provision of nurseries.

What happens in inner cities, as in any other areas, is to a considerable extent a particular articulation of problems and policies which exist more widely: of national economic problems and the nature of national economic strategies, of general policies on the relation between public and private, of anti-racist strategies and of strategies for dealing with the enormous changes currently under way in the shape of the labour market. In that sense, and very importantly, the tendency must be resisted to treat 'inner cities' as 'an issue' which can be dealt with in isolation from other policy-areas.

THE NECESSITY FOR THE LOCAL

None the less, there is also a specifically urban dimension. Both the economic role of cities within our society, and the internal organization of urban areas, are changing quite radically.

To some extent these changes are due to the rediscovery of the inner city by certain elements of capital, to which we have already referred, and in some cases by upper-income groups. For the Conservatives, then, a number of issues coincide very happily: there is a possibility of invading the inner city through the investment of outside capital and through new social groups, thereby both providing new arenas for investment and breaking up, they believe, some of the existing solidarities of Labour areas. It is in this context that it is necessary to understand the form of the Government's policies. They are not centrally about job-generation, relieving poverty, or improving the social infra-structure. The function of Urban Development Corporations (UDCs) in particular (and where they are within urban areas) was to create greenfield sites within cities, safely circumscribed places which have been cleared of all local influence, both economic and political. The Conservative Government is in this sense quite adroitly seizing the moment. And it is therefore important to recognize that on certain terms they may well be able to claim, by the time of an election in the early 1990s, that their policies are beginning to succeed. There will be a 'before-picture' of dereliction juxtaposed with a picture of property-development. And to local people who have for years seen nothing but dereliction, and even to local councils in an increasingly desperate need for income, this may look tempting. If that is the case then it would be wrong to respond simply by saying that the policies have failed. Of course, they *will* have failed in the important sense that they will not have challenged in one iota any of the mechanisms which have produced the problems in the first place. But there may well be development, of particular types, and in small areas, in some inner cities. And they will have blue signs outside, claiming a central government contribution to funding. The policy may *look* as though it is working. And what that means is that what must be challenged are the terms of its so-called success. As at national level, it is the *nature* of growth which must be criticized. And it must be criticized for (at least) three sets of reasons.

First, and in a sense least importantly, it has to be pointed out that many of the new developments in city centres, and certainly those in the areas controlled by UDCs and Enterprise Zones, are not taking place unaided. They are happening on the back of very considerable state subsidies. The London Docklands Development Corporation is the most glaring example. It has already absorbed hundreds of millions of pounds of central government money, and its appetite for public-sector funding is growing rather than decreasing. But in other areas too, neologisms are a cover for the real nature of policy. 'Leverage' is simply another word for subsidy.

Spending public money to revitalize inner cities is of course necessary. The problems with the Tory strategy are: first, that public money is being spent in these schemes to subsidize private capital in projects which, as we shall see, bear often minimal relation to the local area or population: second, that this money is spent on these high-visibility schemes while local authorities in the same areas are being starved of resources for the provision of basic services (a redistribution of funds which can only exacerbate social polarization); and third, quite simply that the strategy gives the lie to the notion that the basis for urban revitalization lies in the market and entrepreneurship. Once again there are political parallels in the United States: 'Nowhere has government support for private business interests been more visible than in the subsidization of urban real estate . . . This agenda was far too important to business to be held hostage to any ideological consistency. The watchword of the era may have been laissez-faire, but urban redevelopment was too big a matter to be conducted without government assistance. Thus, as they did for the military build up, conservatives closed their eyes and jumped in to help business in a major way' (Harrison and Bluestone, 1988, pp. 104–5).

The second way in which the apparent success of current policies must be challenged is in terms of the very definition of 'the problem' in the first place. It is here that the term 'inner city' has itself become an obstacle to clear thinking. The Conservative Government (and it is not alone in this) defines the inner-city problem as a geographical problem; as a problem of place. Thus, if there is some physical development, and if new social strata are brought into the area (promoting 'social mix' and thereby fitting in nicely with the political project of breaking up old collectivities and bases of resistance), then the problem has been solved. But 'the inner-city problem' is *not* a problem of place. What the term refers to, or should refer to, are problems of poverty, unemployment, and deprivation, of a declining industrial base, of increasing inequality. The policies of the Conservative Government may well make a difference to inner cities; but they will not solve *these* problems.

As it stands, government policy will provide relatively few jobs for local people. Moreover, this is not because of detail such as the lack of local-recruitment clauses. It is because on the whole, as we have seen in the case of the LDDC, these will not be jobs which local people can fill. It is not economic development *for* local people. This is not a policy which builds on local needs and local skills; the role of local people is in construction (possibly) and in servicing the new development once it is built. The third way, therefore, in which the apparent success of these policies must be judged is by asking the question: for whom are they designed? As they stand they are likely to increase polarization, in social and income terms, within the inner city. They are likely to exacerbate a trend already under way for some of the worst urban poverty and deprivation to be found in areas *outside* the inner city, most particularly in the outer estates. There is already considerable evidence which indicates that this is happening (Meegan, 1984). Once again the terminology of 'inner city' is unhelpful. And as they stand current policies look set to reproduce, particularly in the inner areas of the northern cities, the problems of branch-plant economies. The Government's policies, in other words, are more about increasing centralization than they are about generating indigenous growth. Economically, Conservative polices are about clearing the ground for big capital. For all the talk of partnership, local industrial capital could get less of a look-in under these policies than if the policies were genuinely designed at local level. Indeed, local industry may well be adversely affected in some parts of the country, and there has been evidence of it getting nervous at the possibility of more direct central government intervention in their areas.

In fact, it is important to notice that this attempt to eliminate local influence, either economic or political, is not working. A newly contrite LDDC is now recognizing the necessity at least to pay lip-service to the need for social projects for the local community (though it could be argued that what is needed is more *economic* projects for the local community) and the need to consult with local interests. Moreover, outside London a number of Urban Development Corporations are far more aware of the need to team up with local representatives, including the local authorities. In at least one case the local authority has been selected as the planning agent. All of which makes a nonsense of the 'need' for UDCs in the first place. (The difference a UDC makes in this case is first, that local planners now have to submit their plans to its unelected board, rather than to the local authority, and second, that there is more money, for while the UDC receives central government cash the local authority is being starved of resources.)

This quite noticeable shift in emphasis between the LDDC and later Urban Development Corporations, however cosmetic, reflects an important point: that there *is* a need for a strong local dimension to urban policy-making. What we are facing is a rapidly changing urban hierarchy, not one single urban crisis (Massey, 1987a). While the causes of change are not simply local but have their roots in a wider systemic restructuring, the way that that restructuring works itself out, and the implications for the future of different cities, are highly varied. There is a need to have an equivalent space at the political level for this specificity to be expressed. This emphatically does *not* mean that local activity alone can solve the economic problems of local areas. Just as local

specificity is a product of the combination of wider forces and
local influences, so both national and local strategies are necessary,
both to challenge the wider forces and to respond to the particular
local conditions in which they operate.

So there must be strong, genuinely locally based policies. Such
policies, moreover, as well as being city-based, must be city-
wide. Trying to solve the 'inner-city problem' outside the context
of the city as a whole is doomed to failure (unless pushing the
problem elsewhere is deemed success). It might even be that
serious regeneration needs urban policies which go wider than
single cities. The cities of the north of England, for instance, are
struggling to revitalize themselves (with some success) in the
context of a worsening North–South divide. It might well be that
for them to establish an effective countervailing force to London,
a *network* of northern cities would provide more strength (Murray,
1988). It is certainly necessary that some action is taken to curb
the vast expenditure by some areas simply on advertising themselves in competition with other areas. This costly merry-go-
round creates no new jobs and has no rational outcome from
either an economic or a social point of view. The winners are
either the areas which are anyway the most attractive to investment (i.e. nothing is changed) or the areas with the best advertising
campaigns (hardly a good basis for deciding the distribution of
jobs).

A whole set of national-level policies, other than those already
mentioned, must also be introduced to lay the framework for real
local economic planning. The local authorities must play a major
role, as employers, purchasers, and investors, as well as in their
role as planners, and there need to be changes to national legislation
to widen their powers, duties, and financial bases. There could be
stronger national legislation to encourage developments on sites
which have already been used, and subsequently abandoned,
and actively to discourage development of greenfield areas. A
dereliction charge could be levied on industry which would be
waived when a company redeveloped a brownsite area. But
beyond all these things, it is necessary to intervene actively to
regenerate local economies, and it is here that local authorities
have made great strides over the last decade (and in spite of being

stopped at every turn by the Government) either through new departments set up for the purpose, or by the establishment of separate agencies which are often referred to under the generic title Enterprise Boards.

ENTERPRISE BOARDS

The problem here is 'what's in a name?' The experience so far of Enterprise Boards and related forms of intervention has covered a very considerable variety of approaches (Cochrane, 1987). There are important issues of strategy and principle to be addressed.

The basic impetus for all these approaches comes from a general recognition that local authorities must do more than provide the general environment in which the private sector can make a profit. Such a policy would neither guarantee regeneration nor exercise much control over the form of it. Moreover, the argument goes, the problems of British industry are deeper than this. They concern the organization of the economy itself. It is necessary, therefore, to intervene more directly in the economy of the local area. The question is 'how?'

One approach is to operate more or less as a public-sector investment institution. It is an approach which has been adopted in a number of areas and, within its own terms, operated with some success. None the less, it is a highly circumscribed approach, and there are a number of fundamental questions which should be asked of it.

First, it rests, of course, on an assumption that a major problem of local economies (and in our case here particularly those of inner cities) is a lack of finance for investment. At the extreme, it rests on the assumption that this is *the* major problem for the local economy in question. Now, it does seem to be the case that there is a lack of finance, in some parts of the country and for certain types of projects, even where investments are potentially commercially viable. It is certainly well established that the availability of venture capital varies quite considerably between different parts of the country; there is well-documented evidence of its relative scarcity in the North, for instance, though recent indications are that the gap may now be narrowing. Second, however, it is a lot less clear that lack of finance is *the* major problem of industry, which the local public sector ought to be tackling. This 'finance-gap' argument is a local version of the one at national level that it is British banking which has been uninterested in investing in British production, and the argument is subject to the same qualifications. One has to ask why the investment opportunities in British industry are insufficiently attractive. It is difficult actually to demonstrate an overall shortage of finance for really attractive investments, either locally or nationally. Indeed, in recent years there have been large amounts of cash available, but even manufacturing interests in Britain have been putting it into finance and other sectors, and certainly not into long-term restructuring and expansion. In other words, the shortage may be (and indeed the evidence points in this direction) just as importantly a shortage of the right kind of investment looking for finance. This implies that our fundamental concern should be with production rather than with finance, and raises hugely difficult issues about how to generate good projects for invest-ment and restructuring. The two concerns (production and finance) are of course not necessarily mutually exclusive, but in the context of an Enterprise Board they can pull in conflicting directions. For one thing, as the argument above implies and as the experience of at least some Enterprise Boards strongly cor-roborates, it is not so much that there is an absolute shortage of finance, but that there is a shortage of the *right kind* of finance. What is needed is 'patient money', long-term investment either for thoroughgoing restructuring of some of the dilapidated sectors in our inner cities or for the establishment on a firm footing of new sectors of growth. Third, and at a deeper level, what this approach is arguing is that part of the private sector (an element of 'the market'—in this case for investment funds) is not working perfectly, that the public sector can do the job better, and that it is the role of the public sector to do the job better. It is indisputable that the private-sector supply of investment funds does not work like a perfect market. It is also true that in many ways the public sector is better placed to recognize and respond to commercially viable local opportunities. Its local base, its links with trade unions, and a host of other characteristics have frequently and persuasively been argued to its advantage over a highly concentrated, risk-averse, London-based private sector. The real question is whether the role of the public sector at local level *should* be to use local resources simply to plug the gaps left by the private sector, in other words to make 'the market' work better. It implies that the crisis of the inner cities of the last twenty years, and the changes currently under way, are a 'mistake', a result of the malfunctioning of the system. Of course they are not; they are part and parcel of the way the system works. Fourth, and to raise immediately one reason why such a strategy may be inadequate, an operation based on plugging gaps left by other people cannot set its own priorities. It inevitably has to operate in a response mode, rather than being able to design and implement its own strategy for the local economy.

In practice, these arguments may not be such tight constraints as at first appears. The idea of a 'finance gap' can be used as a way to get in to the local economy, to gain some bargaining-power with companies, a manœuvre which can in turn open up the space for a more thoroughgoing restructuring of production. It is on this basis that a number of Enterprise Boards have worked quite effectively. Among the more evident characteristics of British industry are a sharp divide between international capital on the one hand and regional/local capital on the other, and the backwardness of much of the latter. Much of what remains of regionally and locally owned British industry is pretty moribund, not only in physical but also in managerial terms. There is, in other words, a failure in 'the market' of industrial development as well as in that for investment funds. And this, like the 'finance gap', provides an opportunity, though again limited, for intervention at local level. But a focus on production implies further requirements of the policy framework, and raises its own issues. As we have already argued, it implies that the investment is long term. But more than that, at least some of the experience of Enterprise Boards has shown that it is often impossible to put in long-term investment and expect the company to get on with the agreed restructuring. (The market in managers clearly does not work perfectly!) In case after case the public sector has had to move in to do the job itself. And in order for this to be possible it has been necessary to have both a controlling financial interest and real day-to-day influence over what is happening in the company. Inexorably, by the logic of the arguments for intervention themselves, if the Enterprise Board is to achieve anything meaningful (i.e. to make a serious difference) it is pulled away from being a public-sector copy of a merchant bank/venture capital house/financial institution towards being an actively interventionist public-sector holding company. Simply being a merchant bank is inadequate because the economy is 'not working' in a far deeper sense than the maldistribution of investment funds.

All these arguments about the economy 'not working properly', the 'inadequacy of UK capitalism/capitalists' etc., are subject to the point made above. The collapse of the former economies of inner cities may be especially bad in some places because of the particular failures of the UK economy, but those failures do not provide a total explanation. 'Uneven development', an unequal and periodically shifting geography of growth and prosperity, is endemic to a capitalist economy. With the system working perfectly (in its own terms!), and with every capitalist behaving optimally, some communities and places will, from time to time, be faced with economic annihilation because they are no longer, for whatever reason, profitable places for economic activity. This means that it is important to be clear about how to use the market-failure argument. The aim must be, not simply to plug the gaps (for although this might do some good it would by definition probably be limited in its effects), but to use those gaps as a way to gain some sort of social control over the market. Such a strategy implies, none the less, that there is a margin in which social intervention of this type can be compatible with 'normal' (capitalist) criteria of commercial viability.

This applies *a fortiori* if intervention is not simply to mirror the results of the private sector. As we have seen, the current re-structuring of urban areas in Britain (and the USA) is resulting in rapidly increasing social inequality. The question, as we said, is not just growth, but what *kind* of growth. The ultimate futility of going for 'jobs at any price' has been demonstrated in many other places. Perhaps most dramatically there is the case of the regional policy of the 1960s and 1970s, which so failed to provide a basis for long-term growth. A central question then must be to what extent, and how, is the Enterprise Board to be an instrument of social change? To what extent will it aim to improve the quality of employment? to fight racism and sexism in the workplace (and not by just the obvious means but by changing, for instance, who does which jobs and how jobs are evaluated?) To what extent will it aim to give people more control over their working lives, to introduce democracy in the economy? These are huge issues and cannot be addressed seriously here (for fuller discussions, see Mackintosh and Wainwright, 1987; Massey, 1987*b*), but the questions they raise are fundamental. What is to be the relation between so-called 'commercial' and 'social' objectives? How can conflicts between different groups be dealt with? What kind of rate-of-return will be looked for and will it be on individual investments or for the porfolio as a whole, allowing deliberate cross-subsidization?

Once again, it may be possible to use market openings to gain a foothold for further intervention. When the Greater London Enterprise Board pioneered its social strategies in the early 1980s, crèches were barely on the agenda and, to the extent that they were, they quite definitely figured as part of its 'non-commercial' (ie 'social') objectives. Today, with the current shortages of labour in the South East, and the so-called 'demographic time-bomb' forcing employers, in that region at least, to think the previously unthinkable in terms of whom they will employ and under what conditions, crèches and childcare-facilities generally are clearly becoming part of the necessary infrastructure of a local economy. Moreover, and more generally, there will also often be considerable room for manœuvre in which social change in the organization of production will be compatible with the need for financial viability and competitiveness. The opposing strategies towards 'flexibility' mentioned in the opening discussion of the nature of economic growth are a case in point. Mrs Thatcher's downgrading-and-deregulation version of flexibility is no more competitive (and is most probably in the medium term far less so) than a flexibility geared to quality and training (and remember that none of these local economic strategies stand a chance of serious success without a concomitantly progressive and supportive national strategy). There will, then, be a degree of compatibility between the achievement of progressive social aims and remaining commercially competitive, even at an individual-plant level.

None the less, there will remain serious issues about combining objectives. Social changes of this type will not always cost money, but they will often do so. How then is this to be reconciled with the (usual) commercial objective of producing 'viable' jobs (which in this terminology means jobs from which a profit can be made)? One solution which has been adopted is to separate 'commercial' and 'social' into distinct 'investment' and 'grant' budgets. This, however, again raises further issues. Far from challenging the currently given distinction between 'the economic' and 'the social', it explicitly reinforces it. The economic is left to carry on as normal, and we subsidize some social add-ons. Nothing is done to change the social way the economy works. Further, it will not always be *possible* simply to separate social costs from commercial investment funds. But most importantly in this context, if social changes are to be subsidized though grant-money then there are again implications for the overall nature and project of the Enterprise Board. Once again it implies a long-term involvement with each enterprise. Properly drawn-up social plans take a long time to put into operation, and if their operation is subsidized and continuing, the Enterprise Board cannot simply withdraw from investments when it has established them, or turned them around commercially. Once again it must be involved in building up a gradually expanding portfolio of firms. And it may also be involved, perhaps over the long term, in a programme of subsidy. What is at stake is the kind of employment we are going to have in our cities. As we saw earlier, Mrs Thatcher has no hesitation at all in subsidizing the kind of economy *she* wants to see in the cities of the future. The ten-year holiday from rates, for instance, which goes along with being in an 'Enterprise' (!) Zone and would pay for a lot of social improvements in the workplace.

This, however, runs very much against the view, expressed in some quarters, that Enterprise Boards should be, above everything else, commercially oriented venture-capital houses. The immediate aim of this approach is to go for a high rate-of-return through turning investments around quickly. The high rate-of-return results from the increased sales value. In the longer term the aim is to demonstrate the ability of the public sector in this arena, and to begin to establish a significant public-sector role in finance. We cannot take over the City, so we need a big government operator to establish control over a large part of the investment function. Enterprise Boards can be one means to this end.

Once again, this is in its own terms a viable strategy and one which, in its own terms, may be operated with a degree of success. But it is important to recognize its implications. It is a question of aims. The aim here is to establish a 'respected' public-sector financial institution. This is a different aim from that of achieving social objectives through extending public-sector influence within the rest of the local economy. And these aims have been seen to conflict. The survival and the rate-of-return of the Board takes precedence over the impact on the local economy. Other means of making money are adopted—not in itself wrong, but again potentially contradictory. In one case the rate-of-return has been boosted by selling off land. It was land bought relatively cheaply when the local land market was in a slump. This allowed the purchase of some sites at a reasonable price, and the aim was to integrate them into the industrial strategy, and to preserve them from socially undesirable changes of use. But precisely because it was at the margin of change of use, this land was highly saleable. As prices have risen, planning permissions have been sought and the land sold. The Enterprise Board has profited, but at the expense of social change in the local economy. Its financial aims have been satisfied, but at the cost of its production aims. Further, it has already been shown that restructuring production and achieving social objectives require long-term commitment and high degrees of public-sector control/influence. This is incompatible with the fast-turn-around finance-house view. It is an ironic point since the argument for the *need* for a public-sector financial institution itself derives in part, as we have seen, precisely from the lack of long-term financing. But the fundamental point is deeper. In these days of Thatcherism our aim cannot be simply to pull things into the public sector. Rather, we have to justify (as we are always being told) having anything in that sector at all. That is very difficult to do if your aim is to be only 'as good as' the private sector. The point of the public sector is that it is *different* from the private sector. It should have different aims and achieve different objectives.

DEMOCRACY

It would seem then that we are at some kind of historical turning-point for cities in this country. Their shape, and their roles, are changing and the frameworks laid down now and in the next decade stand to have an influence for many years. There are fundamental questions, and potential conflict, over such things as who will be housed there, what sectors of industry will dominate their economies, and within those sectors for whom will they operate? Cultural industries are likely to be increasingly important, for instance. But what will this mean? Are cities to be yuppie playgrounds where the unemployed cannot go? Studies have pointed to the increasing disenfranchisement of the poor from urban life: 'the police move you on if you don't have money to spend'. Or are our cultural industry strategies to be more like those developed in recent years by radical left–Labour authorities?

By the virulence of her attack on Labour local authorities, Mrs Thatcher has clearly indicated the importance of who has influence over the development of urban economies. But the Labour party must also face up to the issue. In many ways, the Labour leadership has been as fearful of and as antagonistic to real attempts to devolve power as have the Conservatives. Attempts to make the local state an enabling state, to experiment with popular power and popular planning, to have respect for the autonomy of other organizations outside the party, have all too often been derided. The leadership has all too often acquiesced when experiments in giving real control to local groups have been dubbed 'loony'. Such experiments are fraught with difficulties, and many mistakes have been made (but they have also often been recognized) and in many ways the process is necessarily conflictual (for an excellent discussion of many of these issues see Mackintosh and Wainwright, 1987). Elements of the Labour hierarchy and politicians of the old guard used to running 'their' cities view such developments with alarm. So, equally, do the middle-class professionals the whole basis of whose class position rests on their claim to expert knowledge, and technical neutrality.

But the issue of the future of the economies of inner cities is not one for which there is a technically neutral solution. Mrs Thatcher won in 1979 on the basis of an attack on an outmoded, centralist, statist, labourism. She has for a decade now been treating us to her alternative. The nearest thing to a competing vision from the Left has come from the radical local authorities, many of them in urban areas and up against the most enormous problems. If only the national party dared see it.

References

Boddy, M., Lovering, J., and Bassett, K. (1986), *Sunbelt City? A Study of Economic Change in Britain's M4 Growth Corridor* (Oxford).

Cochrane, A. (ed.) (1987), *Developing Local Economic Strategies: Some Issues and Ideas*, (Milton Keynes).

Davis, M. (1987), 'Chinatown, part two? The "Internationalization" of Downtown Los Angeles', *New Left Review*, 164, 65–86.

Harrison, B., and Bluestone, B. (1988), *The Great U-turn: Corporate Restructuring and the Polarizing of America* (New York).

Mackintosh, M., and Wainwright, H. (eds.) (1987), *A Taste of Power: The Politics of Local Economics* (London).

Massey, D. (1987a), *The Roots of Urban Crisis*, Centre for Local Economic Strategies, Occasional Paper 1, (Manchester).

—— (1987b), 'Equal opportunities, the GLEB experience', in A. Cochrane (ed.), *Developing Local Economic Strategies: Some Issues and Ideas* (Milton Keynes).

—— (1988), 'A new class of geography', *Marxism Today*, May, 12–17.

Meegan, R. (1984), *Outer Estates in Britain: Interim Report. Preliminary Comparison of Four Outer Estates*, CES, Paper 23 (London).

Murray, R. (1988), *Crowding Out: Boom and Crisis in the South East* (Stevenage).

Sassen-Koob, S. (1984), 'The new labour demand in global cities', in M. Smith (ed.), *Cities in Transformation* (London).

Index